Terrorism Awareness

Terrorism Awareness: Understanding the Threat and How You Can Protect Yourself provides readers a foundational understanding of the threats that face us every day. The goal is to introduce readers to different tactics and techniques used by terrorists—both international and domestic—to better understand personal protection concepts and, if necessary, take actions to make themselves "hard targets" that terrorist organizations will want to avoid. This includes providing a background on understanding how terrorists operate, and, more specifically, how to recognize the pre-incident indicators associated with terrorist operations.

Coverage includes situation awareness of the phases of terrorist operations, common attacks, surveillance and targeting tactics, kidnapping and hostage situations, bombings and blast effects, hijacking, armed assaults, and more. With such awareness, readers can be alert to common cues to avoid dangerous situations, as well as familiarize themselves with various actions they can take to better protect themselves. Sometimes certain events may arise which are unavoidable and, in those cases, learning how to best mitigate those scenarios can mean life or death and provide the best opportunity for safety and survival.

Terrorism Awareness is a helpful guide to provide anyone working or traveling in the United States or overseas—particularly in potentially volatile places subject to terrorism or civil unrest—the tools they need to recognize potential threats and to keep themselves, and those they are with, safe.

Robert H. Deatherage Jr. (Bob) spent over 22 years in the U.S. Military, serving in both the U.S. Marine Corps and U.S. Army Special Forces, and working in several different positions and groups. He retired as the Noncommissioned Officer in Charge of the Antiterrorism Training Detachment, D Company 2nd Battalion 1st Special Warfare Training Group. Since retirement, he has worked as a Security Manager for international construction companies in Iraq, Israel, the West Bank, and Gaza. He has also worked as a DOD contractor with the DEA in Afghanistan and as a Corporate Security Tactics Manager in the commercial Nuclear Industry, overseeing security tactics at multiple commercial nuclear power plants. He currently works as a consultant in the security industry and still conducts training seminars for the Military, including Special Operations units, and Civilian Law Enforcement organizations throughout the United States on a wide variety of subjects in Antiterrorism, Defensive Driving, Security, and PSD operations. Bob has a Master's in Business and Organizational Security Management.

Terrorism Awareness
Understanding the Threat and How You Can Protect Yourself

Robert H. Deatherage Jr.

CRC Press
Taylor & Francis Group
Boca Raton New York London

CRC Press is an imprint of the
Taylor & Francis Group, an **informa** business

Designed cover image: Shutterstock

First edition published 2023
by CRC Press
6000 Broken Sound Parkway NW, Suite 300, Boca Raton, FL 33487-2742

and by CRC Press
4 Park Square, Milton Park, Abingdon, Oxon, OX14 4RN

CRC Press is an imprint of Taylor & Francis Group, LLC

ISBN: 978-1-032-27418-8 (hbk)
ISBN: 978-1-032-27416-4 (pbk)
ISBN: 978-1-003-29264-7 (ebk)

DOI: 10.4324/9781003292647

Typeset in Sabon
by SPi Technologies India Pvt Ltd (Straive)

"Terrorism is a global threat with global effects; ... its consequences affect every aspect of the United Nations agenda from development to peace to human rights and the rule of law. By its very nature, terrorism is an assault on the fundamental principles of law, order, human rights, and the peaceful settlement of disputes upon which the United Nations is established. The United Nations has an indispensable role to play in providing the legal and organizational framework within which the international campaign against terrorism can unfold."

Kofi Annan
UN Secretary-General
4 October 2002

Contents

Preface

This book's intent is to provide a basic understanding of terrorists and terrorist organizations and the information you need to make yourself UNDESIRABLE as a target for anyone, and UNPREDICTABLE to any threat that you may encounter regardless of your location. No matter where you are, any time you suspect anything, REPORT IT to someone. Whatever suspicious activity you see, it needs to be reported to someone; do not hesitate or think someone else will do it. How many times have we seen on TV where someone would say, "*I thought something wasn't right*," "*he just didn't act right*" after an incident has taken place? I want you to use the things discussed in this book to move the threats crosshairs off of you as a hard target.

And finally, you always need to remember that we as potential targets always want to be INFORMED about the threat, be as LOW PROFILE as we can be, be as UNPREDICTABLE as possible, and always be ALERT to what is taking place around us.

Introduction

Throughout history, people have been committing acts of violence for personal, political, and religious reasons to help further their own agendas. Many of these acts of violence appear to be conducted at random with no planning or thought put into it, and many times, it seems they are committed for no reason other than to kill people or destroy property. If you can work your way through the propaganda, put out by both sides of the problem, you will begin to see that the people who commit these crimes are usually sane, very rational, and committed to their cause. The acts of violence they use are carefully planned to promote their agenda; for most of these individuals, their commitment to their cause is so strong that they feel justified in what they do. They are willing to use any extreme measure in order to achieve their goals. These acts are called

TERRORISM

This word is in the mainstream of daily life for everyone around the world; it is amazing how this one word can produce so many different types of reactions: anger, fear, annoyance, apathy, and hope. Terrorism is usually defined by the people who it is being used against, so those in power and the established government decide what terrorism is, regardless of why those particular people or organizations act the way they do. Countries around the world cannot even agree on how to define terrorism, or what constitutes a terrorist act—nor what should be done about it. The Irish Republican Army (IRA) had been considered a terrorist organization by Great Britain and Ireland was considered a guerrilla movement or insurgency by the U.S. Government. The same could be said of the Russia-Chechnya problem or, to retrace U.S. history, the Contras of Nicaragua. They were considered terrorists by the Sandinista government but freedom fighters by the United States who supported them in their bid to overthrow the established government. This was when the phrase "one man's terrorist is another man's freedom fighter" was used to describe the Contras.

With all this confusion and debate surrounding what is and isn't terrorism, what are and are not terrorist attacks, and by whom, it's no wonder that the world is having such a hard time dealing with the terrorist threat as it encroaches into the daily lives of people around the world. In this book, I hope to give people a better understanding of terrorism, why it happens, who is doing it, what they do, and how to protect themselves whether at home or while traveling. I want to give everyone a chance to look at this problem from different perspectives so they can strip away the layers that surround the works of those labeled terrorists, get past the propaganda, awe, and the fear and the mystique created by them, and look at the actual reasons and circumstances of their actions. After all, you cannot fight a problem if you don't know how the problem developed or why the problem exists.

CHAPTER 1

Introduction to Terrorism

So, what exactly is terrorism? And who is a terrorist? These two questions are central to everything that is done to work against and defeat those who employ terrorist beliefs and tactics. How you define your enemy or threat against you is going to decide how you intend to combat that threat and mitigate their ability to hurt you. Right now, there are over 100 different definitions of the word terrorism. The world has been trying to define terrorism for a long time; the League of Nations Convention in 1937 had the following definition "*all criminal acts directed against a state and intended or calculated to create a state of terror in the minds of particular persons or group of persons or the general public.*" The people of the world, and most governments, are continually trying to put terrorism into a definition that is usable by everyone, but is that possible? If we look around at some of the definitions used today, we see that there is still no single way to define it or make it fit everyone's criteria; the American Heritage Dictionary definition from the early 2000s is "*the unlawful use or threatened use of force or violence by a person or an organized group against people or property with the intention of intimidating or coercing societies or governments, often for ideological or political reasons.*" The current American Heritage Dictionary online definition is "*The use of violence or threat of violence, especially against civilians, in the pursuit of political goals.*" Both of them sound good, but does it really cover every person or organization that is being called a terrorist today? Let's look at the U.S. Government definition contained in Title 22 of the United States Code, Section 2656f(d) which defines terrorism as "*premeditated, politically motivated violence perpetrated against noncombatant targets by sub-national groups or clandestine agents.*" Another interesting way to look at it, but it is still vague; defining it seems to be very hard. The Joint Chiefs in Chairman of the Joint Chiefs of Staff (CJCS) handbook 5260 define it as "*the calculated use of violence or threat of violence to inculcate fear; intended to coerce or to intimidate governments or societies in the pursuit of goals that are generally political, religious, or ideological.*"

DOI: 10.4324/9781003292647-1

While all these definitions are adequate and have some of the same ideas present, I prefer to use the definition that is used by the Antiterrorism Training Detachment located at the John F Kennedy Special Warfare Center and School (JFK) Special Warfare Center and School. It is,

> The calculated use of violence or threat of violence to attain goals, political, religious, or ideological in nature. This is done through intimidation, coercion, or instilling fear. Terrorism involves a criminal act that is often symbolic in nature and intended to influence an audience beyond the immediate victim.

All of these definitions show how organizations look differently at the problem of actually identifying what terrorism is to them, but they all have some common elements, and I want to discuss those a little more in depth to help us define terrorism for ourselves.

First, *Violence, Fear*, and *Intimidation* all three are used every day to influence others to get what people want. It is used by criminals, bullies, police, politicians, governments, and militaries and is used to induce terror (fear) in victims who experience these three; but, when does it cross the line into terrorism? They are a necessary part of a terrorist's arsenal of weapons since terrorism is one of the few ways people not in power have to otherwise gain influence.

Second, "*the calculated use of violence*" means that the acts of violence that are carried out are planned in advance and are designed to achieve a goal of the person/group and to influence a certain area of the population; so what some see as random acts are actually planned acts aiming toward a goal of that person or organization. This also means that there is a plan in place by these people/groups, and they are trying to implement it by coordinating their actions with other members of the group or other organizations to all work toward the same goal.

Third, "*symbolic in nature*," when they plan their attacks, these people or organizations want to get as much attention as possible: the need for the local populace to know it happened, the government, the world, etc. They want as many people as possible to see this action and this will draw attention to their cause; they are hoping to gain support and extend their reach through the use of media. and the best way to do this is to attack targets that symbolize what they are fighting against or have a significant meaning to those they oppose. By using symbolic targets, they magnify the effect of their actions, giving a greater impact on them and, in turn, requiring the use of fewer of their limited assets in the process.

Fourth, "*influence an audience beyond the immediate victims*": when a terrorist incident is planned and executed, the perpetrators are not necessarily looking at whether the victims of the incident are affected, unless it is an assassination for a symbolic reason. They want to affect the wider audience, the whole population, the government, by making them see what they did and what they can do. They want to see how everyone is reacting to it. After all, the effectiveness of the incident isn't measured by how much property is destroyed or how many people are killed, but by the population's and the government's reactions to it. This could include more aggressive prevention measures, such as checkpoints, ID checks, house-to-house searches, etc., which is what the terrorist wants to happen since it will show the people their government acting oppressive. It happens all the time. A car bomb goes off, so the government puts a curfew on all vehicles except for government vehicles. A government official is shot, so all weapons are forbidden and confiscated even from law-abiding citizens. Look at the effect on the government's international policies in just two examples. The bombing of the U.S. Marine barracks in Beirut, Lebanon. occurred on October 23, 1983. After the attack, the public outcry in the United States was so great that the U.S. presence in Beirut was done away with. How can anyone forget 9/11 which changed how we use public transportation, how we screen at airports, and so many other domestic policies and international cascading effects? There are multiple examples of terrorist acts that have influenced our daily lives, too many to list all here.

Fifth, "*a criminal act*": we have to remember and remind everyone that the acts that are perpetrated by terrorists are criminal in nature and that this fact takes away their ability to have some type of moral legitimacy for their cause and their actions. By treating them as criminals and holding them to the rule of law, we deny them any special consideration for their actions or their cause and keep them in the spotlight of what they truly are—common criminals.

We have spent a lot of time discussing what terrorism is and/or isn't, so what is a terrorist group? Basically, any group of people who use the tactics of terrorism to commit criminal acts as the main way to accomplish its organization's goals and/or objectives.

The whole concept of what is or isn't terrorism, who is or isn't a terrorist and what is or isn't a terrorist organization comes down to the matter of perspectives or different points of view. Usually, the label of terrorist is put on those who are against the established government or those in power; when it comes down to it, the label of terrorist is a political label that uses the moral viewpoint of those in power as the measurement for who is or isn't a terrorist. In many cases, it is a very subjective distinction and most people always try to put their enemies or opponents in the worst possible light, giving them the ability to claim the moral high ground in their fight against their opponents and/or enemies. Those who are considered the opponents or enemies of those in power do not think of themselves as terrorists; they consider themselves as soldiers for the people, trying to further the cause of the people against those in power. They will label themselves with such names as freedom fighter, revolutionary, vigilante, paramilitary, guerrilla, rebel, jihadi, and mujaheddin; this is done so they can align themselves with others in society who are fighting for the greater good. And they may be, it is easy to forget that in history those who have been labeled terrorists by some have later been considered as liberators of their countries; Nelson Mandela is a good example. He was considered a Communist and a terrorist in his political beliefs by the government of South Africa because of his fight against apartheid. He was convicted and spent 27 years in prison for his involvement with armed resistance groups. Eventually, there was a switch in policy brought about by both the armed resistance and the peaceful political efforts, and he was released in 1990 and, in fact, won the Nobel peace prize in 1993.

The Afghan Mujahideen were freedom fighters that were supported by the U.S. government against an occupying Soviet army and the government that was installed by the Soviets to oversee Afghanistan. The United States gave money, arms, intelligence, and training to these freedom fighters to help them fight the Soviets and eventually push them out of their country, but now when the Mujahideen are fighting against another foreign power that has installed in their eyes another puppet government, they are labeled terrorists by the same U.S. Government that used to support them.

I use these examples not to be divisive but to point out how important perspective is when trying to decide who is a terrorist and why they are doing the things they do. Most people get locked into their own perspective, which can be clouded by emotion, and never take the time to step outside their comfort zone and try to look at something from someone else's perspective and/or try to understand their reasoning. I could write a lot more about former friends and allies that were later called terrorists by the United States and the same can be said of many other countries and their dealings around the world. These reasons and difference in perspectives are why no one, not the United Nations, not the U.S. Government, or any other country in the world has been able to come up with one definitive term for TERRORISM.

When we look at all the conflicts taking place today, many could be called terrorist acts. Look at the Israelis bombing in Palestine and the West Bank and U.S. Military attacks that have hit schools and wedding parties in Afghanistan and Iraq. When we look at the acts and have to make a decision, we should take into account the moral objective behind the attacks. Most often, collateral damage is unintentional. When the Israelis fire a rocket and kill a bomb maker and innocents are killed, the intent wasn't to kill the two innocents but to kill a threat to their nation. However, when a terrorist goal is to blow up a bus filled with school children that was the intent, the killing of innocents to make a statement. We need to focus on what the moral intent of the act was when considering how to judge another's actions.

A BRIEF HISTORY OF TERRORISM

> A man does what he must – in spite of personal consequences, in spite of obstacles and dangers and pressures – and that is the basis of all human morality.
>
> *John F. Kennedy*

How long has terrorism been a force in the world? Since recorded history, violence, threat of violence, and intimidation have been used widely as a tool in every age to get what the perpetrators wanted. It would be impossible to talk about all the incidents in history, so I will try to hit some highlights of what I think illustrates the use of terrorism throughout history. Terrorism and its use as a tool of state can be traced back thousands of years to the Greek historian Xenophon who lived 430–349 BC; he wrote about the effectiveness psychological warfare had against enemy populations before, during, and after conflicts. Julius Caesar in 50 BC would take the children of the leadership of defeated enemies as hostages, they were treated well, educated, etc., but held to ensure their cooperation; this allowed him to use his military more efficiently and it ensured the next generation of leaders from those defeated enemies would be trained, educated, and taught Roman values, so when they returned to their people, they would help institute change in favor of the Romans. Other Roman emperors used intimidation, including the threat of banishment, taking of property, and execution, as a way to limit the opposition to their reign. And, let's not forget about the Roman games, where people would be accused of crimes and sentenced to death for all to see; this was an excellent form of intimidation to keep the opposition in line.

A whole book could be, and has been, written on the history of terrorism throughout the ages—of all the transformations it has undergone over the years to evolve into the deadly and effective tool it is today. But, I will focus on what is termed modern-day terrorism; this is the post-World War II era. During this time, several events happened that proved that in certain cases terrorism tactics worked and helped people achieve their goals.

- First were the successes of the Communist insurgent movements in China, Cuba, Rhodesia, Angola, and Nicaragua. These insurgencies proved that small, undermanned, poorly equipped movements with a plan and proper leadership could defeat the larger established power, its law enforcement, and military. After these new regimes were in power, they provided footholds in their respective regions for the spread of communism and insurgencies to other countries, providing help for those who wanted change. But, more importantly, these countries served as training areas and launch points for the spread of terrorism, throughout those regions and the world. (It should be noted that after 20 years of occupation and war, the United States and their allies could not ensure the safety of the Afghanistan people from the small poorly equipped terrorists, militias, and the insurgency that took over the country in 2021).

- The Arab–Israeli conflict is another of those conflicts in the Middle East that dates back to early recorded history. But the Israeli defeats of the Arabs in the 1960s and the 1970s demonstrated to them that they could not stand toe-to-toe on the modern conventional battlefield with the Israelis and defeat them. So, they had to resort to other tactics; from Yasir Arafat's perspective, the Palestinians would resort to those tactics used by the United States and the Israelis to get rid of the British and he was committed to doing whatever would help them in their plight. What Yasir Arafat would later call "George Washington tactics" in a speech at the United Nations, we call terrorism. These tactics became the basis by which Arab nations could attempt to destroy Israel through surrogacy since they could not do it on the battlefield.
- The Afghanistan war was fought between the Afghan resistance and the Soviet Union Army which invaded in 1979. The Afghan people declared this war to be a Jihad (holy war) against the infidels who had invaded their country and conducted a 10-year campaign against the Soviet army which withdrew in 1989. But, this country of conflict was the breeding and training ground for many of the people currently leading and conducting terrorist acts around the world in the name of their cause. They took their experience in Afghanistan to other places to help fight the infidels, as they deemed them. The most wanted person in the world, until he was killed in 2011, Osama Bin Laden is one of those Afghan rebels recruited from Saudi Arabia to fight in the Afghan war against the Soviets. It was where he was trained by the United States and gained his experience and the contacts that he used until his death. (Certain portions of the Afghanistan people continued this war against the United States and coalition forces who after 20 years of occupation left the country in 2021, allowing them to take over the Government again.)
- Then, during the Vietnam War, there was civil unrest that was so pervasive around the world during the 1960s and the 1970s;

it attracted many young people to different radical causes against the established government. The issues used to draw people were those that appealed to the younger generation, such as civil rights, environmental concerns, political radicalism, and the anti-Vietnam war fervor amplified these feelings. Most of the domestic terrorist groups in the United States were created during this time, including the Symbionese Liberation Army (SLA), an offshoot of the Students for a Democratic Society (SDS), the Weathermen which later broke off into the weather underground, etc. (*members of these organizations who wanted to overthrow the U.S. Government now teach at universities throughout the country and some have held political office in the United States*). But this civil unrest was not only happening in the United States, but also in Europe and other locations across the globe; such groups as the Red Army Faction (RAF in Germany) and the Japanese Red Army (JRA in Japan) were started by college students who wanted to make changes in their society. In fact, many of the terrorist organizations still around today are a direct result of student protests and youth movements of this turbulent era.

- But, in my opinion, the greatest cause of the rise of terrorism and its impact in the world has been the influence of modern electronic media. For the first time in history, we have the ability to communicate instantaneously anywhere in the world. This is a great tool for terrorists; these instant communications and getting on the news is something that the terrorists have quickly capitalized on. Now, any act of violence, anywhere in the world will attract millions of television viewers, giving them a worldwide stage to present their cause; it also plays into their hands by allowing them to intimidate entire populations and cause fear worldwide. This also benefits the television networks which seek to increase their ratings, the number of viewers, and their profits; remember, the news says "if it bleeds it leads." So, now we can watch as friends, family members, soldiers, and innocent people are being slaughtered before our eyes—thousands of miles away live. Think back how many people remember that five United States Congressmen were shot in the House of Representatives by three Puerto Rican nationalists? It happened on March 1, 1954; most people don't remember because they heard about it on the news hours after it happened, but didn't see it. Imagine if it happened today live on TV, could you forget? The use of media has grown since this time as evident in the bombings of U.S. embassies in Tanzania and Kenya, or the coverage received by the Tupac Amaru Revolutionary Movement (MRTA) when they seized the Japanese Embassy in Peru. And let's not forget the one that galvanized our nation: the attacks on 9/11, as we watched live the second plane flying into the World Trade Center, the fires, and the death. It changed us all watching it live and the reruns over and over again on the television news networks; would it had that effect if we saw a 2-minute spot on the evening news after it was over? There are many other uses of modern technology and the news that terrorists have embraced wholeheartedly in the cause, these include the use of the Internet. All of the major terrorist groups have webpages, groups, and personal pages on various platforms across the Internet. They post statements, videos, etc., and they use this forum to recruit and send out messages to followers; it helps them in gaining financial support for their cause.

- It should be noted that recently it appears that the news media and platforms on the Internet have started taking sides when it comes to what is or is not a terrorist/criminal act and who is or is not a terrorist or criminal. It appears as if political ideology and beliefs caused what used to be a mostly unbiased news media to morph into a biased media and only supporting "their side." Media platforms have started banning speech that "they" deem inappropriate or not true. Unknown people who are called fact-checkers determine if what you write or post is allowed to be viewed, with no references or guidance as to why what you post is not allowed or false. The greatest information source of our time has been hijacked by the ideology of those who control the flow of information; it appears as if there is no such thing as unbiased media in modern times.

Terrorism has been around forever, but where is terrorism taking us now and in the future? What forms will it take, with changes in technology, weapons, the ever-shifting makeup of the world, and its politics? One day, will it be feasible for terrorist groups to obtain or build a nuclear device, biological weapons, or other weapons of mass destruction? And would it be in their best interest to use it if they could? How would the world react; what could they do to an organization that would commit such an act, with no country claiming responsibility only a group of people bound by ideology? Can the world, or for that matter civilization as we know it, withstand the continued onslaught of terrorist attacks? Can western society maintain an open culture in the face of this threat? Truthfully, I don't know; there are no easy answers or solutions to these questions, and judgments that are made will be an attempt to quell the rising violence of the terrorist threat, but at what cost to freedom? The one thing we can be assured of is that as long as we align our policies and tactics with the sound principles our country is based on and never lose sight of them in an attempt to make ourselves safe, we can win the war against terrorism. On the flip side, if we allow ourselves to be manipulated by the terrorist threat and the news media into adopting repressive, population control, police-state tactics, and policies that strip away our principles and rights, then the victory will belong to terrorists who will have achieved their goal.

PERSPECTIVES OF TERRORISM

The major reason terrorism has been so difficult for anyone to define is that different people can view the same criminal act of terrorism and each will interpret it according to his or her own experiences, prejudices, beliefs, and value system. This problem is compounded when we consider national and international political agendas, social and cultural differences between different countries, and the history between nations. We cannot forget the reporting bias in the media in modern times; is it the whole story or a selected narrative? I have mentioned it in this book already but we have all heard it in other places the phrase "*One man's terrorist is another man's freedom fighter*" is used frequently, and it is quite true since it depends on which perspective you are viewing it from. President Ronald Reagan himself used the term "Freedom Fighters" when discussing the Contra rebels in Nicaragua, who were considered terrorists by that nation's government.

For the most part, there are generally three perspectives to a terrorist event:

First is *how the terrorists see themselves*; they have an opinion about themselves and their cause; they do not view their cause, their actions, or motives as being criminal, evil, or negative from a moral or social standpoint. They truly believe that the society they live in, in its current form, is evil and requires radical and violent action to change it for the good of everyone, even if everyone does not want change. So, because they are working for the greater good, the violent destruction of property and the maiming and killing of innocents are not only morally justified but also necessary to bring about change. From the terrorist's perspective, the inevitable end they are working toward justifies the violent means they feel they must use to attain it. In their eyes, they are legitimate combatants and freedom fighters, soldiers for the people who cannot fight, struggling for a just cause and representing oppressed peoples in the hopes of a better life.

Second is *how the victims of terrorism view the terrorist act*. The victim, whether he is directly touched by the act, is a family member of a direct victim, or is a victim of the measures taken by a government to stop these acts, sees no moral legitimacy in the deaths of innocent people, destruction of property, or being forced to give up freedoms to face this threat. They feel victimized from a criminal standpoint; this type of act hurts them, intrudes on their lives, and is wrong. So, to the victim, the terrorists are immoral criminals, working outside the rule of law to achieve their own goals to benefit themselves.

The third, last, and probably the most important perspective is that of *the general population and how they view these criminal/terrorist acts*. The terrorists know that the population of their target area will determine how their acts are viewed by those in power; if they disagree, then they will eventually pressure the government to act to protect them. Or the local population will take action against the terrorist group to stop their attacks by withholding support, reporting to police, etc. How the general public reacts to terrorist incidents and demands will determine the success or failure of the terrorists' objectives. The population will always be divided, and a portion of them are always going to be for the terrorist and a portion will be against them. Acts of violence, killing of people, and destruction of property do not usually elicit a neutral response from people. But one thing is certain, terrorists know how to use propaganda and the media, and they will spend a great deal of time, effort, and money attempting to project a "*Robin Hood*" image of themselves to the general public to gain their trust and support.

LONG-RANGE OBJECTIVES OF TERRORISM

Every group or organization has a goal or objective they want to accomplish, that is what they are working toward, so what do terrorists hope to accomplish through acts of violence? Well, it is hard to think what each individual terrorist is thinking or wants for his future, but generally speaking, the long-range objectives of terrorism can fit into at least one of three broad categories.

If someone is using terrorist tactics or a group is discussing the use of terrorism tactics/methods with the intent to bring about the complete overthrow of the existing government in their area of operations, then this group's long-range objective is labeled as REVOLUTIONARY. This threat can take place with groups that are either internal or external to the area of operation against the established government. This is the case in Colombia, where the Armed Revolutionary Forces of Colombia (FARC) are an example of an internal threat to the legitimate government. A good example of an external group would be the case of Israel and the Popular Front for the Liberation of Palestine (PFLP), which, while not based in Israel, wants to overthrow their government. Just because a group is not from the area of operation and works or has support from the outside to overthrow the government doesn't mean it won't be successful. There is an example this type of terrorist-insurgent group that was successful and that is the Sandinista Liberation Front's (FSLN) overthrow of the Samoza regime in Nicaragua in 1979. Normally, these types of groups or organizations, when they become a threat to the security of the government, are referred to as insurgent or guerrilla movements. The most recent example of this goal being reached was in Afghanistan in 2021. The Taliban conducted a successful campaign that started in 2001, leading to the withdrawal of the coalition and finally United States' withdrawal from the country, leaving the Taliban in charge of the Government in 2021.

If terrorism is used by an organization, but it only wants to influence a government into making changes to its policies or laws and not replace the government, then the long-range objective is called *SUB-REVOLUTIONARY*. Usually, the changes the terrorists want to make will be political, social, or economic in nature. Many nationalist movements around the world are in this category. For example, the Euskadi ta Askatasuna (ETA) of Spain perpetrates violence against the governments of Spain and, to a limited extent, France because they want a Basque "free state" in the Pyrenees mountains; they do not care about who is in charge of the government in Madrid except as it affects their one specific cause, a free homeland for themselves. (In 2018, the ETA declared a definitive end and officially dissolved.) We also cannot forget those organizations, some of them labeled domestic terrorists, environmental terrorists (eco-terrorism), or anti-abortion violence; the long-range goal of these special interest groups is to change government policy and public opinion on a particular issue, that is, abortion, animal rights, or environmentalism.

Finally, we get to the last one, which is when terrorism is controlled or condoned by an established state, it is labeled as *ESTABLISHMENT TERRORISM*. The use of the violence of terrorism would be directed against enemies of the regime either domestically within its borders or overseas as in the case of Libyan hit squads that traveled throughout Europe in the early 1980s attacking those who spoke against Qaddafi. Domestically, the use of terrorism was used to destroy or kill opponents or counterrevolutionaries such as the policies used in Mao's China in the 1950s and the 1960s or to promote and spread through the use of terrorism a revolutionary fervor in an attempt to indoctrinate the population with the government's ideology as in the case of the Khmer Rouge in Cambodia/Kampuchea in the 1970s or during the French Revolution in 1791–1793. There was also the use of the right-wing death squads that were so prevalent in El Salvador in the early 1980s prior to the Duarte regime and in Noriega's Dignitary Battalions in Panama; all these groups were considered establishment-type terrorists that worked against their own people. The U.S. State Department has four countries listed as State Sponsors of Terrorism: Cuba, the Democratic People's Republic of Korea (North Korea), Iran, and Syria.

MOTIVATION THAT BINDS PEOPLE TOGETHER INTO TERRORIST GROUPS

There is much speculation about what causes people to commit acts of terrorism, let alone come together into groups whose sole purpose is committing terrorist acts. A lot of this has to do with their own personal perspectives of life, and how that draws others of similar thinking together to practice what could be termed their IDEOLOGY.

Ideology is defined by Webster's dictionary as "*a manner or the content of thinking characteristic of an individual, group, or culture.*" This is a great "general purpose" definition but does not go far enough when attempting to describe terrorist organizations; this dictionary's definition implies that all members of a group believe in the professed ideology of that group, but this assumption cannot be made about contemporary terrorist groups, so a change to the classic definition is required to make it closer to the what is actually taking place. So, with that in mind, "*an ideology is a system of beliefs that supports and lends legitimacy to the actions of an individual or a group.*" This is more accurate for our use of the term ideology as it applies to modern terrorist organizations.

The second definition helps us understand terrorists and their different mindsets since being a member of a terrorist group does not always infer deep and absolute commitment to the cause of the group. Many people who join and actively participate in terrorist organizations do so because of reasons other than pure belief in the cause; they *do so for the rewards for such participation such as money, drugs, or prestige*; they are basically mercenaries in the cause of terrorism, regardless of belief. There are many examples of this, one is the international terrorist for hire Ilich Ramirez Sanchez (Carlos the Jackal), the Venezuelan-born who worked for any group for any cause if the price was right, and we also have the SLA leader Donald DeFreeze (Commandante Cinque), of the 1970s, who used his acts of terrorism to get money, to help pay for his lifestyle and drug habit. We also have those hostages who have been released or who have escaped from Beirut during the mid-80s, when there were numerous kidnappings, such as American journalists Charles Glass and Jeremy Levin. Many of these hostages have commented in debriefings that the groups that held them seemed to have been motivated more by how much money they could get for their captives than by the symbolism of kidnapping an American or for the groups' stated cause. This trend of doing the work for money, drugs, etc., continues today in South America, more specifically Colombia, in Mexico, and is spreading around the globe.

There is now a new term used—Criminal Terrorism: these are people or groups who are motivated by profit; they use this profit from criminal activity to support their movement or other movements. These groups use terrorist tactics, violence, and other criminal activities to fund themselves and others. The major labels for these groups are narco-terrorism and cyber-crime terrorism. The funds gained by these criminal activities fund their activities. It should be noted that traditional terrorist organizations are now using cyber programs offensively, such as the Iranian government who has sponsored cyberattacks against other governments and private sector organizations. So has the Jemaah Ansharut Tauhid (JAT) in Indonesia, who are known for conducting cyber hacking for funding.

Then, we have the fact that terrorist groups want to foster the belief that they are working from *the moral high ground and their claims and concerns are legitimate* and for the good of the entire population, they are fighting for them, and sacrificing for them so any violent act especially one that targets or kills innocents will more than likely evoke a negative reaction and a backlash from the public who they need to garnish support or sympathy from in order to help their cause. So, any claims of the group's beliefs, and their working with a higher morality and the legitimacy stemming from a political or revolutionary cause, may minimize this effect. Usually, terrorists who are caught will claim political affiliation and moral justification to try to counter criminal prosecution by the state. But by defining terrorism as being criminal in nature, we have stripped away any claims of moral legitimacy they may have had.

Politics is an ideology that motivates many terrorist groups; these ideals range from the far left to the far right of the political spectrum. Politics from the *extreme left* comes in many forms.

- *MARXISM* is based on the writings and beliefs of Karl Marx, a nineteenth-century German philosopher and economist who studied the social, economic, and political problems of his day. The essence of Marxian ideology can be found in the following two works: *THE COMMUNIST MANIFESTO*, which he coauthored with Friedrich Engels (published in 1848), and *DAS KAPITAL*, which appeared in 1867. Marx disagreed with the utopian socialists; he believed there could be no compromise between the exploited workers (proletariat) and the capitalist factory owners (bourgeoisie). Marx felt that all problems endemic to the modern capitalist society stemmed from the fact that the workers were alienated from the things they produced because they did not own the finished product or the means of production for those products. He believed that society was dominated by, and the workers were exploited by, the owner class. Further, he considered the state as merely a tool for this dominant class. Marx felt there were three groups in particular that were evil: the politicians, the police, and the military, and he felt that to improve society, the state must be destroyed; and in order to destroy the state, these three specific groups must be eliminated. Since this change could never come about peacefully because the state dominated by the bourgeoisie would not give up its power, it would be up to the proletariat to rise up and overthrow the state by violent revolution.

- *MARXISM–LENINISM*, Vladimir Ulyanov, also known as Lenin, is the one who adapted Marxism to the living and political conditions in early twentieth-century Russia. He stated that the development of society to the state of communism was not inevitable; according to Lenin, the revolution Marx predicted in Europe did not occur for several reasons, he maintained that Marx could not have foreseen the rise of trade unions in the industrialized nations throughout the world, nor could he have predicted the manner in which capitalist imperialism played a part in bettering the conditions for workers in industrialized nations at the expense of the Third World. Lenin also felt that the proletariat was not educated well enough or politically aware enough to understand their own plight and needed a leader to show them the way.
- *MAOISM*, Mao Tse-tung developed a kind of Marxism, which came to be called Maoism after Chinese Communists took power of Mainland China in 1948. His thought processes were complicated but so was his situation; he took a Marxian-type analysis with Leninist structure and then combined those with the fundamentals of Chinese culture and their thinking process. What he came up with was a permanent revolution with a constant scrutiny of party leadership by the people who are the principal tenets of Maoism. The most obvious difference between Maoism and other Communist beliefs is that Maoism is a peasant type of Marxism; he had to change from an industrial-based society used in Marxism, because China was mainly rural with an agricultural-based society, and a poor, largely uneducated peasant class comprising the membership of the Communist movement and the revolutionary army. Mao also had to change the basic concepts of Marxism–Leninism to suit the basic belief and family situation where it would work in a country where family and cultural motivations were deeply ingrained in the individual. Usually, the terrorist groups that follow the Maoist ideology tend to be much more violent than those that follow other ideologies.

For those ideologies on the far right, we have:

- Benito Mussolini first used the word *FASCISM* in Italy in 1919; the Italian word “fascio” which literally means a bundle of rods with an ax in it. This was an excellent way to symbolize the word as Mussolini used it: the power of many, united and obeying one will and the authority of the state, which was the supreme source of law and order. Fascism is characterized as a joining of all aspects of society, economy, culture, government, and military beneath a single leader who is morally and legally authorized to make all decisions for the good of the state. This authority usually comes from a legitimizing background of belligerent nationalism that uses all ethnic and social groups outside their own as scapegoats and as mechanisms to stimulate revolutionary and nationalistic fervor. There are several examples of regimes that used this either in name or in practice: they include Hitler in Germany and Franco in Spain. And, it is sad to say, that these beliefs can increasingly be found today in Fascist-oriented groups such as the Aryan Nation, a right-wing organization centered in the northwestern United States, but there are similar belief-oriented groups and movements afoot in Europe and other nations around the world.

Next, we have the strong belief in a national identity or *NATIONALISM*; this is a powerful motivating ideology for people, especially those of the same ethnic background and identity, who have often been bound together by the nationalistic urge to establish or regain a homeland they believe is theirs. Sometimes, nationalism is used in conjunction with another ideology, such as Marxism–Leninism; this allows it to appeal to a broader spectrum of supporters.

RELIGION is also a powerful ideology that motivates people to bind together into groups for all kinds of purposes. Throughout the recorded history of man, a person's religious belief has provided a reason for many of history's most violent excesses. The are many historical examples which include the crusades of the eleventh and twelfth centuries; we also have the Spanish Inquisition, which officially lasted until the mid-nineteenth century when it was terminated by a papal edict.

There are many other ideologies that motivate people to bind together into groups which can be labeled *SPECIAL INTEREST IDEOLOGIES*. These special interest groups include the radical splinter groups of many legitimate nonviolent causes such as antiabortionists, environmentalists, and antivivisectionists (groups against experimentation on animals), there are almost too many, too name.

MECHANISMS USED TO LABEL TERRORIST GROUPS

There are several mechanisms which are used to label terrorist organizations; one of these ways is by *labeling them by the support mechanism* they use. It is important to be familiar with these terms and how they are applied not only because they will aid in your understanding of terrorism but also because these are the descriptive terms commonly used by analysts and authors who study and write about terrorism.

The first label used to describe terrorist groups by their support mechanism is *STATE DIRECTED*. A state-directed terrorist group's activities are conducted primarily at the direction of a state's government. The group may even be an element of that state's security organization. When considering these labels, along with the long-range objectives, we have already discussed previously, the descriptive lines start to blur and become unclear. A terrorist group can be labeled by different mechanisms to help provide a better understanding of it. Just as a group that acts as part of the controlling state's security forces can be described as being *state directed*; it can also be described as being an "*establishment*" in its long-range objectives. An example of this is the terrorist group As-Sa'iqa, a military unit that is supported, manned, and led by elements of the Syrian Army but operates out of Lebanon. Some sources indicate that the Hizbollah movement and its subunits, such as the Islamic Jihad, are state-directed terrorist groups because of their close ties with Iran.

A *STATE-SUPPORTED* terrorist group receives substantial support from one or more governments but whose actions are not directed by any government; they are autonomous. In some instances, the supporting state attempts to place requirements on the terrorist group for the purposes of receiving aid, but a state-supported group will not let this happen. If it does, we term it a state-directed group. The single most important characteristic of a state-supported terrorist group is its willingness to accept support from any government or source as long as that aid is not linked to specific direction. Examples of state-supported groups include the Provisional Irish Republican Army (PIRA), the Lebanese Armed Revolutionary Faction (LARF), and the Basque Freedom and Homeland (ETA).

The support label placed on some terrorist groups is that of *NON-STATE-SUPPORTED*. These non-state-supported terrorist groups do not receive substantial support from any government and whose actions are totally autonomous. Because of this, these types of terrorist groups must gather support from many different and various sources. These groups are usually insurgent movements that operate virtually with no external support mechanism and, if they are successful in their operations, pose the most serious threat to the stability of the established government. These types of groups, which include the New People's Army and the Sendero Luminoso, are some of the most dangerous of all contemporary insurgent movements since they are able to stand alone and—being Maoist in nature—they have planned on protracted guerrilla warfare with battlefield re-supply.

Terrorist groups receive the majority of their direct support from auxiliary cells they have established for that purpose, but it also receives indirect support, such as propaganda and contributions of money, time, and other material support to the cause, from passive supporters. What are passive supporters? They are people who donate money to what they perceive as a worthwhile organization for a cause they believe in but they are unwittingly donating their money or support to an organization that is really a "front" for a terrorist group. The news media, it could be argued, are also passive supporters of terrorism, in that they take advantage of the violent acts of terrorism to capture the public's attention to increase their ratings or circulation. You can also say that the population of a given area are also passive supporters of terrorist groups and their motives when they "pass the word" about terrorist activities that have taken place; this only serves to increase the level of fear that the population has of the terrorists, which in turn helps increase the effectiveness and power.

IMMEDIATE GOALS AND CHARACTERISTICS OF TERRORIST GROUPS

All terrorist organizations, like any other organization, have a plan that consists of both immediate and long-range goals. We have already talked about their long-range goals which were described as revolutionary, sub-revolutionary, and establishment. But before a terrorist organization, group, guerilla, or insurgent movement can make a working bid to accomplish their long-term objectives—or for them to have enough power or hope to become a serious influence on a government's long-term policy—it must have some smaller victories and accomplish its more immediate goals, that eventually will lead to their long-term one. So, each act of terrorism is designed to accomplish something specific to their plan that is actually a part of their overall strategy of the conflict. These immediate or short-term goals usually include one or more of the following:

- The need to *obtain local and worldwide recognition* of their cause: They need this publicity to advertise their movement, its goals, and what they want to accomplish, and this recognition is of great importance to the group. This publicity will focus national and international attention on the group's grievances, attract money from supporters, foster international sponsorship, and recruit members for their cause.
- To *cause overreaction by the government*: This is one of the basic principles of militaristic revolutionary strategies such as those described by Castro, Guevara, and Marighella. They want an overreaction to their acts because this overreaction may result in the government implementing more oppressive and restrictive population control measures, such as instituting special

antiterrorist laws that allow searches without warrants, detention of citizens without charges, curfews, and travel restrictions, limiting gun ownership. Then, people will see these measures as violations of their rights, and this type of overreaction will also lend an element of legitimacy to the grievances of the terrorist movement, creating an atmosphere more sympathetic to the terrorists' cause; because now everyone sees and feels the heavy hand of the government and experiences the government's intrusion into their lives, when they have done nothing.

- They want to *harass, weaken, or embarrass government security forces*: They will use tactics like calling in false alarms, assassinating law enforcement and other security personnel, and conducting raids and ambushes. These tactics are used to reduce the effectiveness of security forces, wear them out, and take away their own confidence in their abilities and the abilities of their leadership. They also erode the public's confidence in the government and the leadership after implementing such tactics. The rationale being, if the government forces cannot protect their own people and resources, how can they protect the civilian population?
- The want to *obtain money and equipment*: Terrorist activities are commonly used to steal or extort money, support, equipment, especially weapons and ammunition, which are essential for them to be able to continue on with the struggle. Also, any major successful terrorist incidents or a successful terrorist campaign against the government can also attract support from foreign governments that support such causes or other terrorist groups. People do not realize how profitable some terrorist acts can be. Here are some examples: the largest known ransom ever paid for a single individual is $14.2 million. It was paid in 1974 by the Exxon Oil Corporation for the release of Victor Samuelson, a company executive working in Argentina who had been held for 144 days by the ERP (Argentine People's Revolutionary Army); a German industrialist paid 60 million dollars for the release of his two sons, the Juan and Jorge Borne, in 1975 to the Montonero Peronist movement in Argentina; in December of 1975, Carlos the Jackal masterminded the raid on the Organization of the Petroleum Exporting Countries (OPEC) Oil Headquarters in Vienna in which he and three others took over 60 hostages, eventually he received a ransom of 25 million dollars and was given asylum in Algiers. The four-person team Carlos used included Gabriele Krocher-Tiedemann, a terrorist from Algiers, and Hans-Joachim Klein, a known member of the Baader-Meinhoff group from German.
  - There are now various other methods of financing that are used by various terrorist and criminal groups. Not only

narcotics, but ransomware attacks, bitcoin mining, donations. Just about any (largely illicit) venture that can be utilized to obtain money and funding.

- The want to *destroy facilities and disrupt the media and other lines of communication*: By doing this, they hinder the government's ability to control violence, both militarily and politically. It helps to create a chaotic atmosphere within the general population. In some remote areas, segments may be entirely isolated from government influence for brief periods, making them susceptible to intimidation and propaganda by terrorists. It also shows, once again, the inability of the government to protect its population.
- They want to *discourage foreign investments or assistance programs*: They want to do this while they are not in control but while the government they are fighting against is in control, so the economy of the target country will be affected, causing an increase in unemployment which causes hardship among the general population and a decrease in government revenues, which effects government programs to help people. This leads to a loss of government prestige in not being able to do things for the population, which in turn can lead to internal dissent. It is the characteristic of movements worldwide to use foreign investors, foreign corporations, and foreign government assistance as symbols of their cause against capitalist oppression and imperialism. If the terrorist attacks are successful and these corporations lose confidence in the host government's ability to defend property and protect their people, they will cease operations and leave—moving to a friendlier or otherwise safer environment. When this happens, there is a sudden jump of unemployed people in the geographical region surrounding the plant. If the country has no or a limited social support system, these people now have no way to feed themselves or their families and often turn their aggressions against the government and the corporations that fired them. This population of disaffected people now becomes a recruiting pool for terrorist organizations. EXAMPLE: In January of 1986, the FARC demanded 100 million dollars from Shell Oil Company to continue operating in the middle Magaleas valley, but the firm suspended its operations in the region instead of meeting the demand.
- Influence government decisions, legislation, or elections: There is little doubt that the bombing of the Marine barracks in Beirut influenced our government's decision to eventually withdraw the Marines, just as the deaths and capture of soldiers in Somalia influenced our decisions there in 1993. In Colombia, the FARC repeatedly assassinates public officials in successful attempts

to influence law enforcement and judicial processes regarding terrorism. President Jose Napoleon Duarte of El Salvador had a hardline approach to dealing with terrorists; he refused to negotiate with them. After his daughter and her friend were kidnapped by FMLN (Farabundo Marti National Liberation Front) operatives in September of 1985 his stance changed. He angered the military by sending his family to the United States for safety and negotiated for the release of his daughter Ines Duarte and her friend Ana Cecillia Villeda. He also negotiated the release of 25 mayors and government officials in exchange for 101 war wounded guerrillas. He was seen as powerless after this and lost much of the backing of the military and security forces, his government became unstable and was seen as ineffective, losing in the next election.

- They want to free *prisoners and group members* who have been captured: This is a frequent demand made by terrorists, especially if there is a negotiable item involved such as hostages.
- They want *to satisfy their need for vengeance* against the government or individuals: Terrorist groups reserve the most brutal acts of terrorism for informants or other traitors to the cause. The Irish Republican Army (IRA) has been brutal in carrying out acts of vengeance against what it deems to be internal security threats. "Kneecapping" is a favorite tool used by IRA security personnel. The victim is shot in either one or both knees and left as a permanent example and a reminder to other potential informants about what will happen. There have also been executions that have taken place in Iraq and Afghanistan, among other occupied and previously occupied regions because they worked with or gave information to those they consider foreign invaders. Vengeance can also be international in nature; the Madrid train bombing was carried out by an Islamic terrorist group for Spain's participation in Iraq. There were also the London bombings when a series of coordinated attacks struck London's public transportation system. The attack was carried out by an al-Qaeda cell. There are also past examples such asthe December 1985 massacres at airports in Rome and Vienna were carried out by Abu Nidal terrorists to avenge the October bombing of the Palestine Liberation Organization (PLO) headquarters in Tunis by the Israelis.
- They also want to *turn the tide in a guerrilla war/insurgency*: Terrorism and terrorist tactics are an integral part of all insurgencies. They are used in rural areas to punish government supporters, government workers, political leaders, security forces, etc., while in urban centers, they can be used, in addition to the

goals previously mentioned, to bring government security forces or military troops from the countryside where they are needed to fight insurgent movements. When the government starts winning in the rural areas, the terrorists start attacking the urban areas to force the government to pull the troops back to protect these urban centers with its denser population and facilities.

As terrorist groups are trying to achieve the immediate goals of their long-term plans, they have certain defining characteristics that are common to all terrorist organizations.

- *Promote fear*: They seek to intimidate populations, the only way they can by promoting and spreading fear. This tactic is used on a daily basis in Iraq, where murders and executions take place despite the efforts of the government. It is also used in the Philippines where assassination and kidnapping are used by New People's Army. It is also used to intimidate tourists and other potential visitors such as when it was used in Egypt, November 17, 1997, when six terrorists attacked tourists visiting the Hatshepsut Temple in Luxor, Egypt. By killing 58 foreign tourists, 3 police officers, and 1 tour guide, they were able to attack the economy of Egypt by negatively impacting tourism.
- *Militarily weaker*: Terrorist groups will always be militarily weaker than the government they fight against and even though some groups have achieved a high level of sophistication, training, and experience, and are heavily armed, they still remain weaker than the governments they fight; after all, if they were as strong or stronger than the government, they could overthrow it militarily. This means that they have to resort to hit-and-run guerrilla tactics and will do everything possible to avoid taking up a static defensive posture against the stronger enemy, unless they possess a "bargaining chip" such as a group of hostages.
- A terrorist group *does not compare tactical success to mission success*: They will have different levels of success because even though the act may fail to achieve its desired result or the group may suffer significant losses, it would still be considered a success if it achieves good publicity for their cause. A good historical example of this is the M-19 raid on the Palace of Justice in Bogotá, Colombia, in 1985; they lost 35 operatives which hurt the organization since it was a loss of a large number of trained "hard-core" personnel. However, they destroyed court documents and they killed several high-level court officials. They also received a lot of propaganda and publicity generated through the media that helped the group's tactical and strategic objectives.

- Terrorist organizations are *usually urban-based*: They do this because the urban environment offers access to multiple types of transportation, banks, hospitals, money-laundering mechanisms, communications systems, and international contacts. It gives them a great chance to blend in and hide while conducting their daily business, especially in high-density urban areas. Even rural-based insurgent movements will have terrorist cells based in urban centers so that they still have access to the support systems in an urban environment and can provide special support to the movement.
- They are *highly mobile*: With being urban-based, terrorist organizations have access to the multiple transportation systems and the international contacts they need which allows them to obtain the documents needed to travel frequently to other cities and countries for operations or in search of safe havens and to gather more support for their cause.
- They usually *operate covertly*: Most large terrorist organizations have overt politically oriented contingents which act as their public face; the active military-oriented operational cells that carry out terrorist acts maintain strict security and operate in a covert posture for extended periods to avoid compromise or capture. The clandestine nature of terrorist groups helps contribute to their flexibility and effectiveness, but it can also be a problem for them. These groups have to maintain and support an intricate operational system complete with personnel and assets. This is accomplished in the underground of normal society hidden from public view and from the security forces that are actively and constantly seeking them and their networks.
- Terrorists as well as criminal organizations are masters of using social media, the Internet, and other forms of information sharing to spread the message of their organization—as well as using it to promote themselves, obtain financing, and spread misinformation against their targets. They exploit this media for their own gain but can also use it to gather information on those entities and persons they intend to target.

THE TYPICAL INTERNAL ORGANIZATION OF TERRORIST GROUPS

Because of the clandestine way that terrorist groups must operate, there is not a great deal that is known about their internal organization, except what has been gleamed for captured documents, interrogations, etc. What we do know is that many groups today have copied the cellular structure of the Tupamaro organization that was active in Uruguay in the early 1970s, so we have enough information that we can make an educated guess that the basic operational unit of a group is the cell. For the typical terrorist organization, there are normally three types of cells found in a well-organized terrorist group:

- *Operational cell*: This is the cell that conducts all operational activities for the group; it is the action arm, so located in this cell are the people who conduct the raids, kidnappings, and assassinations and plant the bombs. In the more sophisticated or experienced groups, the operational cell will become specialized toward one specific type of attack; you will have a cell that consists of nothing but the bombers, another for assassins, and one for kidnappings, etc. In the newer, less experienced groups, the operational cell may have to conduct all of the terrorist acts and may also have to provide intelligence and support functions.
- *Intelligence cell*: This is the cell that acts as the eyes and ears of the group. It will perform all of the reconnaissance and surveillance on potential targets, which will be used by the leaders in their operational planning. Since these operators are constantly out in the public, they are highly compartmentalized and follow strict security measures. The personnel in this cell are very valuable to the organization because of (a) the amount of training and experience they have or (b) because of where they work or (c) the areas they have access to, so the group tries to minimize their exposure to compromise. The group will not allow members of this cell to participate in the actual acts they are collecting intelligence for; these personnel are protected by the group because it takes a long time to train and place personnel into positions where they can produce information beneficial to the cause.
- *Auxiliary cell*: This is the cell that performs logistical/supply functions for the organization. It is usually made up of professional people, such as doctors, lawyers, food service, or commerce people such as people who own hardware stores or car dealerships; these people are dedicated to the ideals of the movement and believe in its ultimate goal, but not to the extent that they will sacrifice their professional status, besides they may be more useful to the movement in their current status than if they were a gunman. Other professions that are in this cell include doctors and dentists who provide medical support and money to the group, bankers provide money-laundering or transfer services, and grocers provide the group with food. Non-professional

support personnel provide services such as screening new recruits, collecting funds, distributing propaganda, and establishing safe houses. These auxiliary cells are normally larger and less compartmentalized than the other cells, and in some cases, may consist entirely of terrorist sympathizers rather than active cadres.

The size of the different cells varies depending on different factors but a working figure of three to five people per cell is generally used. The total number of cells and the overall structure of their organization will depend on several factors.

- The *actual function* of a cell is one of the determining factors in its size. A cell that has been specifically organized to make improvised explosive devices may consist of not more than one or two people with special training, but generally, they will not plant the devices they make or pick the targets. Nor will they participate in any other function of the organization. They will be compartmentalized and protected due to their skill set. On the other hand, you can have a cell that is set up to conduct kidnappings; this type of operation requires a large number of personnel because of the transportation, holding, and security requirements inherent in that type of operation. In some instances, you will have several cells acting in conjunction with one another in support of the same operation, sometimes without knowledge of any other element; this is done when diversions are needed for something like a kidnapping or when hitting multiple targets.
- The *security measures* used by the government, law enforcement, and military in a group's operational area are also a determining factor of the size of a cell. From the terrorist point of view, it is much more difficult to track down, capture, and break a small cell of two to five people with a decentralized command-and-control mechanism than it is to find and break up a group with a large and often cumbersome centralized group. Basically, the smaller the cell, and the more compartmentalized, the safer they are from being discovered.
- The *sophistication and experience* of a group are another factor that determines its size. If the group is sophisticated and has years of experience, this means it probably has a working clandestine communications network in place, so it does not have to rely on face-to-face meetings to pass on communications for any messages, planning, or coordination. This allows the group to take advantage of the decentralized control aspect of its organization and organize its cells into very small, yet efficient, units. But, a young inexperienced organization that does not have a dependable clandestine communications system in place has to

> rely on face-to-face meetings for almost all aspects of operational planning and coordination; this increases their security risk and chances of compromise and discovery. So, the only logical structure for a group like this is to organize into a few cells of larger size. This then reduces the number of times that operational or planning information must be transmitted and minimizes the chance of exposure to security forces and lessens their chance of compromise. And as this younger organization gets older and more experienced, its communications systems will develop, and the cells decrease in size accordingly.

As I have discussed before, the most basic unit of a terrorist group is the cell, which lies at the bottom of that group's organizational structure. For security purposes, the entire organization is protected from compromise by a secure and clandestine communications system that depends on cutouts and other secret techniques to transmit information to each level of the group, and this communication works both ways from higher headquarters down and from the cells up. The cells are set up so that a cell member knows and meets only the people in his cell, those he has direct contact with. The leader of each cell knows only one person outside his cell and that is usually the person who recruited him into the organization, but the cell leader will never see his recruiter again; after recruitment and training, the cell leader will receive all future communications in coded message format from dead drop locations, newspaper advertisements, or phone calls. By communicating this way, if the security forces do manage to capture a member or an entire cell, the damage to the group as a whole is limited because they only know the people in their cell and no one else; so this ignorance about the rest of the organization is a layer of security for the organization as a whole; after all, they cannot divulge what they do not know even under the most rigorous interrogations.

A well-organized group may also have a national command element that is responsible for the organization's ideological and political direction, as well as operational planning at the strategic level as well as the organization's long-term goals. This type of group will be further divided into subcommands usually responsible for geographic regions in which commanders direct and coordinate the actions of a group of cells in their designated area of operations.

TRAINING PROGRAMS USED BY TERRORIST GROUPS

Terrorists, like any group, have special purposes and needs to have training programs. Since these groups are paramilitary in nature, these training programs are oriented to the missions, the physical characteristics of the area of operations, such as urban, rural, mountains, jungle, etc., and the security measures being used in the operational environment in the area of interest. Much of this type of training will be somewhat standardized; after all, there are some things such as communications and first aid that everyone needs to know. Discipline is strictly enforced during the training, and the trainees are closely monitored for any signs of weakness in their abilities or in their ideological commitment to the cause.

The *internal training* done by the group is conducted at the cell level by members of the group who have expertise in the area being taught; the training takes place in the country of operation and always in a clandestine fashion. It is exactly like what is called hip-pocket or squad-level training in the U.S. Military, where one person possesses a particular expertise (e.g., communications, marksmanship, and employment of the RPG-7 antitank rocket) and trains the remainder of his unit locally. If the group has secure areas available to them, then they may build permanent facilities in which to conduct training. But if they do not have a secure environment available within their operational area, all of the training will be conducted in safe houses in a clandestine manner.

For *external training*, this would be conducted by non-local group members who come from outside the operational area and it can take one of two forms. In the first type, the operatives selected for training will travel to another area, even to another country. They will travel individually or as a group, to terrorist training camps or to other permanent institutions for their training. Once they have completed their new training, they will go back to their home territory and operation cell to put into use for the movement. In the second type of external training, an operational cell from the terrorist group will travel as a unit, to the external training area which is located in another country. Usually, this training will be designed for a specific operation, for example, an airport attack; there the training will be conducted on mock-ups of the actual attack site. Once their training is complete, they will move the training location and deploy directly to the operational area to conduct the terrorist act they have been trained for.

There are countries that provide this training to terrorists from around the world, most of which are on the U.S. State Department's list of state-supporters of terrorism. This includes Iran, Cuba, North Korea, and Syria. The former Soviet Union had established two locations where terrorists from around the world could be brought and trained in the art of terrorism; these were the Patrice Lumumba Friendship University in Moscow and the Lenin Institute in Leningrad. Both of these schools have served in the past as a "graduate" educational institutions for many international terrorists such as Ilich Ramirez Sanchez (Carlos the Jackal).

For the common areas of training discussed earlier, a typical individual terrorist training program can last up to a year in some of the different training camps or training cycles; the leadership training for those selected to oversee the movement can take several more years. The type of training involved includes the following:

- *Individual physical and mental conditioning.* They need this training to ensure that the individual terrorist will be able to withstand the rigors of the anticipated activities that they will be engaged in, as well as to help them complete those missions. It also puts the individual terrorist in the proper mindset when they are placed in stressful situations and helps them resist interrogations in the event of capture.
- *Weapons and explosives training.* This type of training is a basic factor for all individual terrorists since they need to know how to employ a variety of weapons in a split second. The employment of conventional and improvised explosives is also taught. This allows them to commit bombings by either recovering explosives from cache sites or purchasing them from commercial establishments, stealing them, or from battlefield recovery—thereby allowing them to make their own explosive devices.
- *Political/religious indoctrination* is continued in their training. This is intended to plant or reinforce the ideals of the group within the individual member and make them true believers. Also, basic seminars on ideology and advanced theoretical classes for the intended leadership can be expected, since it will be their responsibility to reinforce the beliefs of the group to the individual on a regular basis. The ideological instruction will include many different books depending on the ideological beliefs of the movement. These books can include The Communist Manifesto, Das Kapital, and writings of revolutionary leaders like Mao Tse-tung, Che Guevara, Carlos Marighella, and Fidel Castro, among others.
- *General tactics and combat techniques*: Each individual of a group will need this type of training which is taken from military manuals such as the *Minimanual of the Urban Guerrilla* by Brazilian terrorist Carlos Marighella, in the hopes of enhancing the effectiveness of the individual member which will increase the effectiveness of the group. Any terrorist organization that is planning to conduct an operation such as a hostage barricade will certainly want to know how to employ their personnel and weapons effectively, what techniques the authorities may use against them, and how they can best counteract those techniques. It is not a secret that terrorists and other criminals are known to capitalize on the openness of our society and our willingness to publish anything, including potentially damaging materials

such as the *Anarchist's Cook Book*, *Poor Man's James Bond*, and military manuals which include versions of the *Special Forces* and *Ranger* operational manuals. If they are so easily available, then anyone can order these books through open sources or purchase them from a book store, gun show, or even download them from online sources, We have to assume that terrorists have also acquired them, studied them, and are actively using tactics outlined in them.

- *Tradecraft* is basically training the terrorist to do those things we normally associate with intelligence agents and agencies. It teaches the terrorist to do things like emplacing or recovering caches for use in operations or opening someone's mail, then photographing or copying the contents, and resealing the envelope without the victim knowing it. It also teaches how to gain surreptitious entry into a victim's home, office, or vehicle, things such as wiretapping, the use of scanners to intercept cell phones, hacking computers, surveillance, and surveillance detection may also be learned to enhance the individual's operational capability.
- *Psychological warfare* is taught to enable the terrorist to select his desired target and ensure the message of the attack reaches the right audience. For example, the terrorist may select a specific target to send a message to—a very specific audience or segment of the population. This training will allow him to plan his operation and instill fear in that specific group while eliciting sympathy for his cause from the general population.
- *Survival* is another subject taught, but this does not always entail what many associate with survival training, such as the hardships in deep jungles or searing deserts. It also pertains to operations within towns, villages, or major urban areas within the targeted country. A terrorist will have to know how to blend in with the local populace, speak the language, know how to use public transportation, phone, taxi, banking, and medical aid, and not stand out while he is there risking the chance of compromising the operation. Many terrorist groups will have points of contact set up with sympathizers and safe havens already established in the targeted country. They may even have people who will act as mentors when the terrorist first arrives to teach him how to blend in.
- *Communications* is taught so the terrorist operator can transmit documentation, intelligence, orders, money, and supplies; communications is the cornerstone of any good operation. The terrorists must know how to use various methods of communications, from the basic telephone, Internet, encryption, dead drops, and other means of clandestine communications, including satellite

phones and ham radio. They also need to know how to communicate without being traced, so they communicate with authorities and the media about terrorist incidents.

- It should be noted that, increasingly, people who turn to crime or join terrorist organizations have a military or law enforcement background and bring with them knowledge and skills that can be utilized by terrorist or criminal organizations. In line with this, some terrorists have received training in weapons, explosives, and military tactics from the U.S. Military, when it trains members of host nation military or law enforcement organizations, such as the military training given to those Iraqis or Afghans who wanted to join their nation's military. This training is invaluable to terrorist organizations and gives their members, who have received it, experience in dealing with foreign nationals on a daily basis.

CHAPTER 2

Terrorist Operations

> America has a message for the nations of the world: If you harbor terrorists, you are a terrorist; if you train or arm a terrorist, you are a terrorist; if you feed a terrorist or fund a terrorist, you're a terrorist, and you will be held accountable by the United States and our friends.
>
> —*President Bush, Ft. Campbell, November 2001*

From our brief overview of the history of terrorism, we know that terrorist acts have included assassinations, executions, maiming, hostage takings, and other atrocities designed to force others to some objective that meets the political, religious, and ideological or personnel goals of the terrorist. The terrorist acts committed today are every bit as violent as those of the past; some are even more so because of the use of area weapons that kill more than one person. They have also become more sophisticated because of the advanced technology available to modern terrorists. Groups around the world have pioneered new techniques of assault, use of improvised explosive devices (IEDs), using the Internet, social media, and the taking and holding of captives, when these techniques prove successful, then other groups around the world will imitate them, and in some cases, receive training from the very group that developed that technique to further enhance their own groups' capabilities. The knowledge and understanding of how a terrorist picks his target and what goes into the planning and conduct of a terrorist operation are vital if we are to defend ourselves against terrorist attacks in the future. Knowing your enemy and how he operates has always been the key to limiting his ability to conduct operations and eventually defeating him.

CHARACTERISTICS OF TERRORIST OPERATIONS

Operations conducted by terrorists have to have certain elements in them to be effective and to meet the needs of that individual terrorist or group. Terrorist operations have to be dynamic to grab the public's attention.

DOI: 10.4324/9781003292647-2

Their operations will be relatively simple so they can limit their chance of being discovered. Their operations are also offensive in nature, usually hit-and-run type attacks, and they are designed for their impact not just on the immediate victims but on society as a whole. Let's discuss each one of these more in depth to give us a better understanding.

Dynamic

Terrorist operations need to be dynamic to gain attention; the more dynamic they are the better chance they become instantaneous media events and are broadcast around the world not only on the news but also on social media so they can have a more immediate impact. The following are examples of how dynamic they can be.

Simple

Terrorist operations are simple because they need to be relatively easy to command, control, and support. After all, it is easy to see the problems a terrorist group would encounter in attempting the command, control, and support operations of a large number of military or paramilitary forces in the conduct of any type of operation. So, the terrorists always try to keep their operations relatively simple and limit their numbers to a small group of well-trained and dedicated individuals. These considerations serve to enhance the planning for each operation as well as the actual conduct of the mission planned.

Offensive

Terrorist operations are always offensive by design, using hit-and-run type attacks. They will always try to avoid any type of static or operation that would put them into a defensive posture because they do not have the manpower, weapons, training, or logistical support to stand and fight in a prolonged manner with either law enforcement or military personnel. Even when they are in a hostage barricade or kidnapping scenario, the terrorists are still in an offensive posture. During hostage situations, they have something to bargain with—affording them with at least a chance of receiving safe passage. This hit-and-run principle often makes the terrorist seem invincible, allows them to maintain pressure on their opponents at reduced risk, and creates the impression that the group is larger and more efficient than it really is.

Designed for Their Impact

Terrorist operations have had a major impact on all our lives, even if you have never been an immediate victim of one of their operations. Our tax dollars will be used to finance the U.S. Department of State to harden existing U.S. embassies and military installations. Additionally, 175 existing embassies will undergo renovation, our tax dollars also go to support the airline industry and the upgraded security measures that are needed there, and for military operations taking place around the world against terrorists, increased border patrol operations, and internal surveillance and monitoring. But it's not just money, the heightened state of security and new procedures we must all now deal with in our daily lives, such as the increased scrutiny when entering government buildings, searches, and items that you cannot carry on at the airport, random bag searches and being questioned when riding the metro, new rules when mailing a package; all of these increased measures impact our lives in some way.

Examples of terrorist attacks against Americans

- On October 23, 1983, Beirut, Lebanon, a vehicle loaded with the equivalent of six tons of trinitrotoluene (TNT) crashed through the barricaded gate of the U.S. compound at the Beirut Airport, drove through the front entrance to the Marine Battalion Landing Team headquarters building, and exploded. Almost immediately, media assets from around the world began to relay the incident to their audiences. The impact back home in the United States of this bombing and the loss of 244 American lives closed the political debate in the United States regarding the involvement of the U.S. military in Lebanon. The U.S. military was withdrawn, and U.S. power and prestige in the Middle East suffered a major setback at the hands of a small group of fanatics.
- On Tuesday, June 25, 1996, at 21:49 local time, a fuel truck drove down the street and parked next to the northern perimeter fence at the Khobar Towers, Dhahran, Saudi Arabia. This facility housed U.S. and allied forces supporting the coalition air operation over Iraq, called Operation southern Watch. The Air Force Security Police conducting a check of the closest building, building 131, spotted the truck and suspected a bomb as they observed its drivers fleeing the scene in a nearby car at a high rate of speed. They immediately began alerting building occupants by running down the hallways and knocking on doors. Although alerted by the sentries, the Security Police Command Center had

not contacted the Wing Operations Center to activate the warning system by the time the bomb exploded at 9:55 PM. At the time of the detonation only the top three floors had been evacuated, resulting in nineteen U.S. Air Force fatalities and approximately 500 personnel wounded from the attack.

- On February 26, 1993, a bomb in a yellow van in the parking garage of the World Trade Center in Manhattan, New York, exploded killing six people and injuring more than 1,000 others in, at the time, the worst terrorist incident in U.S. history. The Materials and Devices Unit conducted hundreds of examinations and numerous crime scene searches. It was determined that an approximately 1,200-pound urea nitrate bomb was detonated at the 110-story twin towers of the World Trade Center. Over 100 latent prints, including prints developed on bomb-making manuals seized from convicted World Trade Center bombing suspect, Ahmed Ajaj, were identified as the fingerprints and palm prints of Ramzi Ahmed Yousef. Eyad Ismoil's fingerprints were also found on a telephone directory and a manual for surveillance equipment found at the site where the bomb was constructed. The damage caused by this blast was severe: six civilians killed, over 1,000 injured, 105 firefighters injured; five admitted to hospitals, steel-reinforced floors almost 30 inches thick blasted away on three levels below grade, plus a concourse level floor, leaving a crater about 150 feet in diameter at its largest point. On the B1 level, the operations control center of the Port Authority Police Department (and the fire command station for the complex) was heavily damaged and rendered out of service. On the B2 level, various walls of elevator shafts and fresh air plenums were severely damaged, allowing smoke to enter and rise through the cores of both towers. Numerous concrete walls were destroyed or damaged, and 200,000 cubic feet of water poured into the lowest grade from damaged refrigeration unit supplies (from the Hudson River), sewer lines, fresh domestic water lines, steam pipes, and condensate return. Water was 1.5 feet deep across the B6 level, 124 parked cars were destroyed and 102 damaged. Partition walls were blown out onto the PATH train mezzanine, numerous telephone conduits collapsed from the ceiling onto cars (but phone service was not cut, miraculously). Fire alarms, public address systems, and elevators were out of service, and water-cooled emergency generators were shut down due to overheating when their water supply was cut. This disabled the emergency lighting, sprinklers, and standpipes out of service; 2,500 tons of rubble were removed; the cleanup effort involved 2,700 workers per day, plus a total of 160,000 gallons of cleaning fluid and 200,00 gallons of detergent; restoration cost was $250,000,000, and tenants began moving back into tower 2 on March 18, 1993, and into tower 1 on March 29, 1993.

- On September 11, 2001, five terrorists hijack American Airlines Flight 11, which departed Boston for Los Angeles at 7:45 AM. One hour later, it was flown into the north tower of the World Trade Center in New York City. Five terrorists hijack United Airlines Flight 175, which departed Boston for Los Angeles at 07:58 AM; at 9:05 AM, it was flown into the south tower of the World Trade Center; both towers collapsed, killing approximately 3,000 people, including hundreds of firefighters and rescue personnel who were helping to evacuate the buildings. Shanksville, Pennsylvania—terrorists hijacked United Airlines Flight 93 from Newark international airport to San Francisco International Airport. While the hijackers were heading the plane in the direction of Washington DC, the hijacked plane crashed into the Pennsylvania countryside, killing 44 passengers and crew. Washington DC—hijackers took control of American Airlines Flight 77 from Dulles International Airport to Los Angeles international airport. The hijackers flew the plane into the west side of the Pentagon, destroying the left side of the building, 64 passengers and crew, and 125 military and civilian personnel, were killed with another 80 injured.
- August 03, 2019, Patrick Crusius opened fire in the Walmart located in El Paso, Texas. He killed 22 individuals and wounded 26 more.
- April 15, 2013, two homemade IEDs detonated near the finish line of the Boston Marathon. Three people were killed and 264 wounded. The people responsible learned how to make these IEDs by reading an online al-Qaeda magazine.
- November 05, 2009, Fort Hood, Texas, a U.S. Soldier entered his workplace on the military installation with a pistol and started shooting; he killed 13 and wounded 30 others.
- November 01, 2013, Los Angeles International Airport. Paul Ciancia approached a checkpoint at the airport and fired a rifle, killing one Transportation Security Administration (TSA) officer and wounding six others.
- December 2015. A cyberattack was conducted against SONY pictures. Embarrassing private emails were published.
- June 12, 2016, Orlando, Florida, Omar Mateen opened fire at the Pulse night club, killing 49 people and wounding 53 others.
- June 14, 2017, Alexandria, Virginia, James Hodgkinson opened fire at a congressional charity baseball game; he injured six people.

- December 06, 2019, Pensacola, Florida, Naval Air Station Pensacola. A Saudi aviation student opened fire, killing three U.S. Navy Sailors and wounding eight others.

Other Characteristics of Terrorist Operations

Terrorist operations are very *meticulously planned* down to the smallest detail. They do this to ensure the success of each operation, because they cannot afford to fail. Their operational planning is supported by information and intelligence gathered during surveillance and through the use of other information-gathering techniques such as the Internet and social media platforms. To ensure the plan is sound, terrorists will rehearse a planned operation under conditions as close to the operational environment as possible. They may use sand tables or simple drawings during these rehearsals to reinforce the plan; sometimes, they will go so far as to construct scale models of the target and attack site. If the local security environment permits, they may conduct the rehearsals at the actual attack site. The terrorists will go to great lengths to plan their operations and conduct rehearsals because they cannot afford to fail, because when they do, they will lose credibility—since the failure will be played up in the media by those they attacked. This will cause doubt among its membership, supporters, and the populace which would lead to a decrease in the support a terrorist organization needs to survive.

Operations by terrorists are *conducted by the smallest element* possible to increase security and lessen the chance of compromise; these specially trained elements are tasks organized for operations designed specifically to allow their training and other abilities and knowledge to be used in the most efficient way. Usually, there are at least three elements involved in the execution of any terrorist act: the command element is the element that is in charge, plans the operation, and decides when to conduct it; the action element, which carries out the actual act itself; and the security element, which is responsible for the security of the entire operation from beginning to end. By using these three basic elements, the terrorist organization is keeping within the principles of simplicity, strict security measures, along with the principle of conducting offensive operations using hit-and-run-like tactics.

Terrorists and their organizations *must employ strict security measures at all times*, especially during the planning and preparation for an operation; after all, they are criminals who have to always be on the lookout for law enforcement and military. To ensure this high degree of security, terrorists use the principles of compartmentalization, which is to say each element is separated during the planning and rehearsal stage to prevent information leaks and penetration by the opposition. This also prevents compromise of the organization and its people if one person gets caught: if you only know your one job and don't know the whole plan or the other personnel you can't give any information to the police. This also extends to the use of social media or secure messaging applications used today, to ensure that information passed is not compromised.

Multiple targets are always considered when planning an operation; usually, the primary target is not selected until the last possible moment, to prevent someone from betraying the act and if they are under observation to throw off those law enforcement personnel until the last possible minute. Sometimes, they may, in fact, hit multiple targets simultaneously without individual teams knowing about the other operations. When attacks are done in this manner, it is so that one attack group will be acting as a diversion for the main target, by pulling security forces away, tying up emergency communications, and forcing friendly forces to react to this diversion. The planners thereby increase the possibility of having a successful operation against their primary objective.

Surveillance and intelligence trained personnel will not normally take part in the physical attack for the following reasons: first, the intelligence-gathering personnel spend a great deal of time in and around the victim, at his work or other primary area or the attack site. It may have taken months of planning just to get this person in place to get the intelligence needed by the threat, and they do not want to compromise him or her as an asset. In most cases, a planned terrorist attack is preceded by about 30 days of surveillance. If those people brought in to conduct this surveillance were to participate in the actual attack, chances are great that someone would recognize them and furnish a good description to the authorities, or they would be in some of the security videos around that area or have had a parking ticket or had their picture taken. While a lot of information can be gained from the Internet nowadays, on the ground, intelligence is the best way to verify and ensure information is accurate. Second, it takes time and money to train intelligence personnel more so than other operatives. It may also take time and money to place them in positions where they can do the best so the leaders do not want to take the chance that the intelligence personnel might be killed or captured during the operation or compromised in some other way. In some cases, they may be recalled sometime prior to the operational elements' arrival, once the threat has established the pattern of the target and know his routine (and is, thus, predictable). This lessens the possibility of the surveillance personnel being spotted at the last minute by the target's security elements and of the authorities being alerted. This would cause an upgrade in the security of the target or target area and the compromise of surveillance personnel.

Probably, the most important characteristic of any terrorist group's operation is that its *targets will be undefended, unaware, and have the weakest security profile*. Terrorists usually go for the easy, soft target; this increases their chance of success while minimizing the threat to their personnel and the organization. So as long as the target that is picked will provide the desired results, it is a success.

Phases of a Terrorist Operation

There are four basic phases of every planned terrorist operation; if there is a negotiable item that becomes involved in the operations such as a hostage, a fifth phase is added so that negotiations take place so they can exploit their negotiable item.

The *first phase* is called *the pre-incident phase*: What takes place during this phase of the planning is that the terrorist leadership will decide on what type of operation will be conducted and what their goals are in terms of what they want to gain from the operation. This is also when they will determine the type of attack they want to use. The attack and tactics used will play to that terrorist organization's strengths, experience, expertise, and what they have done in the past with success. A lot will also depend on the type of security and law enforcement they have to work around, their funding, logistics, and local support. Their target could be purely symbolic, such as a statue or monument, or a more practical target to intimidate or cause fear such as police officers, military, government leaders, or the judiciary. The operation plan is based on all information gathered by any means such as open-source documents, Internet personal social media accounts, and intelligence gathered by extensive surveillance of the proposed targets. This is the phase in which the terrorist will have total control of their operational environment and are the most secure and confident in their abilities to function. But because this is the decision phase and target selection phase, it is also the best time for a potential target to prevent any incident from happening. This is done by practicing effective individual protective measures, including surveillance detection techniques; surveillance is the first visible hand of a threat. By spotting the surveillance and practicing good visible security measures, you will give the perception of being that hard target and an aware person who has a strong security sense and this can cause them to pass you over for a softer less aware target. This does not always work, as it depends on the value of the person or facility being targeted. The group could feel that any risk is acceptable and go ahead with plans of striking that particular target for its symbolic value, the prestige they might obtain from a successful operation, to prove a point, or for revenge. Just because you are aware and have a strong security presence doesn't mean you can let your guard down. During this phase, all required elements for the operation have been completed and planned with extensive rehearsals, and dry runs taking place. Only when they have eliminated all the "what ifs," possible actions during the attacks, and looked for flaws in the execution and planning will they move to the next operational phase.

The *second phase, the initiation phase*, marks the movement to begin the planned operation. This is usually the point-of-no-return since they have to commit personnel and assets and expose themselves by moving these items into place for the attack. From here, the attack is going forward unless a preplanned mission-abort clause has been placed into the operations plan in case it is compromised prior to the mission taking place. For the terrorist, this is the most dangerous phase of their operations cycle; until now, they have been in complete control of their operational environment by staying in areas they control and remaining in the background and out of view of local security forces and law enforcement. Once the physical movement begins, they no longer have the complete control they are used too. Now, they are moving in an environment where they have no control, probably carrying illegal items such as weapons or explosives and are exposed to local security, law enforcement, and possible compromise by any local who turns them in for being suspicious. Regardless of what happens prior to the attack, once the attack begins, they will do everything they can to accomplish their predetermined goals for that operation; for contingencies, they will have several alternate plans of action preplanned in case something goes wrong at the attack site such as a kidnapping attempt. If this fails, then they will implement their contingency plan, which could be an assassination. So, now, they can still claim a successfully planned and executed operation by saying they assassinated their target instead of saying they failed at a kidnapping.

The third phase of a terrorist operation is *the climax phase*, this phase has no set time schedule for it to end and can come about in several ways. It may immediately follow the initiation phase of the operation such as in the case of an assassination, bombing, or an overrun attack on the target. If the terrorists happen to obtain a negotiable item during the operation, then the climax phase may last from several hours to several days, weeks, or months as in the case of hostages and negotiating their release through various intermediaries. In a case like that, then the climax phase actually includes the negotiation phase. The terrorist security will peak during the climax phase, and they will begin closely monitoring the law enforcement radio frequencies, social media, and civilian media/news and may even put surveillance at the site to observe what is taking place outside and passing that information to those carrying out the operation; this phase, the climax phase, is also the signal for the end of the incident. *EXAMPLE: During the Iranian Embassy take over in London, England (May 5, 1980), the terrorists inside learned of the coming assault by the Special Air Service commandos and the means of entry they would be using, because live television coverage of the incident was shown on three of the four British stations in the capital city area.*

The *last phase* is *the post-incident phase*. This phase is extremely important for the terrorist and their organization, as it is during this phase that the terrorists will regroup all the operational elements that conducted the planned incident and discuss the operation from start to finish to determine what went well, what could have been done better or differently, or what went wrong with the operation. They will take lessons and learn from them; they will share these lessons learned throughout their organization. Also, these lessons learned are often shared with other terrorist groups so that they can learn from them and improve their operational skills and learn new tactics and techniques. If there is no negotiation phase, then the terrorist will begin to exploit their act in the media during this phase, using the media by giving statements, videotapes, etc. They will also flood social media with their statements and videos, etc.

The last possible phase happens when, in an operation, the terrorists have taken a negotiable item such as a hostage and item of value. An extra phase, *the negotiation phase*, begins. This phase is characterized by terrorist demands, deadlines, talks, trade-offs, etc., such as during a hijacking or during the takeover of a residence or facility. The terrorists will want to prolong this phase as long as possible so they get the maximum amount of news coverage and publicity for their cause. It is more than likely that during this phase they will maintain some type of communication with their headquarters or command element to help provide them with guidance as well as additional information about the overall situation, and what is taking place on the outside, such as views of the local populace and actions by law enforcement, security teams, and the international community. The terrorists will probably make numerous demands for things to advance their agendas and organizational goals. The one demand that will always be present is the request for transportation to a safe haven or location such as a country that is sympathetic to their cause.

Common Terrorist Acts

The most common terrorist acts used are bombings, arson, armed assaults, assassinations, maiming, sabotage, threats/hoaxes, hijacking, skyjackings, kidnappings, and hostage barricades situations, with bombings being the most prevalent way to accomplish a terrorist's agenda: this will probably remain so for the foreseeable future. While hostage-taking incidents can grab media attention for a longer time, taking any hostage demands a much higher degree of expertise, training, planning, and preparation, and it is usually done by groups that have evolved to a higher degree of proficiency through experience or training. We will discuss all these common terrorist acts in much greater detail shortly, but first, there are a number of steps in every terrorist act that are common to all acts, and there are also some steps that serve only one purpose, so are specific to particular acts.

The common steps are as follows:

Selecting a target: Target selection is based on the terrorist group's objectives for the operation and the capabilities of the group planning the operation. They will ask themselves questions such as: Do they want to destroy a symbolic target such as a statue or monument, for media attention or do they want to pursue targets, such as policemen or government officials, to instill fear and intimidate those organizations? Can they gain access to the proposed target and/or target area and still remain uncompromised so that they can complete the mission as planned? Do they have the necessary resources and support such as documentation, weapons, transportation, and an available support network to conduct such a mission?

Conducting surveillance of the target: Surveillance of the potential targets must be conducted to gather all information and intelligence necessary to select the target with the lowest threat to the group so they will have a greater chance to successfully complete the operation. Terrorists have two things they are looking for to help their planning efforts: they want to establish your daily routine and predictability, and they are trying to determine your overall security posture and awareness.

Planning the operation: Planning of the operation will be based on the information and intelligence gathered from all sources. This will be evaluated and choices made to ensure they have a plan with the greatest chance of success, while keeping the risk to the organization as low as possible.

Conducting rehearsals and dry runs: To ensure the plan is sound and workable, terrorists will conduct rehearsals, walk-throughs, and dry runs to ensure that everyone will know what their job is, where they are supposed to be, etc. This also allows them to work out any kinks in the plan they didn't foresee and to make minor changes to ensure the operation's success. When possible, they will do walk/talk-throughs at the actual operational site to allow operators to become familiar with the environment, but this depends on the level of security and law enforcement operations directed at them and the level of security at the proposed site.

Carrying out the act: Conducting the attack on the selected target or targets as planned and rehearsed.

Escaping from the target area: This is important in the scheme of things for the terrorist to escape the target area after the attack so that they can exploit the act; this also serves to show how incompetent the government security forces and law enforcement are in allowing them to escape. By escaping, they also take away the government's ability to use the media in a positive light and talk about how they captured the attackers. When the terrorists escape, this gives those conducting the attack more confidence and experience for conducting future operations.

Exploiting the act: This is how the terrorists get their message out to the entire world about what they have done and why they have done it. They will flood social media with their successes. They release photos and videos along with statements explaining the position, ideology, etc. The media usually broadcasts everything that is sent or released to them because violence gets people to watch the news and sells newspapers. Even without media organizations, to get the incident and subsequent information out, the terrorists are now using the Internet and social media to their advantage, uploading videos of attacks, propaganda, and press releases. How they exploit the act is unlimited in today's information age.

BOMBINGS

Bombings have been a favorite weapon of terrorists since the gun powder was discovered and continues to be the weapon of choice in terrorist activities, due to the low risk to the terrorist, the fear it creates, and the increased media exposure. The terrorist can control the time of the explosion and place it where it will do the most damage to the intended target. Bombs continue to be the favored mode of terrorist tactics and attacks, and they have accounted for almost half of all recorded terrorist incidents. Using bombs is a relatively safe tactic for the terrorist, a bomb, while taking an expert or someone with training to make, requires no skills to place and arm and requires few people to do so, and it is inexpensive to make and does not take a lot of resources from the organization. A bomb can be made with crude devices and minimal detection and will still work and achieve the desired effect; after all, they gain the best media coverage, because they are so dynamic. A bombing has the primary purpose of gathering headlines; even if it kills no one, it will still make the news. It is also used to create fear in those who oppose the terrorists and their objectives and in the population in general, and of course, it is used to destroy personnel or property. Target selections for bombings may be either symbolic—to those who oppose the terrorists and the government or system they are conducting operations against—or they can be a practical target, such as government personnel, equipment, aircraft, diplomatic installations, or personnel. They can even be used against the general population in order to create fear. Using this method of attack is also an excellent way for a small, relatively weak organization or a lone-wolf or lone-attacker to attack their targets. Depending on the tactic, IED, vehicle borne improvised explosive device (VBIED), mail bomb, etc., the attacker can often bypass the security measures employed by their target. Examples of this were seen frequently in Iraq and Afghanistan: car bombs, IEDs, and VBIEDs. Such tactics are no longer limited to war zones as can be seen with the Madrid train bombing, the London Subway bombing and Oklahoma City bombing, and the Boston Marathon bombing. It can happen anytime and anywhere that a terrorist can get too.

NOTE: The major problem that bomb squads, first responders, and rescue workers face when approaching a bomb incident is whether they might also be targets of other possible secondary devices in the area waiting to be detonated. Another major problem for authorities is if a terrorist organization has conducted several successful bombing attacks against targets, they now have the option to call in a hoax bomb. Since all bomb threats are considered real, they will have to be handled as a bona fide bomb, wasting resources of the government or law enforcement to deal with it, causing stress in those people and others effected by the hoax (buildings evacuated, roads blocked), while wasting very little of their own resources and achieving almost the same results of media coverage and keeping their organization in the public spot light. While terrorists may have not taken swatting themselves, such incidents have risen dramatically based on a similar end game of using authorities to waste public funds, draw attention, and target unwitting individuals.

Steps of a Bombing

Selecting the target: The terrorists will select their targets based on their capabilities, support, and material resources.

Conducting surveillance of the target: The terrorist will have surveillance personnel in place observing their target for prolonged periods of time, and they will be placed in such a way so as to not seem out of place. The goal of the surveillance is to observe the victim or the target location to discover routines and their level of security awareness and effectiveness of security. They will also observe for items that can be brought into the targeted site or the attack site without raising the suspicion of the target security, local law enforcement, and the local populace.

Conducting rehearsals and dry runs: After getting the surveillance report on what items can be brought into the attack site without interference, they will start gathering these items such as briefcases or other containers that can be used for holding bombs and can be taken into the potential attack areas and be left in that area under the observation of the surveillance team. They will make note of the time it takes for someone to notice the object itself and how long it takes to alert the security forces, then how long it takes them to respond and what their actions are when they get to the object. This tells the terrorists approximately how long they can set the timer delay—so that the terrorist placing it can get away—how much damage they can cause, and other ways they can exploit the target and use its discovery/response tactics against them.

Gathering materials and constructing the device: Making a functioning bomb is a very specialized skill, so most terrorist groups have a specially trained bomb maker in their organization whose only responsibility is to make the bombs. This person probably received specialized demolitions training at one of the terrorist training camps in the Middle East, South America, North Korea, or received training from other groups who sent out people for the specific purpose of training other terrorists. They might have received their training when in the military or working for the government before turning to terrorism, or he may simply be a disgruntled person with knack or training in chemistry or electronics such as the Unabomber. Several terrorist groups currently post instructions for making explosive devices online for their followers, which people have used to make a functioning device such as the perpetrators of the Boston Marathon Bombing.

Planting the device: The expertise of the bomb maker is too valuable to risk losing him, either to the authorities or to an accidental detonation, so he will normally not be used to place the bomb. The devices are usually made very simple to set. Since there may be limited time to train the person placing the bomb, some devices have actually been placed by individuals who had no knowledge of the container's true content, with the device was set to go off at a predetermined time or to be command detonated from another location.

Escaping from the target: Normally, the person placing the bomb will want to get away from the attack site and, hopefully escape, notice. He does not want to make security suspicious, so that they increase the level of security and start searching for a device. He does not want to be compromised with the device or be seen placing it, then running like hell, alerting others to the device. He wants to get away, so that he can conduct more operations for the organization and exploit the act in the media to its fullest extent. I said normally at the beginning because this does not apply to suicide bombers. I will discuss them in more detail later.

Exploiting the act: Telling everyone what they did, why they did it, to get their ideology in the forefront, to get people to realize their opponents are wrong, and making sure the media gets the details out and gets it right. Now, with social media platforms and the Internet, the terrorist will video tape the incident and then release the video and photographs online themselves, sending links to the media. Many times, there will be a delay in claiming responsibility for an act; this is to determine if the general public is outraged by the attack. If the terrorist operational and/or political objectives were not achieved, they will either deny their involvement, blame the act on another group, or simply remain quiet about the incident.

Other Techniques of Bombings

Courier bombing: The Provisional Irish Republican Army (PIRA) has used a technique in the past by which the person placing the bomb has their name and address attached to the safe arming wire that must be removed to activate the bomb after it is placed. The courier has to make the decision, he has to either activate the bomb and remove the evidence of his involvement or risk arrest by authorities when the device is discovered and is deactivated with his name on it.

Proxy bombing: This is a technique called which has been used both in Ireland and in the Middle East with great effect. A terrorist group will kidnap a family member of a legitimate employee of the intended target and then the terrorists threaten to harm that hostage unless the employee, using their legitimate identification, passes through the security checkpoints, breaches the defenses, and delivers the bomb to his place of work or another facility to which his identification documents will grant him access. This tactic is designed to bypass those security measures put in place by the target, since most facilities allow unlimited, unrestricted access to its trusted employees. This exact type of "proxy" bomb was used effectively in the 1983 bombing of the French Embassy in Beirut.

Decoy/hoax bombs: These devices and tactics have been employed in the past with devastating results to first responders and rescuers. The terrorist will set off the first device after it explodes, this draws their true targets into the area that they have prepared. If it is a HOAX device, they will call it in and observe again to get their intended targets into the area that they have prepared. They will observe the area waiting for emergency services, police, and onlookers to congregate in the blast area, then they detonate a second device; in some cases, they have even used a third device. They also set off decoy bombs in order to observe how the target and local emergency services react, learning their tactics, and thus allowing the terrorists to increase the lethality of their attacks.

Suicide bombers: This phenomenon started in earnest within the last 40 years, and it has developed into a common attack used by terrorist organizations. This tactic of terrorists mounting suicide attacks has caught the governments, law enforcement, and media interest worldwide as they try to figure out how to deal with this devastating and effective form of precision bomb delivery and detonation. The problem everyone faces when dealing with this tactic is that it is difficult to combat because the people who carry out these acts are so dedicated or are filled with such despair or want revenge so badly that they are not concerned about their own survival, just accomplishing their mission. Normally, people, including terrorists who are using explosives as part of their operations, will plan a safety margin as part of the operation by planning escape routes for those placing the bombs, ensuring that their personnel are clear of the danger area and attack site, and detonate the device using remote control devices, a victim-activated device (trip wire), or a time delay mechanism. The suicide bomber, when he conducts an operation, only needs to identify his victim and get as close to their target as possible before detonating the explosive device. The people who practice this tactic of suicide bombing are typically Islamic terrorist organizations and religious extremists; in recent years, there has been an increased use of the suicide bomber tactic by politically motivated groups as well. Still, the groups that use this tactic are based in two primary locations, the Middle East and Sri Lanka, although Al-Qaida operative's throughout the world have used suicide bombings to strike targets.

A suicide bomber is basically a person who carries out an attack with an IED, with the intent to destroy or kill their intended target, while knowing they will die when they activate the device. Suicide bombings are actually divided into three basic categories: *Type I*, a bomb-actuated IED that is carried in a bag, box, or other objects. *Type II*, a bomb-actuated IED worn concealed under clothing or inside the clothing of the attacker. *Type III*, an IED concealed in a vehicle that carries the main explosive charge.

Suicide bombers can be found around the world and they are often motivated through extreme religious beliefs or nationalistic or separatist ideas. Because of the strong religious ties, the suicide bomber exhibits patterns of indoctrination, anger, and resistance to authority of their opposition. The Islamic extremist suicide bombers are usually selected at a very early age because they can be molded for this task, and it is easier to focus them along this path while their beliefs and perceptions are being formed. While other suicide bombers are selected from radical groups when displaying a willingness to learn, and a strong dedication to the cause of the group—a willingness to do anything to help promote its goals and objectives. Let's not forget also about domestic terrorism. There are many domestic groups in this country and they should not be discounted because most show a disregard for our government, our laws, and target various establishments within our society. They have the ability to get its members to do what is necessary to promote their goals and agendas.

KIDNAPPING

Kidnapping is the ultimate operation for a terrorist group and is probably the most difficult operation for any terrorist organization to successfully accomplish. This type of operation needs to have the necessary security for the kidnappers during the negotiation phase while they are conducting their operational plan and contacting the authorities to issue demands and ultimatums in an attempt to achieve their goals. A kidnapping operation that is successful can achieve many goals for the terrorists: they can get money, obtain the release of jailed comrades, and receive lots of free publicity for an extended period of time during the negotiation phase of the operation. These types of operations can also cause economic stress for the local area and the country as a whole since it can force large companies with business concerns to cut back on the number of personnel assigned—especially if they have to continue to pay for kidnapped employees or for massive security efforts to operate there. By forcing these companies to scale back their operations, the businesses will generate less revenue for that area, less payroll, and less income for the country as a whole. Using this act in an area may also be used to force a government into granting concessions to the terrorist or giving in to other demands by them that would not normally be considered, such was the case with the kidnapping of the daughter of the former El Salvadorian President, José Napoleón Durate.

There are two ways to carry out a kidnapping once a person has been selected as a target by threat actors. The terrorist can either abduct the individual from a *static location*, or they can abduct him during movement between those static locations which is called an *enroute* kidnapping. A static location is any of the target's primary areas such as the subject's residence, place of work, and any location he frequents on a regular basis, such as a restaurant, gym, country club, golf course, nightclub, or a church. When the target is enroute or traveling between these static locations, he will either be walking or using some means of transportation such as a private vehicle or public transportation. Enroute is when a person is most vulnerable.

Steps of Kidnapping an Individual from a Static Location

Penetrate the target area: A terrorist and his organization are limited only by their imaginations in using different techniques and ruses to gain access to different target locations and attack sites. This penetration of the target area may occur during the pre-incident phase of the operation to gain intelligence and familiarity or the penetration will occur during the actual attack. Terrorists have used many different types of ruses in the past such as posing as repairmen, salesmen, survey takers, policemen, mailmen, deliverymen, or something as simple as a local citizen asking for some type of information, such as a missing pet or to borrow something. If nothing they do to try to gain overt entry into the attack site works, they will use surreptitious entry techniques to allow them to accomplish their mission.

Gain control of the victim: It is vital for the terrorist to be able to physically control the victim, to limit the ability to resist and alert others to what is taking place. To achieve physical control of the victim, some violence may be necessary, do not kid yours the terrorists are quite prepared to do whatever is necessary to accomplish their mission without getting compromised or caught. In some instances, failed kidnapping attempts have turned into successful assassinations when the intended victims resisted too much or attempted to flee. Remember, the example of Ambassador John Mein that we previously discussed: the terrorist must have something to show for their effort and commitment of resources.

Removing the victim from the attack site without being compromised or detected: This is an important part of the operation, if they are detected during the movement of the victim they could be stopped, identified, and the situation would turn from a kidnapping into a hostage situation. To prevent the victim from sounding the alarm, crying out for help, or being able to move in an attempt to escape, the terrorist will bind, blindfold him, and gag him. They may even administer some type of drug to calm him down and make him easier to control for transport. There will be a need to remove the victim from the attack site without drawing suspicion or attention when dragging a body so the victim may be removed from the attack site several different ways, sometimes in an innocent-appearing container such as a large cardboard box, large rolling trash can, and steamer trunk duffle bag. Another technique that has been used is to roll the victim inside a carpet.

Transferring the victim: An important and vital part of the plan is for the terrorist to cover their tracks by changing their appearance and their vehicles, so that they cannot be tracked or identified when transferring the victim from the attack site to the holding area. In an attempt to lessen the chance of compromise, the operational plan could call for the change of custody of the victim from those who did the actual kidnapping to those who will be responsible for holding the victim. These people will then transport the victim to the holding site. This will further minimize the possibility of the holding area being compromised, since those who carried out the attack will have no knowledge of who is holding the victim or were. *EXAMPLE: In February 1988, Lebanon, U.S. Marine Corps Lieutenant Colonel Higgins who was stationed there as a member of the UN peacekeeping force was kidnapped as he was driving on a highway outside the city of Sidon, by the Hizbollah; it was reported by the U.S. Military and the Amal security forces that the attackers drove him away from the attack site in a brown Volvo, later witness's reported that the kidnappers had several other brown Volvos staged there that sped away in different directions to confuse pursuit and security workers.*

Steps to Kidnapping a Victim Enroute

Selecting the attack site along the route: The terrorists during the surveillance of possible targets will also be doing a route analysis of those targets, deciding among other things who is predictable during movement. With this information, an attack site is selected according to the security posture and routines of the selected victim. They will plan their attack around the weakest point on a predictable route, where they can channelize the victim as much as possible controlling the attack site. But, the attack site also has to meet other criteria for the terrorist for them to be successful. Is there cover and concealment for the attackers themselves? After all, they will need a way to blend in with the surrounding environment prior to the arrival of the victim and will need a believable reason to be lingering in that area to avoid raising suspicion and being compromised. Is the site conducive for the planned attack? Are there visual obstructions that could interfere with them or give the victim a place to hide, take cover, or receive help? Is the attack site well defined and does it permit the attacker to limit the target's actions and possible responses so that they can gain control of the victim with a minimum threat from security? Can the attackers quickly and easily escape the area after the attack? Is there unobstructed access to major routes of movement? Is there alternate means of transportation they can use?

Isolating the attack site: There will be a need to isolate the area of the attack to keep those not involved, that is, pedestrians, other traffic, vendors, out of the way. Some methods that have been used previously—to limit the number of extraneous people in the area—include false alarms to security forces prior to and during the attack (to tie up phone lines and send them to locations away from the attack site), fake police roadblocks, bombings, and other diversionary tactics such as auto accidents. The method they chose has to be believable by everyone so as not to arouse suspicions of either the locals, people in and around the attack site, and law enforcement and security forces. And, most importantly, the victim.

Stopping the target vehicle: Conducting an attack on a stopped vehicle is much easier than conducting one on a moving vehicle and you have a better chance of getting the selected victim out alive and unhurt, so stopping the vehicle the selected victim is in is a must. There are a number of ways to do this. Some that have been used in the past are very normal for some operational areas: military or police roadblocks, traffic accidents, hitchhikers, placing traffic signs to change the traffic pattern, ramming the target vehicle forcing it to stop, policemen pulling the victim over, and a baby carriage being pushed in front of oncoming cars causing everyone to stop and blocking the victim's vehicle in, pedestrians stepping in front of oncoming traffic to stop the flow of movement, etc. Remember, they don't have to specifically stop the victim's car if they can stop the flow of traffic the victim is traveling in. Then, he will be stopped as well, and since it was not directed specifically at the victim, he could let his guard down.

Neutralizing the security detail: The terrorists need to find a way to neutralize any security with the victim. The attackers do not want a sustained firefight that would allow law enforcement to respond before they could get away, and they want to minimize the chance of the selected victim being wounded or killed accidentally. They are always careful to direct their fire away from the victim and to concentrate on taking out the security personnel before they have a chance to fire back, hit a panic button, or call for help. They could use radio jammers or other such equipment to block any signals from going out from the victim to call for help.

Gain control of the victim: Just like anytime there is a victim the threat actors will need to gain control of them, usually because of the shock, fear, and violence of action might have them where they are very easy to control, or they could be freaking out and hard to control. Gaining control could involve physical violence, such as pistol-whipping, drugs to control the victim, or it could be as simple as pointing a gun at the victim.

Escape from the attack site: After gaining control of their victim, just like in the case of the static location, they now need to get away from the attack site with little or no interference. This clean escape is important because if they are followed or compromised, rescue forces will then try to recover the victim and none of the planned goals for this operation will have been met. Also, just as important to the group is to keep the personnel and materials used in the attack available to conduct more missions in the future; with limited resources available to the terrorist, keeping these resources free and available are of vital importance to the cause.

Transfer victim: Transferring the victim to another vehicle and/or another set of personnel after the attack is a way of compartmentalizing the operation. This way even if the personnel who conducted the enroute kidnapping are compromised and caught, they will not be able to reveal anything about who has the victim or his location.

Example of an Enroute Kidnapping

Aldo Moro was the former Italian Premier (1974–1976) as well as the leader of the Christian Democratic Party in Italy. He was trying to form a coalition government with the Italian Communist Party. Recently, he had obtained the official support for a coalition government from the Communist Party and was due in the Italian Parliament that morning to vote on it. The terrorist organization the "Red Brigades" were opposed to this idea, and had planned on kidnapping the head of the Italian Communist Party, Enrico Berlinguer. During the pre-incident phase surveillance, it was discovered that his security profile was too high to guarantee a chance of success, so they considered the secondary target, Aldo Moro, whose security profile was lower than that of the primary target and he had become very predictable in parts of his daily routine.

Moro was a religious man and had some methodical habits established; for the past 15 years, he basically used the same route from his home to his office. He did this because every morning he stopped for a few minutes at the church of San Francisco d'Assisi or at the Chapel of Santa Chiara. The morning of the attack he stopped at San Francisco d'Assisi at 8:30 AM, leaving 30 minutes later at around 9:00 AM, the motorcade left the church and continued along the route to parliament. Sometime during this movement along the route, a white Fiat 128 station wagon with diplomatic license plates moved in front of the lead vehicle in Moro's motorcade, also two other vehicles, a blue and a white Fiat sedan, moved in behind the motorcade. Around 9:05 AM, as the motorcade approached a stop sign, the station wagon stopped suddenly in front of Moro's car which had been traveling at a considerable speed and tailgating the station wagon. Moro's car struck it in the rear but Moro's second security vehicle was also tailgating so it rammed into Moro's car, which caused Moro's car to become pinned between the two vehicles.

NOTE: During the pre-incident surveillance, the terrorists had discovered that the driver of Moro's vehicle and the driver of the follow vehicle had a habit of tailgating and driving too fast, so they incorporated this into the attack plan and used that to their advantage. The terrorists had picked the attack site carefully and had also parked a car along the curb next to the planned accident site to ensure that Moro's car would be blocked from possible escape by driving on the sidewalk.

After all was said and done, the whole operation lasted around 30 seconds and involved at least 12 terrorists who fired between 80 and 90 rounds, killing the entire security element and kidnapping Moro, whose body would be found on May 8, 1978, after 54 days of imprisonment.

It was a military-like operation that used excellent reconnaissance, deception, and detailed planning with rehearsals, along with operational concepts such as surprise, violence of action, superior firepower, as well as planned escape routes from the area for the different elements. All these elements made this one of the most successful and studied terrorist incidents of our time. The terrorists made the effort to limit the number of innocent bystanders in the area prior to the attack and had plans in place to confuse the police before, during, and after the operation, increasing their chance of success.

HOSTAGE BARRICADE

A hostage barricade operation is the seizing of a targeted facility with whatever people are inside; this is different from a kidnapping because a kidnapper hides his victims and negotiates without working face-to-face, but in a hostage barricade situation, the hostage taker uses his victims to confront the authorities. The hostage barricade is an overt seizure of one or more people or other negotiable commodities to gain the attention of the authorities and news media. They will then use the hostages as a bargaining chip to obtain publicity for their cause, to obtain money, have members of their organization released, or other concessions in return for the safety of the hostages and their eventual release. There is generally a goal that is established as part of the operational plan for the hostage barricade incident; they will target specific facilities, areas, or people that the group wants to force into negotiations. These types of operations increase the level of risk to the terrorist organization by forcing them into a defensive situation where they are stationary and in a known location for them. To successfully complete an operation like this, the terrorist organization will require experience planning, operations, logistics, and intelligence capability. NOTE: Not all hostage barricades are planned; think of criminal activities such as bank robberies that go wrong, family disputes, and employee who is seeking revenge. These are all unintentional by the perpetrator and, since they did not plan and allowed their original intended operation to fail, they are nervous and panicky; these are the types of situations we see mostly in the states.

Select the target facility: The terrorists will look for a target that will fit in with their abilities and will achieve the goals they want. They will look at facilities or a place with a certain type of people that will force the government or the established power into a negotiation with them that they cannot otherwise get them to do. It must be a place they can have access to, with enough area so they can have some type of observation and control on the outside; they must also be able to seal the facility to keep security forces from getting in or hostages from getting out; must be able to control communications into and out of the facility; and it cannot have so many potential hostages that the attack element will be overwhelmed.

Isolate the targeted facility: The facility has to be controllable by the attackers; they have to isolate it completely and still maintain 360-degree security around the exterior perimeter—complete control of the inside and control of all communications into and out of the building. This means that they must have enough personnel to do this for the size of the facility targeted. They have to information-proof the targeted facility so that security forces, when responding, will not be able to gain any intelligence about what they are doing, how they are doing it, where they are doing it, and exactly who they are doing it too.

Neutralize security at the site: Whatever security the site had, including guards, security cameras and alarms will have to be neutralized by the terrorist(s) in order for them to be able to control the facility and thereby control the situation.

Gain control of the hostages: After they control access to the facility, they will need to gain control of all the hostages inside the facility, they must have a general idea of how many people will be there at the time of the attack, they will need to account for everyone then, isolate them render them harmless to their operation. They may have to use physical force, threats, and some type of restraint to control the hostages for the duration of the incident.

Negotiate: This is the whole reason for the operation and the terrorists will have a plan on how they want the negotiation to go, what they hope to achieve, and how. They will open lines of communication with government forces and begin making demands which will be countered by the hostage negotiator, this will continue until either the terrorist demands are met, or the government forces storm the facility and end the incident.

Escape from the facility: The terrorists will always have an escape clause or safe transportation out of control of those they are negotiating with; they will also try to have planned emergency escape routes in case the situation goes bad and the government forces storm the facility in a rescue attempt.

Three examples of hostage barricade situations for those interested were (1) the 19th of April Movement (M-19) group in Bogota, Colombia, at the Dominican Republic, Embassy (February 1980), (2) terrorists from the Tupac Amaru Revolutionary Movement (MRTA) in Lima, Peru (December 1996) at the Japanese ambassador's residence, and (3) the infamous and tragic Beslan School Siege in Beslan, North Ossetia, Russia, in September of 2004.

HIJACKING (MOBILE HOSTAGE BARRICADE)

A hijacking is a mobile hostage barricade and is the seizure, by force, of a surface vehicle, its passengers, and/or its cargo. This type of operation produces a spectacular mobile hostage barricade situation, and this offers the terrorists greater mobility and worldwide media attention, especially when hostages are involved. The purpose of a hijacking is to cause disruption in the economy, embarrass the government security forces, attempt to gain concessions from the targeted government, and to gain popular support; the hijacking of trucks or trains carrying food staples, medical supplies, etc., is a tactic used by terrorists, insurgents, rebels who generally distribute the cargo, free of charge, to the local populace and the poor who cannot afford these items. While doing this, they also distribute propaganda advertising their cause and how they are helping the people unlike those in authority that they are opposing. This tactic is in decline due to the likelihood that the perpetrator(s) will be killed without achieving their goals. Depending on the planned operation and what results they want, any mobile platform can be a target of a hijacking to include trains, buses, and ships, although aircraft has historically been the preferred target: a skyjacking, which we will talk about later.

Example of a Hijacking (Ship, Piracy)

A hijacking many people will remember was that of the cargo ship Maersk Alabama off of the coast of Somalia in April 2009. There were 23 crew members on board; while they had previously received anti-piracy training, the ship was taken over by four Somali pirates aged between 15 and 18 years old. This ended with a rescue of the crew by the U.S. Navy. Hijacking and attempted Hijackings still take place around the world to this day.

Phases of a Hijacking

Gain control of the crew: This is vital to the entire operation as controlling the crew means they control the vessel they are hijacking and can take it to any destination they desire.

Control of any passengers: If there are passengers on the vessel, they will need to be controlled also to keep them from interfering with the operation, and so they can be used as hostages during the negotiation phase. This is when threat and violence are used to obtain and maintain their control of the vessel. Hostages will be informed of the hijacking, searched for identification documents, communications devices, and weapons, and then separated so they can be controlled easier. But remember, not all vehicles or ships have passengers, hijacking a truck or train filled with food or medicine or a ship filled with oil, they will only have to deal with the crew.

The confrontation phase: This is the longest part of a hijacking when the attackers start making demands and setting deadlines for those demands to be met. This is where with hostages, there may be beatings if deadlines are not met, hostage release, and more negotiations will take place; this phase could take weeks.

The crisis and culmination phase: This is the end of the event and is usually ended in one of three ways: a planned end set in motion by the attackers, a negotiated end with both sides working to bring it to a conclusion, and the initiated end, which can be unpredictable and violent when there is a rescue attempt by security forces, usually brought about by a deteriorating situation.

SKYJACKING (AIR PIRACY) (MOBILE HOSTAGE BARRICADE)

We know that hijacking is basically the illegal seizing or diverting of a vehicle. But, with flying so popular in our society, it became another prime target for terrorists and criminals. The U.S. government's Federal Aviation Administration (FAA) defines air piracy as: *Any seizure or exercise of control, by force or violence or threat of force or violence, or by any other form of intimidation, and with wrongful intent, of any aircraft [U.S. Federal Criminal Statue (49 USC 1472)]*. Skyjacking is another form of hijacking but involves an aircraft, which creates another type of mobile hostage barricade. In some cases, this enables the terrorists to conduct negotiations in a country sympathetic to their cause, and to move around keeping security forces at bay and limiting their abilities to gather intelligence on the situation and to formulate a plan of action.

Phases of skyjacking

Selecting a target country: Most countries have someone who is motivated to attack them in some way, and though those countries are targets, it doesn't mean that an airline from that country will be the target of the attack. Other airlines can be singled out as a target because they service those countries and will be carrying citizens from the country, countries, or area they wish to target.

Selecting the location and time of the skyjacking: Terrorists will want to determine the location that gives them the advantage for the operation—a place with security that they can bypass, where they have enough people to conduct the operation, and a location that will allow them to achieve their goal. The time or the date of the operation may also be important to the terrorists, either for symbolic reasons or for more practical reasons. They may choose the attack on an important date in the history of the terrorist organization, or the time may be selected to take advantage of the security personnel who are nearing the end of a work shift and waiting for their relief. They could plan the attack to take advantage of a heavy influx of passenger traffic, during the holiday season or other major events like a sporting event or a concert.

Identifying the type of aircraft: The terrorists need to select an aircraft that will meet the needs of their operational plan; they will research and find out the characteristics and capabilities of different types of aircraft before making their decision about what goals they want to achieve, where they want to fly too, and what type of aircraft will give them the ability to control the crew and hostages with the resources they will be able to take on board.

Airplane Considerations: Some of the possible considerations are as follows:

How many aisles does the aircraft have? How many levels does the aircraft have? Where is the communications console located? Is it in the main galley or is it forward by the cockpit? Is the cockpit door reinforced and locked? How many crewmembers are required in the cockpit to operate the aircraft, and how many cabin crews are there? Is the aircraft compartmentalized into first-class, coach, and tourist sections, or can a terrorist see all the way to the rear of the plane from the first-class area without having his view obstructed by partitions? Does the aircraft have a rear door or exit so that the terrorists can observe the rear of the plane while it is stationary on the ground? What is the maximum range and fuel capacity of the aircraft selected?

This is just some of the information that a terrorist will need when planning the operation for a skyjacking. This type of information is what allows him to plan how many people he will need, where he will need to place people to control the aircraft, how to get into the cockpit, where he can fly too after takeoff, etc. Sadly, these days most of this information is likely available on the Internet. They will also need to do a reconnaissance of the airport where the attack will begin at. The intelligence personnel will gather data concerning the security measures employed in the airport and how well trained those operators are in using that equipment, shift breaks, when most people are in line waiting, is there a trusted traveler program in place, are first-class passengers treated differently, etc.

NOTE: The habit of treating passengers differently is always a matter of concern for security; they have different screening standards, etc. Also, the trusted traveler program and similar programs even for aircrew are another danger, it does not take into account that most terrorists who commit acts are not on any law enforcement checklist and have not broken the law, they use people who are "clean" so as not to highlight them to security forces doing checks, by allowing them a way to bypass some security you are opening a door for the terrorist to exploit.

Penetrating security measures at the selected site:

Terrorists will be worried about how they will get their people and the necessary weapons through security and onto the aircraft. A group could try to have one of its members or someone sympathetic to its cause hired to the security force or as someone who is monitoring security equipment, or if possible, a member could work on a crew responsible for servicing the aircraft. Since some of these personnel do not pass through a security checkpoint, or as someone working at a restaurant or store located past security but before the gates, these personnel do not pass through the same security as passengers either. They will also need to get the equipment they will need for the operation past security and into an area they can access it; this includes weapons and explosives which they may try to smuggle onto the aircraft in seemingly innocent items. Once they know what the security measures are that are being employed at the target airport, they will come up with ways to defeat that security by masking weapons or weapon components to make detection difficult. If the terrorists can get other terrorist sympathizers or intimidate people already working at the airport to work for them, then these people can cache weapons on board the aircraft itself, or in a place that the attackers can have access to it past the security checkpoints.

NOTE: Currently, there are two terms used to describe skyjacking:

Skyjacking—illegal seizure of an aircraft while in flight.
Commandeering—illegal seizure of an aircraft while on the ground.

Example of a Skyjacking

On December 24, 1994, Air France Flight 8969 was commandeered in Algiers, Algeria, prior to departing the gate. Four men wearing blue jackets and displaying airport badges boarded the aircraft. They claimed to be security and requested passports to check the identification of the passengers on board. It all seemed normal until the four men closed the passenger door and brought out weapons from under their clothes and from bags they had brought on board with them. Three of the Armed Islamic Group members immediately went to the cockpit to secure it while the fourth stayed in the main passenger area to control the passengers by aiming his AK at them. Immediately upon gaining control of the aircraft, crew, and passengers, they issued their demands for the release of three Islamic Salvation Front leaders (Abbassi Madani, Ali Benhadj, and Abdelhak Layada). Inside the aircraft, each of the hijackers had a role, and it seemed to the passengers that they knew what they were doing and had practiced. The leader of the group stayed in the cockpit controlling the flight crew and communicating with the negotiators. One stayed in the back to overlook the cabin. The third was asking all the questions of the passengers and was considered the interrogator, while the fourth was the man who did all the violence and killing: the executioner. From the beginning, the terrorist had already picked who they would kill. First, they brought an off-duty Algerian policeman and a Commercial Counselor at the Vietnamese Embassy to the front of the aircraft by the door. When the negotiations stalled, these two were killed and thrown onto the loading ramp. The following day in a show of faith, the hijackers released 58 passengers, but as the negotiations continued with their demands not being met, they became agitated and demanded to leave Algeria, when the negotiators refused, another passenger, a chef at the French Embassy, was taken forward shot and dumped off the plane. With this killing, and the threat of more if the plane was not allowed to take off, the French government insisted the plane be allowed to leave so this demand was met t however the auxiliary power unit (APU) had drained most of the fuel to keep the aircraft running during the thirty-nine-hour standoff, so they only had enough to get them to the southern French town of Marseille. After landing, a French counter-terrorism force arrived and set up observation points around the aircraft, all requests for fuel were denied but requests for food and water were met. The observation points noted that the hijackers had dressed hostages to look like hijackers to include masks, uniforms, and weapons; they also noted that two hijackers always stayed in or near the cockpit while two others remained near the rear of the aircraft and that some hijackers had earplugs to portable radios. During this time, the French observed no external support. The hijackers had one real bomb that was placed behind the cockpit and a fake bomb they placed under the first-row seats. The hijackers were talked into clearing the first ten rows of passengers as this would allow a film crew to interview the hijackers, around 5 PM on the 26th. The hijackers requested fuel again and threatened to kill a passenger if they don't get it; the request was denied, and in an act of frustration, the hijackers fired their weapons at the tower. The French counter-terrorist team conducted an assault on the aircraft to end the situation; their assault was fast enough to prevent the terrorists from connecting the battery, that each of them carried to the bomb behind the cockpit. The bomb consisted of 2.2 lbs of dynamite; 14 cm of detonation cord held together by white tape primed with three electric detonators. In all, over a thousand shots were fired by the terrorists and the rescuers; the end result was a successful rescue with all four terrorists dead, nine assaulters wounded, and three crew and 13 passengers injured.

Example 2

On February 6, 2000, in Ariana, Flight 805 was hijacked by a group wanting to escape the harsh life of Afghanistan. This flight was supposed to fly an internal Afghan route but just after the plane took off, 8–10 skyjackers armed with an assortment of weapons took control of the cockpit and passengers. The group of 8–10 skyjackers instructed the crew to fly to England; to fly that far, the aircraft made several stops to refuel. As a concession with negotiators to allow the flight to land and to show good faith in order to get fueled, the attackers released hostages at each stop. The aircraft made its way to Stansted Airfield north of London and landed. At this time, a British counter-terrorist force deployed to Stansted and set up their operation in a hangar to plan a rescue operation, the media showed up and set up across the airfield to record the events. On February 10, the skyjackers negotiated a settlement which released the rest of the hostages. It was difficult sorting the hostages from the attackers since 40 of the hostages were related to them. A total of 78 passengers sought political asylum in the United Kingdom after their escape from Afghanistan.

Example 3

No American can forget September 11, 2001. These skyjackings were not the standard, but a new process in that the planes being taken were going to be used as weapons. American Airlines Flight 11, United Airlines Flight 175, American Airlines Flight 77, and United Airlines Flight 93 were all hijacked on the morning of September 11. The planes were used as suicide weapons. Two were deliberately crashed into the twin towers of the World Trade Center. One was crashed into the Pentagon and one was crashed into a field in Pennsylvania by the terrorist because the passengers were attempting to retake control of the plane. These skyjackings led to the war on terror being started.

ASSASSINATION

Assassination is the murder of a pre-selected victim. It is a tactic that automatically gains media attention with a high level of visibility in the news. This tactic can be carried out in any number of different ways—by a lone gunman, suicide bomber, or a well-planned ambush either with small arms or explosives; it might even be a raid into a facility to get just one target. Assassination is one of the oldest terror tactics in use. It is still effective and is used by terrorist groups around the world. The victims of this type of attack can be anyone who has drawn the attention of the terrorist for some reason. This tactic is used to send a message to those in power, and the population in general, of what will happen by continuing a course of action that the terrorists do not like—or not pursuing a course of action that the terrorist wants to be pursued. This includes killing those who are talking to the police or security forces about the organization, to keep someone from testifying against the organization or its members in a legal proceeding. Thus, anyone who goes against a particular group is a possible target. This tactic can also be used to specifically highlight a particular issue, and is one of the best ways to intimidate people and receive the media attention the group craves; the higher the profile of the victim, the more media attention the attack will garner.

The basic steps in planning and conducting an assassination are the same as for a kidnapping, except now they are focusing on the personnel security measures of the intended victim, and how to defeat them. An assassination is actually easier to carry out since now they do not have to worry about defeating security without killing the target, nor worry about gaining control of the victim. The techniques for carrying out this act range from a lone attacker with a gun or bomb to a well-planned ambush. It is important to know that many assassinations take place near or at the victim's residence as he leaves for work in the morning; this is where a victim is most predictable and more vulnerable.

Steps to an Assassination

Selecting the attack site: The terrorists during the surveillance of the target will be doing a route analysis and trying to decide among other things when the target will be most predictable. According to this information, an attack site will be selected, they will also be looking at the security posture and routines of the selected victim to pick the best form of attack that will achieve their goal of killing the target without having to engage security forces. They will plan the attack around the weakest point in the target's predictable routine. Will they need cover and concealment, and is it available? Remember, they will need a way to blend in with the surrounding environment prior to the arrival of the victim and will need a believable reason to be lingering in that area to avoid raising suspicion and being compromised; is the site conducive to the planned attack, are there visual obstructions that could interfere with them? Or give the victim a place to hide, take cover, or receive help; is the attack site well defined and does it permit the attacker to limit the actions and possible responses of the target? Can the attackers quickly and easily escape the area after the attack? Is there unobstructed access to major routes of movement? Are there alternate means of transportation that they can use?

Isolating the attack site: There may be a need to isolate the area of the attack, to keep those not involved and those that might interfere, away. Some methods that have been used previously, to limit the chance of outsiders interfering, are false alarms to security forces prior to and during the attack—to tie up phone lines and send them to locations away from the attack site—fake police roadblocks, bombings, and other diversionary tactics such as auto accidents. The method they choose has to be believable by all so as not to arouse the suspicions of either the locals, people in and around the attack site, law enforcement, security forces, and most importantly the victim. But, depending on where the attack takes place, they might not even need to use this step. If the victim has no security and a lax personnel security profile, the attackers might be able to walk right up to him and shoot him, then walk away.

Stopping the target vehicle: Conducting an attack on a stopped vehicle is much easier than conducting one on a moving vehicle given that it is easier to hit a standing target than a moving target. There are a number of ways to do this. Some that have been used in the past are very normal for some operational areas, tactics such as military or police roadblocks, traffic accidents, hitchhikers, placing traffic signs to change the traffic pattern, ramming the target vehicle forcing it to stop, policemen pulling the victim over, and a baby carriage being pushed in front of oncoming cars causing everyone to stop and blocking the victim's vehicle, pedestrians stepping in front of oncoming traffic to stop the flow of movement, and so on. Remember, they don't have to specifically stop the victim's car if they can stop or slow the flow of traffic the victim is traveling in, then he will be stopped as well, and since it was not directed specifically at the victim, he could let his guard down. For some types of assassinations, this is not a vital element; when using a bomb or a shoulder-fired weapon like a rocket propelled grenade (RPG), it wouldn't matter if the vehicle was stopped or not.

Neutralizing the security detail: The attackers need to find a way to neutralize or bypass; the detail if there is security with the victim, the attackers need to get close enough to kill the victim and to check and make sure he is dead before they leave the area. They are not worried about a firefight with security other than for their own protection, since it should be very quick "in, hit the target, then out." They are also not worried about the security following them since any security left alive will probably be trying to aid the victim and/or provide aid to themselves.

Escape from the attack site: After the target is killed, the attackers will want to make a good getaway with little or no interference; this clean escape is important so they cannot be followed or compromised. Also, since the group may have limited resources and trained personnel, it is important for them to protect these resources so they can conduct more missions in the future. With limited resources available to the terrorist, keeping them free and available is of vital importance to the cause.

Common Factors of Assassinations

I will give some examples of past assassinations, and they will have several common factors:

The victims of assassinations all had predictable routines or were predictable in a portion of their routine enough that the threat could take advantage of it, by planning and conducting a successful operation.

The victims and their security either ignored or disregarded indicators of terrorist surveillance and attack site preparation along their routes of movement when it presented itself.

The targets ignored or disregarded threats made against them, their families, or the institutions they represented; in some cases, they disregarded threats made directly against them by name.

The last common factor is also the saddest and most worrying, and that is most of these attacks could have been avoided by practicing simple security awareness and having a proactive security element in place. People tend to ignore threats and danger to themselves with the attitude it will not happen to them—"they will not attack me I am too important or too tough"; "stuff like that only happens to the other guy," etc.—attacks can happen to anyone, and your status, nationality, background, and popularity are factors that will not protect you and may even make you a target!

Examples of Assassinations

October 28, 7:00 AM, 2002, Amman, Jordan: Laurence Foley, a U.S. diplomat who was the senior administrative officer with the U.S. Agency for International Development was killed as he left his house and walked to his car. The morning of the attack, the two attackers drove a rental car to the housing area where Mr. Foley lived. They reached the residence around 7:00 AM, one man got out of the car and walked to Foley's house and hid behind his car waiting; this man was wearing blue jeans, a keffiyeh to cover his face, body armor, and had tear gas and a 7-mm silenced gun. When Mr. Foley came out moving toward his vehicle, he stood up, emptied his handgun into Mr. Foley, went back to the rental car, and was driven away. The two were captured in December of 02 and identified as al-Qaeda operatives. The operatives, when questioned, stated that Mr. Foley was not their primary target, they had been sent to Jordan to scan people on a target list. They picked him because at the time he had no security profile, and they had remained in the country to continue watching for opportunities to attack others on the target list.

Example 2

On October 6, 1981, during the 6th October 1973 victory parade in Egypt, Khalid Ahmed Showky El Islambouli carried out a successful assassination of Egyptian president Anwar Sadat. Khalid and other soldiers were in the parade with their military unit; when their trucks arrived at the area in front of the reviewing stand, Khalid and three others jumped from their truck and moved to the stand where President Sadat was standing with other foreign dignitaries. The assassins threw grenades. Khalid ran into the stands and fired his assault rifle into Sadat's body until it was empty. The assassins were immediately captured.

Example 3

The assassination of Archduke Franz Ferdinand of Austria: On June 28, 1914, Sarajevo, the Archduke and his wife arrived in the city by train and were going to be moved through the city in a six-car procession, the vehicle tops were down to allow the crowds a better view of the occupants. There were seven men assigned to assassinate the Archduke, they were staged along the route of travel blending in with other citizens there to see the Archduke and his wife Sophie. The first person in line for the attack had a policeman standing behind the crowd near him, so he chickened out and let the car pass without taking action. The next attacker in line threw a grenade at the car. The driver saw this and accelerated to get by it, after that unsuccessful attempt the motorcade sped up and the crowd's movement didn't allow for any other attempts. At this point, the attempt was a failure, but the Archduke and his wife wanted to visit the victims of the failed attempt and decided to go to the hospital, security decided it would be best to take the most direct route to the hospital but they never told the Archduke's driver who turned on a side street. It was a coincidence that one of the attackers had gone to a café on this street for a sandwich, thinking that the attack was over and failed. When the Archduke's car drove by the café he was in, the driver of the Archduke's car knew he had made a wrong turn and stopped the vehicle putting it in reverse to back up to the main street, as he did this, the assassin left the café and waited as the car was moving slowing by him in reverse, he drew his weapon and fired from a distance of five feet into the car, one bullet struck the Archduke's wife and killed her instantly, one hit the Archduke in the neck. He died about 5 minutes later, while holding his wife. The assassin was captured. Since he was too young for the death penalty, he was given a 20-year sentence and died in prison.

Example 4

On May 25, 1983, in the evening Lieutenant Commander Schaufelberger, the senior U.S. Naval representative at the U.S. Military Group, El Salvador, was assassinated at the Central American University in San Salvador. The Central American Revolutionary Workers' Party (PRTC) was thought to have carried out the act. Lt. Cdr. Schaufelberger was dating an employee of the university. For several months during this time, he had established a pattern of driving to the university in civilian clothes to pick her up after work. He varied the days of the week when doing this but the time was the same, between 1830 and 1840. On the day of the attack, he arrived at his usual time for the pickup and honked his horn: this was the signal to his date that he had arrived; he was driving an armored embassy provided Ford Maverick. His girlfriend exited her building and saw what she thought was a white Volkswagen microbus pull up from behind, stopping near Lt. Cdr. Schaufelberger's car. When the vehicle stopped, three men got out. The driver stayed with the vehicle. One of the gunmen, carrying his weapon went behind the victim's car and approached his girlfriend, stopping her to talk; this drew the victim's attention to them. Meanwhile, a second gunman took up a security position by their vehicle, observing the grounds, and the third gunman ran up to the open window of Lt. Cdr. Schaufelberger's car while he was distracted and fired four rounds of .22 magnum from a handgun into the victim's head. The assassins then ran back to their vehicle and escaped. NOTE: How could they shoot a .22 through an armored car? The air conditioner in Lt. Cdr. Schaufelberger's vehicle had quit working so he had removed the bullet-resistant Lexgard glass on the driver's side to keep the car cooled down while driving. Even though he carried a revolver underneath his right leg while driving, he never got the chance to use it. Lt. Cdr. Schaufelberger was an experienced U.S. Navy SEAL and was security chief in the country for 53 other U.S. military advisers. The moral of the story is that a well-planned and executed attack can get to anyone.

ARMED ASSAULTS

There are two types of armed assaults: raid and ambush.

The raid: So, what is a raid? It is an operation to attack a position, facility, or installation followed by a planned withdrawal. The reason a raid is conducted is to capture enemy personnel, destroy enemy equipment and supplies; to destroy positions, facilities, installations, or other points of strategic or tactical value, to harass enemy forces, to rescue personnel friendly to your cause, and to gain intelligence. In the past, terrorist organizations have used this tactic to take over television or radio stations to put out their message, to embarrass government security forces by destroying facilities and personnel, and taking equipment and other items they needed. This includes money gained from bank robberies and armored car attacks.

Fundamentals of a Raid

Surprise: This is attacking the target at a time when least expected or security is lowest or attacking using an unexpected ruse or method.

Firepower: Having the necessary firepower to counter any security the intended target may have and be able to concentrate it at those critical points to help them in achieving the necessary fire superiority to accomplish their plan.

Violence: Maximum violence in the shortest amount of time is necessary to overcome any security and achieve their goal, this is accomplished by using the first two, surprise, necessary firepower, and aggressiveness in the initial attack and maintaining this aggressiveness until the target is neutralized.

Example of a Raid

February 06, 2007, Acapulco, Mexico: 16 attackers conducted a coordinated assault on two police stations in Acapulco, killing at least seven police officers and wounding an undetermined number. The operation took place just before noon, four policemen were killed at the Emiliano Zapata neighborhood station and three others were killed at the Ciudad del Renacimiento police station. There were eight heavily armed attackers at each station, all attackers escaped without incident.

The ambush: A good military definition for an ambush is a surprise attack from a concealed position on a moving or temporarily halted target, and this applies to terrorists also. A well-planned ambush will seldom fail, especially terrorist ambushes that are well-planned can make use of diversions and are properly rehearsed and precisely executed to use surprise to the maximum advantage. The purpose of an ambush is to kill the intended targets or disable their vehicles and neutralize security so that the terrorists can kidnap them. When they plan for a killing attack, they will usually consider two types: an explosive ambush or a weapons ambush. An explosive ambush—a bomb may be planted along the route the victim travels or placed in a vehicle parked alongside the road; these types of attacks can be devastating and are hard to anticipate since they can take place anywhere. The weapons ambush can be equally devastating and is used when kidnapping is in mind since the terrorist will have more fire control which gives them a better chance of taking the target alive.

Fundamentals of an Ambush

Surprise: This is attacking the target at a time and a place when they least expect it; the idea is to attack in a place where the target thinks no attack is possible and a time when they feel the safest.

Coordinated firepower: Having the necessary firepower to accomplish the goals of the attack on the intended target. Every attacker will have designated targets so they can concentrate fire at those critical points necessary to ensure total coverage of the kill zone. All members of the attack element should know when to start firing; this means the kill zone will be marked or some type of prearranged signal will be coordinated.

Aggressive execution: Using maximum violence of action to instill fear, shock, and surprise, concentrating the necessary firepower and aggressiveness in the initial attack and maintaining this aggressiveness until the target is destroyed or the goal is reached.

In addition to many recent publicized examples from Mexico, as well as daily ambush examples on coalition forces—including the Iraqi/Afghani military, police units, and U.S. forces during the occupations of Iraq and Afghanistan—the Taylor & Francis/CRC Press title *Survival Driving: Staying Alive on the World's Most Dangerous Roads, Second Edition* (ISBN: 9781032065625) details several examples of ambush-style attacks.

STANDOFF WEAPONS

Standoff weapons have emerged as a new threat in armed assaults. These weapons include any type of weapon that can be fired from a distance to hit the desired target, including missiles, shoulder-fired rockets, and mortars. This is a preferred tactic for the terrorist because like a bombing it lowers the amount of risk by not having to directly confront security forces.

OVERRUN ATTACK (DRIVE-BY)

The overrun attack is a form of weapons ambush that is very simple to carry out; it is sometimes called a drive-by. The selected target will have a known routine that the terrorists think they can exploit; the victim of a terrorist attack actually chooses the attack site for the terrorists by being predictable in his routines. The attackers will then choose the best attack site on the target's route, it is vital that the attackers know the capabilities of the victim's car, so they know how to defeat any armor or tactics that may be used during the attack. On the day of the attack, they start by following the victim's car from his home or other known location, and at the selected attack site, they will pull around to pass, as they are going by, they will fire at the victim and continue to drive away, making their escape. This attack can be done from any type of vehicle, including a motorcycle; it can also be done, for example, if a person is moving on foot along a known route, a vehicle can fire as it passes the victim.

Examples of Overrun Attacks

On April 21, 1989, a vehicle overrun attack was carried out by the New People's Army of the Philippines against U.S. Army Colonel James N. Rowe. Col Rowe and his family were aware of the terrorist threat against him prior to the attack, had detected surveillance, and was using measures to increase his security. But, Col. Rowe's office was located in a location that, while he could vary his routes, he had to drive through the same traffic circle to and from work. This predictability in routine was exploited by the threat, on the morning of the attack as the COL's vehicle entered a traffic circle less than a mile from the Military Assistance Group Headquarters, terrorists drove by his vehicle as it slowed and fired on his lightly armored vehicle, killing Col. Rowe and wounding his driver.

U.S. Navy Captain Tsantes, in November 1983, was killed in an overrun attack by the members of the 17 November terrorist group in Greece; Captain Tsantes was in an embassy vehicle with an untrained driver on a predictable route. When his driver got boxed in at a stop light, a Vespa with two people on it weaved its way through traffic, and the passenger shot both Captain Tsantes and his driver, killing them.

The above examples show that terrorist organizations have historically, and continue to, use this type of attack to kill selected individuals in urban areas with a police presence for a long time.

ARSON

This tactic can be conducted by terrorist groups that may not be as well equipped as other major terrorist organizations. It is also used specifically by those whose goal is to destroy equipment, property, and vehicles and use up resources. This is an excellent low-cost tactic, with no technology necessary, and can be accomplished with items that are available in every society. It is also very easily done if they do combine technology with this tactic; it is usually when they make an *improvised incendiary device (IID)*, which has timing devices that allow them to put the IID in place while the terrorists make their escape and it goes off at later predetermined times. Even in areas that have strict control on ownership of weapons and restricted access to explosive materials, there is always access to gasoline, glass bottles, rags, matches, Styrofoam peanuts, propane, and other flammable materials. Arson operations are very simple to conduct with the hardest thing being the ability to gain access to the target—if that is even necessary, since there is always the option of setting something on fire from the outside. This tactic, while basic, allows terrorist groups to gain confidence in their abilities to plan and carry out operations and experience with little or no risk to the individuals or the organization. These types of attacks always gain media attention, while instilling fear in those targeted and destroying property and other resources that might be used against the terrorist group if left alone.

MAIMING

Maiming is a mutilation or physical injury which involves the loss of, or incapacity to use a portion of the body correctly or total loss of its use; it can also involve disfigurement. This type of tactic is often used by terrorists as a means of administering their perception of justice to members of their own groups who have violated their rules, defected, or turned informant against them, or to intimidate the local populace. The effectiveness of this tactic is not in the actual act itself, but in how others in the organization and/or general population will react to it; if the victim lives, then they will have a living example of what happens when you cross their organization and people will see and remember this every time the victim is seen. One tactic called kneecapping is a technique used by both the PIRA and the Red Brigades. In this technique, a bullet is shot into the victim's knee area from the rear of the leg so that the larger exit wound out the front causes more damage to the joint. When repaired, the victim will have a limp and/or walk with a cane or crutch reminding everyone of what happens to those who go against them. Other groups have used sulfuric or hydrochloric acid thrown or poured either on the face or on other body parts. This also has a lifelong effect on the victim as well as serving as a reminder to those who see him.

TERRORIST WEAPONS

Terrorists use any weapon they think will accomplish the mission; this includes weapons ranging from those that are old and obsolete by modern standards to modern state-of-the-art weaponry available in the world market. When they are looking for weapons, the terrorists will choose them according to certain criteria:

Availability: Are the weapons, ammunition, and spare parts available to them on a regular basis? Can they obtain the weapons and ammunition in their home country, another country being used as a base for conducting operations, or in the country where the operation is to take place? This is very important because the harder these items are to obtain, the more difficult it will be to include them into any mission plans; this could limit their scope of operations and restrict what targets they can go after.

Concealability: Is the weapon concealable, does it break down for transport; can it be mixed in with other things to prevent detection when moving to an attack site prior to the operation? Is it easily detectable to untrained or poorly trained security personnel, can it be moved through security checkpoints without detection? All this includes ammunition; the weapons the terrorists decide to use have to be able to be moved to the planned attack site without being detected.

Firepower: The firepower needed will be dictated by the mission planning and the pre-selected target, they will need to have weapons that have the necessary firepower to overcome all foreseen obstacles and achieve the objective of their operation.

Simple: The weapons terrorist groups choose to use are usually very simple in construction and operation, so this makes it easier to teach their use and maintenance to people with little or no education or to people with no prior experience with handling weapons. If the weapons selected have multiple safeties—and other additional safety features or a high maintenance requirement—chances are they will not be used as a terrorist's primary weapon system. The conditions the terrorists live in and the environment they must move through require that their weapons be simple to operate, clean, and easily maintained; they also need the confidence that their weapons will be reliable in any situation.

CHAPTER 3

Improvised Explosive Devices

One of the goals of any terrorist organization, guerilla movement, or insurgency is the need to get media attention to put out their own propaganda, beliefs, ideas so that they can become a known entity and move into the public spotlight. Remember, we said that terrorist's acts are dynamic; few things are as dynamic as something blowing up. So, if you are trying to generate headlines to gain publicity, one of the fastest ways to get such attention is to bomb a place, a person, or a thing that has value. Just like maiming, the impact or physical destruction does not have to be large; sometimes, it may simply be the threat of such an attack such as a hoax, bomb threat, or dud that serves as an ugly reminder of the terrorist's presence. Also similar to arson, the bomb can be cheap, and it gives the terrorists the chance to place it at the desired location with little risk to the terrorist who is doing the placement. Then, they can walk away, building confidence in the organization and its members and gaining support and new members by their ability to conduct such acts. The more success that an organization has using this technique, the more it will be used. But, we must remember that success to the terrorist is not just how many people are killed or how much damage; often, it is the publicity gained from the act and the ability to be in the spotlight. This in turn causes fear among the local population that a bomb can be anywhere, an explosion can occur at any time. Living with this fear can cause the population to resent those in charge because they cannot protect them and, in turn, gives the advantage to the terrorist.

Now, let's discuss all the reasons that the use of bombs is so popular.

REASONS FOR TERRORIST BOMBINGS

To gain attention: As previously discussed, the person planting and using bombs will gain instantaneous publicity of the event and so to their cause. This is a chance to get people to listen to them and view them as

DOI: 10.4324/9781003292647-3

a real entity with real grievances and not just a group you read about in the paper. In some cases, it will attract a worldwide audience to their handiwork, giving them a chance to potentially attract even more people and resources to their cause.

Inexpensive to make: Bombs can be made from just about anything, from various chemicals readily available all over the world that can be found in the local stores. The components of the bomb that detonated in the World Trade Center in April 1993, the bombs made by the Unibomber, the bomb used in the Oklahoma City bombings, and the bombs at the Boston marathon were all made from locally obtained materials.

Bombs can be used in a variety of ways: for example, they can be used to make a small group with limited resources seem much larger and better-resourced. They can accomplish this by planting multiple devices and have them go off at the same time or by hitting different targets on multiple days in a row in different regions of the country. Fake or Hoax bombs can be placed and called in to shut down transportation hubs, interfere with business districts, and tie up vital resources of the government, which makes them look incompetent when it is found out to be a hoax.

Used as a diversion: First responders and security forces will respond to threats as required; by setting off a device in one part of a city, the terrorists could divert these personnel to that area. Then, they could strike in an unprotected area while these forces are engaged elsewhere. They can also be used to attack those first responders themselves by setting off one device or placing it so it can be found, then when first responders, security, and explosive ordnance disposal (EOD) show up to neutralize or move it, other devices that had previously be emplaced could be detonated, killing or wounding these vital personnel and removing them as a resource in the fight against terrorism.

Difficult to detect: Depending on how a device is constructed and placed, it can be difficult to find before an explosion. Likewise, pieces of the device and secondary devices can also be difficult to find after the first explosion is set off. Because bomb makers and the terrorists who use them go to great lengths to hide their devices or to create them so that they blend in, it can take security forces large amounts of time and money to try and figure out how and where the bomb makers have concealed them. This will also cause streets and buildings to be closed, business interruption, etc., until a device is found or an area cleared. Once an organization has established its ability to set and detonate bombs in different locations, they can then start calling in bomb threats and/or hoax bomb sightings to tie up those who respond, to waste resources and to shut off selected business areas, commercial areas, etc. Every reported sighting has to be considered a true report and threat until it is completely cleared by the bomb squad or security forces.

Destruction of evidence: Usually after a bomb has been detonated, there are small fires and other hazardous materials such as spilled fuel in the area. When the fire department arrives, they usually spray the area down putting out the fires and cleaning the potential volatile materials away from the wreckage, what this is also doing is possibly erasing large portions of the evidence left behind after such attacks. This makes efforts to trace the evidence through past events such as purchases, any physical evidence, and the ability to link how a device was manufactured to a specific person or group almost impossible. So, unless a certain person or group claims responsibility, they can get away with the attack.

DEFINE AND CATEGORIZE IEDs

So, exactly what is an improvised explosive device or IED? They were made famous for their use in Iraq and Afghanistan, but they have actually been around for a long time and used by terrorist groups and others during their conflicts against those in power. An IED can be defined as a device, usually a homemade, designed to cause death, injury, or the destruction of vehicles by using explosives that have been hidden and can be set off using a variety of trigger mechanisms. IEDs are nonstandard devices or modified military ordnance or civilian demolition materials. Or, they can be devices which can be fabricated from common materials using explosives; fireworks; or destructive, lethal, noxious, pyrotechnic, or incendiary chemicals.

The main supply of these types of explosives comes from countries that support terrorism and weapons black markets located throughout the world. It is very easy to obtain military explosives, blasting caps, and other materials to initiate an explosion, but this is not the only way terrorists can obtain explosives. They can also acquire them through:

Purchase: Materials are available through the open market—grocery stores, farm stores, gun stores, fire work stands, pharmacies, etc.—that can be used to construct IEDs. In most countries, anyone can buy black powder, smokeless powder, and even dynamite for use with reloading weapons, blasting stumps, for beaver dams on a farm, etc. In many countries, these items are unregulated.

Theft: Explosives and the materials used in making explosives are not that difficult to steal, they are available in mining areas, where explosives are usually stored at the site with little or no security, at demolition sites of construction companies and, believe it or not, from the military which losses this type of material during shipment. This can also include military installations both in the United States and overseas. In Iraq, terrorists had attacked Iraqi military compounds and taken weapons, ammunition, explosives, and other military ordinance in raids.

Battlefield recovery: A lot of explosive material and military ordinance is recovered at attack sites, destroyed vehicles, shot down aircraft, and from disabled civilian security vehicles, law enforcement vehicles, and killed or wounded personnel. Few realize the amount of material recovered from these incidents; I have seen vehicles stripped down to the chassis, everything else taken in less than 2 hours. These materials are then used by the terrorists in their future attacks.

But where do people get the information on what materials they need, learn how to combine them to make an IED, how to fabricate items to set them off, make timers, etc.: in short, how to make a bomb? There has always been information available on how to construct such devices: military manuals, police manuals, even manuals put out by terrorist organizations. Most of these books can be bought at military surplus stores, gun shows, and over the Internet. Today, with the Internet, it only takes a few searches to find out everything you need to know about making a bomb. Several terrorist and militia groups post this information for their members. But, as with any complicated process, learning from a book can be very dangerous. Many would-be terrorists are killed or injured as they try to build their own devices when they start the process of learning the art of bomb making. This is in large part due to the lack of knowledge concerning certain procedures that need to be followed, and the characteristics of the chemicals they are using—in addition to mistakes or errors with the information they obtained.

Bomb makers usually come in three categories of individuals: the first being the **highly skilled individual** who received training in the military, law enforcement, civilian sector demolitions such as mining, quarrying, and some construction jobs or has a background in chemical or electrical engineering, such as Ted Kaczynski, the Unabomber. People in this category can and will construct devices that are very effective and lethal; their bombs will be very sophisticated and will probably have anti-tampering devices or countermeasures designed into it. All of this will show a high degree of skill. Many bomb makers have a signature or a something specific in how they make their explosive devices. If evidence can be found after the blast, it can often be traced back to who constructed it and/or what organization. The next category of bomb maker **is an individual who has been trained** on how to make one type of bomb; the bombs produced by this type of individual will still be lethal, but they will also tend to be less sophisticated in design and effectiveness since they do not have the experience, knowledge, or training to modify the devices they make, so he will be limited in his ability to construct bombs other than the ones he has been taught how to make. The last type of bomber is **the average citizen or the disgruntled individual** who wishes revenge on an individual or company or wants to punish society for his frustrations. With no training, this is the person who uses those publications we talked about or looks for the information on the Internet. These are also the people who most frequently end up blowing themselves up, injuring themselves, or constructing devices that do not work.

DESCRIBE THE EFFECTS OF BOMB FRAGMENTATION AND BLAST

When an explosive goes off, it transforms from a solid into a rapidly expanding mass of gases. The detonation will produce three primary effects that create great damage in the area surrounding the explosion.

The first effect is the incendiary/thermal effect, which is seen as the bright flash or fireball when the explosive is detonated, but unless there are highly combustible materials involved, this effect is an insignificant part of the explosion and is generally the least damaging of the three primary detonation effects.

The second effect produced by any explosion is blast pressure. This requires some science to explain but is actually pretty simple; the average air pressure is 14.7 pounds per square inch (psi). When an explosion occurs, rapidly expanding gases are formed that exert pressures up to about 700 tons per square inch and that travel up to 13,000 miles per hour (mph). This pressure effect causes the formation of the shock front (or shock wave); this shock front is only a fraction of an inch thick and is part of the atmosphere, which then is being compressed before it is set in motion to become part of the positive pressure wave. This shock wave has two separate phases: the first is the POSITIVE PRESSURE PHASE, the shock wave moving away from the point where the explosion went off will crush, smash, or destroy everything it can in its path. What is not destroyed is picked up and moved, which turns them into secondary projectiles or fragmentation. The second phase is the NEGATIVE PRESSURE PHASE when the blast wave was moving outward, this compressing and pushing of air forms a partial vacuum at the point of detonation so that when the positive pressure wave finally dwindles and disappears, a broad partial vacuum exists around the point of the detonation; this displaced air rushes back in to fill this vacuum toward the point of detonation and has mass and power that will strike and move objects in its path and cause more damage.

The third effect produced by an explosion is fragmentation. There are two types of fragmentation resulting from an explosion: primary and secondary. Primary fragmentation consists of the material encasing the bomb, either the casing as with a pipe bomb or items placed on, around, or in the bomb with the purpose of fragmenting (nails, glass, nuts, screws, etc.). The secondary fragmentation consists of those objects that had been picked up in the shock wave (gravel, glass, carpet, splinters, bricks, cars, etc.).

DESCRIBE INITIATION SYSTEMS OF EXPLOSIVES

One of the things any bomb maker must learn is how to set off the explosives or explosive materials he just put together. The military and civilian engineers use blasting caps as the primary method of setting off the explosive charge, but there are other improvised ways to do it, which I will not discuss. A blasting cap is basically a device that contains a type of easy-to-ignite explosive charge; this charge is what provides the initial energy to set off the primary explosion. The type of explosive used in blasting camps is usually highly explosive compound that will explode when exposed to flame, heat, or shock. There are two types of blasting caps that I will talk about: non-electric and electric.

The non-electric blasting cap requires time fuse to provide the flame which detonates the primary explosive. But, time fuse is a cord that is made out of black powder, which smokes, causes heat and a smell that is easily identifiable prior to the explosion. Also, timing cord is difficult to cut to the correct length to get a certain time out of it before the explosion, and if wet or old will burn slower which could cause the timing to be off.

The electric blasting cap provides much more flexibility to the bomb maker in determining the kind of triggering mechanism or time delay he wants to use, which in turn gives them much more flexibility in the type of operations they can plan for. When using an electric blasting cap, the triggering methods used to set it off are only limited by the imagination of the bomb maker. The power source used in the device can be anything that is enough for electrical current to detonate a blasting cap, such as batteries and solar cells. The military M-6 electric blasting cap requires 1.5 amps to detonate, which is not that much; static electricity can set off electric blasting caps if you are not careful. Basically, any device that has any type of switch that can open or close a circuit (turn something on or off) can be used to activate an electric blasting cap.

The person making the bomb will select and construct the activation method according to the mission, the characteristics, routines of the victim. Any particular item that the victim handles or operates can provide the bomber with a variety of options to choose from in selecting an activator. These activators fall in three primary categories: command, victim activated, and time delay.

Command activation: This is simply running firing wire from the bomb to a location where a person can set it off by activating the power source as the selected target enters the kill zone. This can be difficult to do at times. The wire would need to be hidden, and after the IED goes off, it can be traced back to the location of the person who activated it. Also, the person would have to be close to the kill zone since it would be difficult to run out 500 meters of wire and keep it hidden. Command activation also includes using some type of radio transmitter with a receiver such as a garage door opener or a remote car door opener, a cell phone, a wireless phone and with the base station. This allows the person who will activate the device a chance to put more distance between himself and the kill zone. The person detonating the device only needs to be able to see when the victim enters the targeted area, and unlike using a wire for command detonation, it cannot be traced back to his location.

Victim activated: This means an action done by the selected target will cause the detonation of the IED; in other words, the victim sets it off. This is basically what is called a booby trap when an item such as a doorknob is rigged so when an unsuspecting subject opens the door and blows himself up; it is also trip wires across a street or sidewalk, inside a house, or pressure-sensitive devices that will detonate as someone walks on them or drives over them. There is a new more sophisticated way that is being used. It is using infrared (IR) devices, such as the chime that goes off when you enter a store. The device is set up and, when the target passes through the beam, it detonates the IED. The victim activation method allows the terrorist to place it and leave; it also ensures more hits on selected targets since the bomber does not have to be there to set the device off, and it's not someone guessing speed and timing to set it off from a distance. The draw down to this is, it is possible for someone other than the target to set it off. The IR device is even better for the terrorist since they can place it with the device turned off; this allows normal civilian traffic to pass through the kill zone. As the target approaches, all they have to do is turn the device on, ensuring a hit on the target.

Time delay activation: This type of bomb activation means the terrorist does not have to be at the scene when the IED goes off. This is an excellent tactic for them because it lessens the chances of the terrorist being caught since he is not in the immediate area when the explosion occurs. The devices used with this type of activation are usually targeted toward things, buildings, planes, facilities, bridges, etc. It would be difficult to use this type of device against one specific person unless you know down to the second his schedule, where he was going to be and when.

Anti-handling switches are a secondary method of detonating an IED; any disturbance of the device before it is detonated by its primary method will cause it to detonate. These types of devices are usually placed inside the IED's container or underneath it in order to conceal it. A good example would be the attaching of a mercury tilt device to a briefcase bomb, that once it is emplaced and turned on, if it is picked up again, it goes off.

Another tactic used is placing an IED so that it is found. Then, the terrorist will command to detonate it when EOD arrives to disarm or detonate in place. Killing these trained professionals takes away a valuable resource in the fight against terrorism.

HOW THE IED GETS TO THE TARGET SITE

The vehicle itself is the bomb: This is when the vehicle holds a bomb; it is used all over the world and actually turns this type of device into a smart bomb by the terrorists. When driven by someone (suicide bomber), it can avoid security and detection waiting until its target is in range and then ram it and explode. It can drive around obstacles and detonate in buildings or crowded streets. An example of this type of IED delivery was the attack on the Marine Battalion Landing Team 1-8 on October 23, 1983, in which a large yellow Mercedes truck was loaded with the equivalent of 6 tons of TNT, and it destroyed the headquarters building located at the Beirut airport in Lebanon. Another example is when the vehicle bomb itself is taken to a location and parked, to be command detonated when the selected target passes by or parked inside a facility or near a structure and then detonated to destroy it. Examples of this include the Oklahoma City bombing and the first World Trade Center bombings in 1993.

An IED is placed on or in a vehicle: This is used when the terrorists are targeting one specific person and they have access to his vehicle. Basically, the target vehicle becomes his known location; if he has little or no security and is not performing vehicle checks, then the terrorists can have access to it and place the device. Usually, these types of devices are victim activated, turning a car switch, sitting in the seat, etc. These types of devices like most here are used all over the world by terrorists and criminals. A good example is the case of Ian Gow. He was targeted because as a treasury minister he opposed the Anglo-Irish Accord, and he also knew he was on the Irish Republican Army (IRA) death list. However, he never increased his security profile or his personnel security awareness. He had the attitude that if they wanted to get him, they could get him at any time and at any place. On July 30, 1991, his car and his wife's car were parked in their garage, which had no security. His car was scheduled to go to a shop for repairs, so he was going to drive his wife's car to work that day. The device was placed under his wife's car by means of a magnetic contact and contained an estimated 1.5 to 2.5 kilograms of Semtex. NOTE: A no security, fatalistic attitude was a contributing factor to his tragic death. The terrorist gained intelligence knowing when his car was going in for repairs, which car he would be driving, what day, and when.

Letter bombs: Letter bombs or package bombs. These types of IEDs are not used as often as they used to be, due in large part to the training many postal employees receive concerning the characteristics of these devices and screenings currently done at most postal offices. Letter and parcel bombs are *victim activated* even though several different types of mechanisms such as electrical, chemical, or mechanical action mechanisms may be employed in its construction. NOTE: UNABOMBER Ted Kaczynski initially posed as a person or group calling itself "F.C." and sent a number of devices through the mail. In at least two cases, F.C. has preceded the sending of his devices with correspondence telling his victim of a future delivery. In the first case, the future delivery would be a manuscript. In the second case, the future delivery would be a book. None of the victims saw anything suspicious about the correspondence.

IED Concealment Techniques

Once an IED is emplaced at the target site, its success depends on its ability to remain on site and blend in to the surrounding environment, so that it is either goes unnoticed or appears to be harmless. If it is recognized as something dangerous or out of place, then the personnel in the target area will take notice and react to it. This dramatically increases the chance of failure for the terrorists who placed it; another reason for concealing these devices is having an IED configured to look harmless decreases the chances of the terrorists being caught with it during transportation to the operational area and during the final approach to the attack site.

How to Detect a Concealed IED

Depending on the environment you are in, there are several ways to look for a possible a concealed device.

Something missing: Is there a possibility for terrorists to remove something from your residence, office, another primary area or somewhere along one of your routes of travel—and replace it later? More than likely, you will have many things in or around your primary areas to include your residence and your office that have been there for a long time that you don't even notice on a conscious level anymore but are just there in the background. In order to avoid having something removed and modified with an IED, then placed back into your residence or office, you need to try and remember every detail concerning the items contained in these places, including their location, orientation, and how they are sitting.

Something moved: When you are walking around any of your primary areas, you need to keep your eyes scanning. You might notice something different subconsciously, so if you see something out of its normal position, you need to conduct a quick inspection of that object and the immediate surrounding area. If you think it has been tampered with or is not the same object, you need to get out and call your security and EOD. It is always better to be safe than sorry. NOTE: If one of your primary areas has been photographed, interior published in a magazine, or the terrorists have the ability know and see what type of furnishings and/or materials you have inside these areas, then you need to mark easily attainable items in such a way that you can tell if they have been swapped out or not. For items that are attainable in the local area such as stereo speakers, computer monitors, chairs, clocks, phones, lamps etc., the bomb maker can get the same one on the local market, modify it with a device, and then swap it out. It is very important to information proof your primary areas so that this type of intelligence is denied to the terrorist.

Something new: If you see something new in one of your primary areas, in a room, office, house, or car, there is the possibility it could be an IED. The terrorists sometimes like to make an item that might draw your curiosity into an IED, something you will pick up or move to get a better look at it and boom. So, before you pick up anything new, you need to find out whose it is, and who put it there. After all, new things should not be showing up in your car, office, bedroom, etc., without your knowledge of it. If you cannot find out how the item got there, leave it alone; it would be best to call the authorities or EOD.

Terrorists go to great lengths to disguise their IEDs and/or explosive materials used in their construction so as to facilitate their transport into the operational area, passing through security checkpoints. In the past, they have melted down TNT and poured it into craft molds in an attempt to both disguise it as well as give it an innocent appearance. Often, it is shaped into children's toys, statues, and ashtrays. When the IED is already put together, they are sometimes discovered by the initiating system or blasting cap well that is needed to prime the explosives. They have also used gas and propane cylinders to transport IEDs as well as explosive raw material.

METHODS USED TO RECOGNIZE POSTAL BOMBS

First, if you know you are a target by some type of threat, are on a target list, or live and work in an occupation that will make you and your family a target of terrorists, criminals, or other threat actors, then all your mail and packages need to go through the post office. If you are in the United States or an embassy or other official channels, these organizations already have a system in place that checks mail and packages. Your mail box if you have one at your residence should be locked with only the mail man on your route having a key, and it should be away from your driveway and your residence. You should never accept any package that you did not know was coming. Family members should let you know they are sending packages, how big, how they are wrapped, etc. If it is an ordered item, you should know the day of delivery, how much it should weigh, and where it is coming from. You should never have any type of packages sent to your home or office; they should be sent to a post office box or other site. This way if something shows up, you can refuse it or have whoever is delivering it open it at a safe distance from your residence. The same is true of any registered mail or large envelopes: if you are not expecting it, don't know who sent it or why—refuse to accept it.

Letter bomb recognition: Letter bombs can be made to look like anything, from greeting cards, to manuscripts, legal papers, books, and other types of packages; but any type of letter bomb may have one or more of the following characteristics:

Strange or unknown place of origin: The parcel has a post mark, canceled stamp mark, or the stamps themselves from a country and/or state that you have never been, have no relatives, and don't know anyone.

No return address: There is no return address on the letter or package. Most people who send mail, such as family members, put their return address—so that you will know who it is from and the mail item will be returned to them if it isn't delivered for some reason. No return address means that someone doesn't want the parcel coming back to them.

Excessive amount of postage: This happens because the bomber does not want to visit a post office or one of those mailing places to have the exact amount of postage put on. There are several reasons for this. Postal clerks are trained to detect abnormal behavior in people and someone who is extremely nervous, etc., would be remembered or have his letter or package looked at more closely. Also, many of these locations have video surveillance cameras, postal employees are trained to detect letter bombs and some stations have equipment for this purpose, and finally, the person mailing it doesn't want to get caught with the device, if it is detected. So, it is easier to put excessive postage on it and drop it in a mail box so it will be picked up and taken, no chance of the person sending it being caught.

Wires protruding from the item: Because of how the package or letter is handled and how it is wrapped, wiring may end up poking through a seam in the wrapping paper or poking through the paper itself. Sometimes, the device will need to be armed after it is sealed inside and the parcel is ready for transport. These wires could be part of the wires used as the arming safeties forgotten about in the excitement, fear, rush to get the package out or, again, it may just be part of the mechanism for the device.

Misspellings: Words that are misspelled on the package can be an indicator that it was written by someone who is not a native English speaker or someone with a poor understanding of the English language.

Incorrect title: Addressed to an individual with an incorrect title or rank for them. This shows that the person sending it has outdated information for that individual and no personnel or professional relationship.

Addressed to a title only: When a parcel is addressed to a position or a title and not a person, this also can indicate a lack of professional and/or personnel knowledge of the person in this position, which means that the sender does not know who holds that position and indicates a lack of familiarity with the organization.

Visual distractions: These are markings put on the parcel/letter such as personnel, perishable goods, fragile, handle with care, rush, priority mail, etc. These can be placed to draw the recipient's attention to them and not to the package or things that might seem wrong.

Restrictive markings: Are markings placed on the parcel/letter that are supposed to restrict who opens it, such as confidential, personal, eyes only, etc.—so that it goes to the intended recipient only. This is to ensure that the selected target is the one who opens it when the device goes off.

Return address different from the official postmark: The return address is different from the post mark on the parcel/letter, usually they are the same, since the letter enters the postal system from where it was physically mailed.

An unusual smell: A strong smell or odor coming from the letter or package such as shoe polish, almonds, or marzipan, this is a substance known as nitrobenzene, or another type of strong chemical smell. A strong perfume smell can also be used to try to cover up any odors coming from the package.

Unusual weight or rigidity: These devices can have an unusual weight for their size, because of the materials needed to make an IED. It can also be too rigid or hard; the IED components can be built into a device such as a pipe to protect the mechanism and provide fragmentation. If the device is not constructed into something to hold it together, it must be built on some type of hard flat object to hold the components in place and keep them from moving around or bending during transport, this hard flat object will also act as part of the fragmentation effect increasing its deadliness. This hard surface is what makes it unusually rigid and can add more weight to the package/letter.

Unevenly balanced or lopsided packaging: If the components had not been secured properly, they can shift during movement which could cause them to move to one side of the package, throwing the balance off and making it look lopsided.

Springiness: This could be because the activation mechanism that they are using could be a pressure-release type or a break contact type—both would require some type of spring in it to ensure that as the letter is removed from the envelope or an object is removed from a package, the device will go off.

Greasy marks/oil stains: Such as when you have popcorn in a paper bag, or the stain French fries cause on a to-go bag or potato chips on a paper plate. This happens because explosives contain binders to hold the components together; some are petroleum based such as Semtex-h while others are mineral/vegetable oil based like C-4. These types of explosives will "sweat" and the resulting stains will seep through and can be left on the outer packaging of the device.

Looks repackaged: The package/letter appears to have been opened carefully and then resealed. There can also be excessive materials used to wrap the device like too much tape or lots of wrapping paper; this is done to help contain the components and prevent any accidental openings of the device.

When considering whether something is a package or letter bomb, remember that these are common indicators only. A device may have or exhibit none of the above indicators—depending on how it was constructed and who put it together. A package could also have several or all of these indicators and not be an IED. These indicators are mentioned to give you a general idea of what to look for when it is probable this type of attack can be used against you. Do not forget that a parcel can be delivered by many means: personal carrier and private messenger, FedEx, UPS, postal service; it could even be put into a private mail box by someone walking by or placed into a buildings mail slot.

How to protect yourself: While the indicators above will give you an idea of what to look for when screening your mail and packages, there are several other things you can do make yourself less vulnerable to this type of attack. If possible, you need to not accept any deliveries at your residence, get a PO Box, and go there to pick up your mail. At your work, all mail and packages—regardless of how they are delivered—need to go to one place for inspection and distribution. This location needs to be located away from any vital portions of the building, critical equipment and away from any large number of people, preferably this would be in a building away from the main building or offsite. The personnel that work in this section need to be trained in letter/parcel bomb indicators, and, when possible, they should have the equipment necessary to screen mail and packages before they are delivered. There are X-ray machines that can scan packages, mail, or other devices that can detect hazardous items without opening the letter or packages themselves. Many of these devices are expensive; there are field expedient ways to check letters and small packages, such as using a stud finder or a metal detector, it will pick up components of the device such as wiring, batteries, and other materials, and they are inexpensive and easy to obtain. Using these types of devices, along with the indicators, provides an accurate detection system and will help you confirm any suspicious packages faster so that the appropriate authorities can be called. A combination of all we have talked about will increase your ability to search more efficiently and raise your level of security against the use of such devices. Another benefit of having all mail and parcels distributed from one office is that you will always know who to call if a suspicious package is placed in your office while you are away.

Suspect mail assessment:

- Attempt to verify item with recipient
- Is it expected?
- What are the contents?
- Verify sender (was the item sent by who is indicated on the parcel?)
- How was it delivered, who signed for it?

What to do with a suspect item: When you identify a package as suspect, there are several things you need to do to ensure the safety of yourself and others.

- Do not move it from its current position; if holding it, gently place it down
- Take note of its size, shape, and why you think it is suspicious (give to authorities)
- Isolate it as much as possible (without moving it)
- Evacuate the area
- Notify Law Enforcement and building security
- DO NOT put in a confined space or in water
- Prepare the area for an explosion; open windows and doors
- Do not transmit any RF (radios, cell phones, wireless phones) within 25 feet

WAIT FOR THE PROFESSIONALS, IT IS ALWAYS BETTER TO BE SAFE.

VEHICLE BOMB SEARCH

Vehicle bomb searches are covered extensively in the book published by the Taylor & Francis/CRC Press titled *Survival Driving: Staying Alive on the World's Most Dangerous Roads, Second Edition* (ISBN: 9781032065625) but below is a quick overview.

The primary reason to conduct a car bomb search is so you can be observed by the terrorists, and any observers or surveillance personnel, and they will then know that you perform a thorough, systematic search of your vehicle before you enter it. From this, they might logically conclude that you have a heightened security awareness and profile.

That being said, another reason is of course to find a bomb. A good car bomb search should take 5 to 15 minutes: anything shorter means that you will not have enough time to do a good search and anything longer than that and people will start skipping it because it takes too much time. So, before getting into your vehicle, you must first search it for any type of tampering and for a possible bomb. Before you start your car bomb search, you need to look for telltale signs in the surrounding area, such as pieces of tape, wires, scuff marks on the body of the car; any signs of tampering; and any foreign objects on, near, or around the vehicle. This is a tedious thing to walk around and scrutinize things lying on the ground and trying to remember if they were there before but don't get lazy or complacent; your life and the lives of your family members is a high price to pay for complacency or laziness.

Next you need too visually divide the car in half, lengthwise. Begin this part of the search by starting at the middle front of the vehicle and start working to the left (to the right if you are sitting in the driver's seat). Remember to never put your hands somewhere you can't see and use an inspection mirror and a small mini mag flashlight to inspect the darker portions of the vehicle.

- Inspect the grill, the front of the bumper, underneath it, and behind it.
- Inspect the bottom of each tire, front and rear, where it makes contact with the ground you are looking for pressure or pressure-release firing devices. Inspect the underside of each wheel well. A bomb may be attached to the underside of the wheel well by magnets taped to it. Inspect the top of each tire and the coil springs.
- Inspect the whole right length the vehicle, the underside, rear tire, and wheel well.
- When you get to the rear check the trunk for signs of forcible entry or tampering, inspect the rear area and underneath the vehicle to include the bottom and the top of the gas tank. Check the opening of the exhaust pipe for anything inserted into it. You can prevent this by placing a screen over the end of the exhaust pipe or drilling holes through the exhaust pipe with bolts inserted and welded.
- Inspect the gas cap for tampering or for a bomb or incendiary device that may have been dropped into the tank. A technique for detecting signs of tampering is to place a piece of transparent

tape on the gas cap and body. If the tape is broken, it is a sign that the vehicle has been tampered with, another way is to mark the body and gas cap with fingernail polish or tape, just don't tighten the gas cap all the way before you do this; when you check, the marks should still be lined up. If they are not, someone tightened the cap down; you should also consider getting a locking gas cap.

- Inspect the left rear tire and wheel well. Inspect the same way as you did the right side. Inspect the left side and underside. Inspect the same way as you did the right side.
- Inspect the top, bottom, and length of the exhaust system and pipes; also, inspect the top, bottom, front, and rear of the muffler. It is easy to place things on top of these areas.
- Inspect the drive shaft top, bottom, and sides for bombs, especially around the universal joints.
- Inspect the left front tire and wheel well. Inspect the same way as you did the right side; next, inspect the left front grill and bumper. Inspect them the same way as you did the right side.
- Always check inside the car for an intruder, then check the door locks. If you locked the car when you left it and you find it unlocked when you return, don't get inside, move away from the vehicle and go to your destination by other means, and report it. If the car is still locked when you return, and if there is no sign of tampering on the weather stripping around the doors or windows to indicate that a coat hanger was used to unlock the door, unlock it and open the door.
- Once you have the door open, inspect under the driver's seat and the passenger seat for a bomb with a pressure device that will be activated by your body weight. If satisfied, open the hood by releasing the hood latch and inspect under the hood. If your vehicle does not have a hood-opening latch inside the vehicle, you need to install locks on the hood.
- If you suspect that something is wrong with your vehicle, leave it and report it.
- Two people can do a more thorough search and inspection of a vehicle. One man works to the right and the other works to the left, starting from the front middle of the car. Each man makes a complete search of the car, checking everything his buddy has covered and completing the inspection at his buddy's starting point.
- When searching a car by yourself, it does not matter whether you work to the left or to the right, as long as you inspect the whole vehicle. When making a visual search, do not touch anything, as you might detonate a bomb and don't forget to inspect the ground and the area around the vehicle for trip wires or clutter.

BOMB SEARCH TECHNIQUES FOR BUILDINGS

A building search will usually be conducted after a bomb threat or warning has been received and, after reviewing the facts, a decision to search is made. A building search includes the outside of the structure also, so you always search from the outside, then move inside for a floor-by-floor, room-by-room search; the interior search is usually the most difficult because a device could be hidden anywhere and in anything.

Potential IED hiding places in outside areas:
Dumpsters/trash cans
Storage areas
Structures close to the building
Parked cars
Bushes
Street drainage systems

This is not an all-inclusive list; it depends on what type of area the structure is in and what is around it. These areas should be reviewed on an annual basis, to keep the list updated of what to check in case of a threat. You must also be aware of the danger of secondary devices which can be placed around the area; this has happened in the past with abortion clinic bombings.

Potential IED hiding places inside the building:
Mail parcels or letters
Desks or other storage type containers
Trash cans, trash baskets, recycling containers
Utility closets and boiler rooms
Ceilings with movable panels
Areas that are hidden by drapes or curtains
Recently repaired areas, such as walls, floors, or ceilings
Restrooms
Hallways
Vending machines
Shredders and the shredder bags
Refrigerator

Once again, this is not an all-inclusive list; one should be made up that covers your specific building and the rooms within.

After the decision to conduct the search is made, the building needs to be evacuated in an orderly manner; personnel who work there must take their personal items such as bags, briefcases, backpacks, and purses.

There should be a designated search team ready; this team will consist of people from each floor who are familiar with the area with an understanding of what should and should not be there. To make it go quicker and in a systematic way, the facility bomb threat plan should have diagrams of each floor, and room search cards which will be maintained in each room searched; and when the search is completed, they will be filled out by the person who searched it and given to the floor search supervisor.

THE BOMB THREAT PLAN

The first part of the bomb threat plan you put together will be designating who will have the authority to make decisions and will be responsible for the actions that need to take place. Then, you need to have a roster of who will supervise each search, the outside search, the garage/parking area search, the detailed room search and the common area/public area search, and the people who will be conducting the searches at each location. You also need to designate where the command post will be located to carry out any operations required. It should be centrally located, with easy access, good communications to help facilitate the coordination of the bomb search effort. Then, a rally area for personnel who are evacuated out of the building needs to be designated and the people who will be in charge at the rally area or areas to get an accountability of personnel. People should know who is in charge, where they need to go to be accounted for, who and where they report to for search operations, and who has other additional duties and activities that deal with the bomb threat plan.

Evaluation of the threat: Once a bomb threat is called in or notification is given by some other means, someone has to determine the validity of it. This important decision will be made by evaluating all available information concerning the threat to include:

All information recorded on the bomb threat card by the person taking the threat call, and that person's impression of the caller.

Background noises if the threat was made by telephone; these noises could help give some type of indicator of the caller's location and proximity to the threat location.

Target identification, did the threat make reference to a specific location or person in the building? Did he give any information that would indicate he knew about the facility and that it was a valid threat?

Access, if he gave a specific location, is it possible for a device to be placed there?

Recent activity, analysis of recent terrorist activities to include bomb threats, hoaxes, and bombings.

Once the evaluation is made and is considered a valid threat, then action will need to be taken to ensure the safety of personnel first, with damage to buildings, equipment, and data second. NOTE: In the absence of any positive information indicating a hoax or invalid threat, all threats should be taken as valid and appropriate action taken.

The evacuation: There are a number of tools that will help the person in charge to make the decision to evacuate, not evacuate, or partially evacuate the building or facility. The assessment of the threat is one tool, as well as past incidents, past threats, etc. With today's heightened sense of security awareness and physical security now in place at facilities considered at risk, you should consider that the most likely place for a device to be placed is on the outside of a facility in a location to do the most damage, since an evacuation might put employees at risk if you evacuate and have their rally point next to an IED or car bomb. The next place that will be used to place a device would be those areas with easy access for anyone, or the areas accessible to the general public; this includes restrooms, waiting rooms, hallways, building lobbies, elevators, parking garages, or lots, etc. So, when evacuating personnel through these accessible areas, you might be temporarily putting employees at a greater risk. Those designated rally points or assembly areas need to be away from parking lots, curbside parking, or anywhere where there is the possibility of hiding an IED, an open field, a fence line, etc. These rally points should not be public knowledge to keep them from becoming target areas of potential threats.

Once the decision to evacuate is made, the person in charge will have to decide whether to conduct a full building evacuation or a partial evacuation. A full evacuation should be conducted when there is a credible bomb threat that does not list a specific location or target, a partial evacuation is made when the threat is made against a specific target, area, or place or a suspicious item has been found and reported; in this case, the immediate area around the suspicious item and the areas above and below need to evacuated. Evacuating a building can be a very hectic, confusing exercise; it requires a high degree of planning and needs to be practiced on a regular basis, conducting drills and rehearsals so everyone will know what they need to do, how they need to do it will make people more comfortable with these drills and help prepare everyone for the real thing. Once the building is evacuated, access controls should be put into place immediately to prevent people from reentering the building, for the facility to keep people from leaving the grounds until local law enforcement arrives, and to keep onlookers from entering the grounds. When the decision to evacuate is made and completed, all gas, fuel, oxygen lines, etc., to the facility need to be turned off at the main valve outside the building to prevent any secondary explosions in case a device does go off. Electricity should remain on so the search teams have enough light to do their job, but all major machinery needs to be turned off by the operator as part of the evacuation. All elevators need to be sent to the floor right above the lowest level and stopped so that they cannot be used until they have been searched. Or, they can be locked and all search teams can use the stairs, though in a large or high-rise facility, this may be difficult. NOTE: All employees being evacuated need to unlock all desks, drawers, cabinets and take all their personnel items with them, backpacks, purses, lunch sacks, box's, briefcases, laptop bags; this will remove clutter from the work areas and this will allow the search teams to cover areas more effectively.

The search: The search procedures need to be written down and reviewed periodically by those who will be responsible for carrying them out to ensure they are up to date and if people who were involved have left than they have been replaced in the search plan and the replacements are familiar with it, this plan will include floor diagrams, building plans, exterior diagrams, and plans for an outside storage buildings and/or garages; there should also be examples of room search cards, the location for the room search cards should be the same in every room so they can be easily found. The search itself needs to be quick, thorough, and systematic and should be carried out only by personnel who are familiar with the areas being searched. It is important to note that EOD and law enforcement personnel should not take part in the search but be stationed at the control center. They should only be called to a location if a device is found. The searches that will be conducted need to be conducted at the same time: the building search to include a detailed room search, the roof, and public area search; the exterior search to include the grounds, the garage search. There will be one person in charge of each search; all searchers will report to him; he will pass the information to the control center. Two-person search teams are usually the most effective for detailed room searches; it may be hard to have enough trained people to do the outside areas and garage areas. The people on the search teams need to be familiar with the areas they will be responsible for searching, usually the people most familiar with a facility are the groundkeepers, maintenance personnel, and the security staff, since part of the job requires them to enter all portions of the structure at one time or another.

When searching inside the facility, you always start at the lowest portion of the building and search your way up to the roof. You should begin the search on each floor in the public access areas, since these areas have no access control and are available to everyone. This is the easiest place for an outsider to get into and place a device. After you search the public access areas, then you continue with the detailed room search.

Detailed room searches: The search needs to start from the center of the room, with the room being split into halves and divided into three layers. Each searcher needs to know how the room has been divided and what is contained in each section, and the search areas should overlap for better coverage. When you first enter the room, the searcher should go to the center of the room, stop, and listen. There is the chance you may be able to hear a mechanical triggering device since it is the easiest and simplest to make. You need to search each room by height, assigning specific areas for each team member. You need these areas to overlap so you don't miss anything. You should have no more than two people search a room; any more than that will be to confusing and could lead to portions going unsearched. You start at one end of the room in the center with both searchers next to each other. This is where you start each search, then walk to the wall, walk down the wall scanning, turn in to the center walk along the wall; when you meet the other searcher, you walk down the middle of the room back to the start point, you need to concentrate on focusing your scanning to the height level for that sweep of the room. The search team will do four sweeps through the room by layers. All items not necessary to the search should be left outside or turned down such as cell phones.

First layer search: Will begin at the floor level and moves up to hip area. When a device is left, this is the area most often used since it is not in the normal line of sight. During this search, there will be lots of clutter. This will include employees personnel stuff that was left behind to purses, backpacks, briefcases, lunch containers, and also other normal office items such as waste baskets, shred baskets, desk drawers (employees need to unlock before leaving), box's containing papers. Searchers also need to look under floor rugs and mats, etc. The searcher is scanning for any objects that seem out of place or unusual for where they are located. The searcher should also look for signs that furniture was recently moved such as indentations in the carpet when something was moved and not put back in the exact same place.

Second layer search: Will go from your hip to your chin; this layer will include packages on desktops, bookshelves, pictures, anything mounted, hung on the wall and things sitting on top of desks, books cases, etc.

Third layer search: Will go from chin to the ceiling; this is again a sweep around the room looking at all items at this height, hanging plants, speaker systems, emergency lighting, ceiling mounted light fixtures, ventilation ducks, etc.

Fourth layer search: Will be added if the room has false ceilings or suspended ceilings; this layer includes looking up in the ceiling at anything sitting on the ceiling panels at the hung lights, basically anything from the suspended ceiling to the hard surface above it.

Once each area has been searched and cleared, the person who conducted the search will fill out the room search card, sign it, and give it to the supervisor, and he will mark it as searched on his diagram and call it in to the operations center. There needs to be a way to mark it so it does not get searched again in the confusion, different colored chalk needs to be part of the search team kit. If the room has doors, they need to be left open after it is searched and cleared and then tape will be put across the entrance, and on the floor right in front of the door, you will need to write in blue chalk if okay, red chalk if suspect items were found. With a time recorded, doors and windows need to be opened to help disperse any blast pressure if a device does go off. If it is felt that, after a search, that dog teams need to be brought in, then the search teams will accompany the bomb sniffing dogs. When they clear each area, once again a chalk notation should be made and the room search card will be updated and returned to the search supervisor.

Elevators: These are part of the public access areas that need to be searched both pedestrian and freight; when searching elevators, they need to be brought down to the level right above the lowest level and then have their doors blocked open (disperse blast pressure if a device goes off). While the search is taking place at the lower level, the elevator well will be searched and then the underside of the elevator. When searching the inside, all panels that do not have tamper proof locks need to be opened and searched and then the top of the elevator which means you will probably need a ladder. At each level, the doors to the elevator shaft need to be opened and a visual inspection of that area needs to be made by the personnel searching that floor. When you get to the roof, the machinery that runs the elevator will need to be checked. Once all parts have been checked, then the elevator can be freed for use. NOTE: Elevator shafts and the well are going to be dirty and messy. There can be as much as 1–3 feet of grease and dirt buildup along with all kinds of trash depending on how often the maintenance crew cleans up these areas. But the grease and trash still need to be checked by hand; long dishwashing gloves will work best. When doing this part of the search, be prepared to get dirty.

Stairwells: These will need to be searched also; it is better to keep them clear of anything, no cabinets and trash cans, etc., and then these can be checked quickly.

Searching the grounds: The search team for the grounds once again needs to divide the area into search sectors that overlap. You should start the search about 50 feet away from the building and work your way in; the main entrances and exits should be where you start your search teams, working your way around the building. As you are searching these areas, you need to go through the trash cans, dumpsters, incinerators, mail boxes and any water storage, water drainage systems, look in and under bushes, etc. Pay close attention to those areas where people walk on a daily basis and by main entrances and exits, also any areas such as smoking areas or break areas, since a bomb would be set to cause as much damage and fear as possible. Once each area and item are searched, the search team needs to tape receptacles closed and write with chalk on the item, sidewalk, etc., which team searched and when they finished.

Garages and parking lots: The search teams for these areas will be focusing on receptacles inside any parking structures. All drains need to be looked into, drainage systems with grated covers that can be removed and any areas with nooks and crannies around pedestrian exits and entrances. These will probably be the areas they want to strike at unless there is a specific person targeted. Is the access to the building's parking areas controlled? Do you have guards? Are visitors allowed to park on the grounds or in the parking areas that employees use? Are visitors and vendor vehicles searched? If you do not have an access-controlled parking area for employees only, then there will always be the possibility of someone walking or driving into the parking area and placing devices on vehicles or in other places to cause damage.

Suspicious objects: When an object is found that looks out of place or suspicious, HALT what you are doing. DO NOT TOUCH. It needs to be marked so it can be found, and a chalk or tape trail from the entrance of that area to the object needs to be put down, so EOD can find it. Also, the area it was found in needs to have the entrance marked and the floor supervisor needs to be informed and he can inform the operations center. The search does not stop. This is because there might be more than one device planted, or the suspicious object you found is nothing more than some ones lunch The search needs to be moved to a different area, so as not to interfere with EOD personnel. After an object has been found and reported, only then will EOD personnel enter the building to view the object and determine whether it is an IED or not. They may go in at this time with a bomb sniffing dog to confirm the presence of explosives on the suspect object. Once an EOD team enters the building, they are in charge. If they want everyone evacuated, then everyone gets out. If they want to remove the object to detonate it somewhere else, they will do it. If they want to detonate in place, then that will be done, THEY ARE THE EXPERTS; help them do their job.

If the search is concluded and no device is found, then it is up to the person in charge of the crisis team to confer with EOD and law enforcement to decide if there is a need for a bomb sniffing dog search to go through the facility. If it is determined that the physical search was thorough enough, then the supervisor can declare the incident over and allow people to return to the building. ONLY ONE person can make this decision with input from the bomb search supervisors, EOD, and local law enforcement.

HOAX BOMBS

This is a tactic and a device that is used to extort, harass, or otherwise intimidate people, businesses, emergency responders, and the population in general. A hoax bomb device is normally a combination of components intended to simulate or infer the presence of an IED, but there are no explosive components. These types of devices can cause panic, fear, and will tie up first responders, emergency workers, and they have the possibility of shutting down streets, buildings, subways, etc. Why? Well, when a hoax device is found or called in, it has to be treated like it is the real thing until an EOD team can get there and make the determination if it is or not. So, the terrorist gets all the benefits of wasting resources, time, causing fear, etc., without actually having to expend vital resources and nor cause any actual physical harm.

Post incident: After the incident is over, the person in charge needs to decide what to say to the media. It is a good idea to have only ONE person designated to speak to the media so that you can control what information is released. You also need to sit down immediately with the entire bomb threat team and do an after-action review; this is so you can determine what went right, what went wrong, and how to fix any problems to ensure you have a working bomb threat plan.

Bomb Threat by Phone

What do when a bomb threat is received by phone: All personnel who answer a phone on a regular basis need to have a bomb threat checklist maintained by their phone. There should be a procedure that everyone is familiar with about what to do if they receive a bomb threat by phone.

If possible, you should always record the call or have more than one person listening in; you can do this by having a codeword or some other type of signal in place when you need to inform the second person.

The person needs to stay calm, listen, and ask questions which are on the bomb threat worksheet. The caller will probably answer questions or tell you what needs to be done depending on his motivation. If the person answering the call informs the caller that there is not enough time because of people, he might be more specific so you can do a partial evacuation to avoid injuring anyone, etc.

The person making the call will be the best source of information available about the device and its location; also, they will be the best source of intelligence for the investigation, so the person taking this call needs to:

- Keep the caller on the line as long as possible, ask them to repeat the message, write down exactly, or record every word that he says.
- If the caller does not give the bomb location, ask him.
- If the caller does not give the time it will go off, ask him.
- If the phone has a display, write down the phone number it shows. DO NOT HANG up the phone at the end of the call, even if the caller does.
- Remind the caller that the facility has people in it, and that a bomb going off could result in the injury or death of innocent people.
- Pay attention to background noises which may be a clue to the caller's location or identity.
- Listen closely to the voice of the caller; male or female; any accents; speech impediments; mispronunciation of words; speaks loudly or softly; calm, excited; be specific about words used and do not paraphrase.
- If a system is in place and you can report the bomb threat while still talking to the caller, do so. If not, then as soon as the person taking the call hangs up, they will need to GO to the person in charge as designated in the bomb threat plan and make the report directly to them.
- Then, the emergency services need to be called along with the Federal Bureau of Investigation (FBI), Bureau of Alcohol, Tobacco, Firearms and Explosives (ATF), and other appropriate agencies on your bomb threat plan calling list.
- The person who took the call, their notes, and any recordings need to remain in place and kept away from others so their memory will not get cluttered; they will need to be interviewed by all law enforcement agencies.

Written Bomb Threat

When a written bomb threat is received: If the threat is received by any written method, all materials need to be saved: the envelope, any container it came in, etc. If it was delivered, you need to keep the person who delivered it on site, if possible. If not, try to get a photograph. Once the threat is recognized as such, people need to stop handling the item, to keep from contaminating any evidence left; this will help law enforcement in their investigation.

- Rewrite the threat on another sheet of paper and note the following:
  - Date, time, and location the document was found or received
  - Names of anyone who saw this happen
  - Place the original in a bag or envelope

Then, the person who received it should leave someone to watch it and go to the person who is in charge as designated in the bomb threat plan and inform them.

Emailed threat is received: The person receiving it needs to leave the message open on their computer and then notify the site decision-makers. If there is time, print or photograph the message and subject line, noting the date and time.

Verbal threat: If a person receives a verbal threat, they should try to get a picture. If the perpetrator leaves, they need to note the direction the person went. Notify site decision-makers immediately. Write down the exact threat as it was communicated to you. Note the description of the person who made the threat. The following is an example:

- Name (if known)
- Gender
- Body size
- Distinguishing features
- Race
- Type/color of clothing
- Hair and eye color
- Voice (loud, deep, accent, anything that is distinguishing)

What you need to have: Every organization should have a bomb threat plan in place, reviewed on an annual basis. Part of this should be a Bomb Threat Checklist (Figure 3.1).

Everyone who has a part in the bomb threat plan needs to know it. Bomb threat plans:

1. Designate the chain of command for bomb incidents (i.e., who is in charge).
2. Designate where the operations center will be and who will be in it.
3. Have the communications plan, what type of communications are used, phone numbers, etc.

Bomb Threat Check List

Time of call __________

Exact words of caller:

____

____

____

____

DO NOT HANG UP THE PHONE at the end of the call

Question that need to be asked:

When is the device going to go off?__________________________

Where is the device located?________________________________

What kind of device is it?_________________________________

What does it look like?___________________________________

Did you place the device?_________________________________

Why?____

Where are you calling from?_______________________________

Why are you calling?____________________________________

What is your name?_____________________________________

What will set the device off?______________________________

Does it have an Anti-tampering device?______________________

Callers Voice:

Calm	Disguised	Nasal	Angry	Broken	Stutter
Slow	Sincere	Lisp	Rapid	GigglingDeep	
Crying	Squeaky	Excited Stressed	Accent	Loud	
Slurred	Normal				

Is the voice Familiar, Who does it sound like:________________________

Background noises:____

Additional Comments:

____

____

____

____

FIGURE 3.1 A Bomb Threat Checklist.

4. Will designate who makes the decision on a bomb threat, how they have to make that decision.
5. Lay out the procedures to be followed when a threat is received or a device is discovered.
6. Will have the primary and alternate evacuation plan, with rally points.
7. Designate search teams for each area and who is on them by name with alternates.
8. Designates what areas which teams are responsible for.
9. Puts in place the procedure of how each search will be conducted, how it is reported, and how it is recorded.
10. Crisis response plan in the event that an IED does go off before found.

CHAPTER 4

Hostage Survival

The taking of hostages has been used as an effective method for people to gain control of situations when there is a law enforcement or security presence preventing them from accomplishing their mission. Sometimes, the operation is taking hostages to force those in power to deal with them and their demands. It also provides them the ability to negotiate with those in power, since the taking of hostages is basically the equivalent to the setting up of a bargaining position.

REASONS BEHIND TAKING OF HOSTAGES

Hostage taking is unique because it uses the morals of society that places value on human life as the center piece for negotiations with those in power. Whatever the motivation of the person who takes hostages, the basic purpose remains the same; it is a way of setting up a bargaining position to achieve an otherwise unattainable objective.

How They Chose the Victims

A victim may have value to someone. Most governments will not negotiate with terrorists, but this does not mean others will not—for example, the victim's value to his family, his employer, the church, or even himself. There are many examples of private citizens, organizations, churches, and business have met ransom demands, thought this often further promulgates the act, since the terrorists know people will negotiate and pay.

A victim can be chosen because of his *job position*, because of his *status in society*, or simply because of his *nationality* such as being an American. Remember that terrorists like to strike at symbolic targets to strengthen their position and increase the publicity. Holding a janitor probably wouldn't make the news; holding the president of a company would and there is clearly the potential for a higher payout.

DOI: 10.4324/9781003292647-4

The chosen victim may be *hated by his captors*; the terrorists may blame him the person directly for any problems. They may target people who in the near future will cause problems for them, like soldiers, other military or law enforcement, judges, etc., so that they may have some influence on this individual's work. Also, don't forget the taking of a hostage is a means of setting up a bargaining position. They may go after people's family members, kidnap a police chief's child to get him to quit doing searches, kidnap a judge's family to influence a decision. When they hate a person, they hate what they stand for and represent.

Terrorists need *publicity* to get noticed. Because of their desire to get media attention, terrorists are not going to kidnap someone and not tell anyone. The more popular, famous, or the more status the victim has, then the more publicity will be generated over the event, which is exactly what the terrorists want and what they need to further their agenda. *Publicity* is one of the necessary tools of the terrorist.

But a majority of the time, a hostage victim is just an *innocent bystander* of circumstances, usually caught up in an operation that went wrong who is in the wrong place at the wrong time. The hostage takers themselves did not plan for this and have no clue as to what they are doing, which can make it an even more dangerous situation for the victims.

Examples of this happen every day, robberies that go bad so when the police arrive they keep everyone in the building as hostages in an attempt to bargain themselves to a better situation: sky jacking, workplace violence, school violence, etc. There are numerous examples of people who take those in a building hostage to better their situation and try to bargain their way out or to a better resolution.

Different Categories of Hostage Takers

The act of hostage taking by its very nature forces the terrorist into a series of stereotyped responses. The hostage now becomes a pawn who is in a difficult place, caught between the terrorist and the authorities as each tries to control the situation. During this, the terrorist can become violent as he strives to control the situation and move the event toward completion of his objective. While the authorities will be trying to exert some control and limit the terrorist's control, it can cause more violence and threats of violence. By how a victim conducts himself during this situation will either enhance or diminish his chances for coming out of it unharmed. The more the hostage understands about his situation, the people who took him, why they took him hostage, etc., the better he will be able to predict the hostage takers' behavior, his moods, and goals. Having an understanding and feeling of some control can assist to diminish a hostage's level of fear.

Attempts to classify hostage takers by category is an artificial matter, since we categorize hostage takers merely to provide guidelines on how to deal with. The only real way to identify the terrorist is to examine them in the *context of his relationships* to the population, their organization, places, ideas they express in their doctrine, and the historical context with which they are associated. The question that needs to be asked when examining any terrorist operation is, "Does the ideology they have support the actual beliefs of their group, or is it merely a tool used as justification for their actions?"

Terrorist organizations are usually arranged into separate social levels or status levels. At the top level of their social hierarchy is the single person, who was raised and lives in an urban environment, is extremely bright, and a *dedicated idealist.* The terrorists at this layer of the terrorist's social hierarchy comes from professions such as engineers, lawyers, medicine, and business owners. As you travel down through the layers of a terrorist organization, you will find a greater diversity of personality types, and all are needed at some time in the organization. *The disillusioned*—this group is generally made up of the younger members of the group, high school, college, etc. They are recruited from college and university campus and special events that appeal to this age group, they are very impressionable, and can be swayed very easily to a cause they believe is right; *The mentally ill*—sociopaths or people with criminal tendencies, a disregard for authority, following the law, etc. These are recruited from prisons and jails and tend to be the more violent members of the group and are used to commit many of the acts since they often lack the fear of being caught. They also lack society normal values against violence, threats, and stealing; *Ideologically motivated*—these are those people who believe in the organization and its goals, the true believers who feel that what the organization is trying to achieve is the only way it should be; The *mercenary*-style terrorists—these are those people who will work for anyone who pays them. They learned their skills and, having been tested, and now sell them to the highest bidder. The cause is not so important as the paycheck; *Personal revenge*—these are those people who feel those in authority have wronged them somehow, or a company, government, or an individual. They want to right the wrong done against them, any way that they can, since they feel that there is no other option available to them. Most terrorist organizations will form a cross-section of the population from which they emerged, since they draw their followers and supporters from that population mix. So, the selected personnel who perform terrorist acts such as hostage taking will be a representative slice of the organization for that area from which the members came.

These *local slices* of the organization will still conduct their operations in support of the larger organizations.

As a generalization, there are two categories of terrorist organizations that use hostage taking as a routine act that pose the greatest risk to people: these are political extremists and religious fanatics.

Political extremists: This type of group will often operate with an organization structure very similar to the military. In doing so, they have a greater degree of physical control over their members and more discipline. This control may hold any violence within the planned operational limits that had been set out in the operations planning phase. But, within any group, there may be one or more of those terrorists whose lack of self-control and their propensity toward cruelty will make them more dangerous to the hostage. These types of people will need to be identified early in the captivity to help you in staying out of their way as much as possible and avoid any confrontation that might encourage them to do violence. While the group leader may be able to hold this type of person in check through his established control of the situation, the group leader will not always be there.

The average age for the political terrorists ranges between 19 and 35. Their youth and lack of experience heightens their fanaticism for cause; it also blinds them to any reasonable dialogue about their beliefs and insulates them to any attempt at appeals based on morals, decency, or fear for their own safety. These political extremists are often prepared to pay the ultimate sacrifice for their cause, but they are not necessarily suicidal, and rarely plan an operation without any chance of survival. So, when their chances for a successful operation start to diminish, their primary concern often changes to one of self-preservation and escape.

This type of terrorist organization usually only takes hostages when they have some control over the operational environment where the incident will take place, or they have a country friendly to their cause or a neutral country that will provide them shelter. The taking of hostages and other incidents by this type of group can be used as a barometer of the political extremism that is present in a given geographical area.

Religious fanatics: This group of terrorist's usually has three subcategories that they fit into. They are usually *members of a recognized religion or a radical offshoot of that religion*, a *member of a cult*, or a *religious loner*. Throughout history, not one religion has been without its excesses in promoting itself above other religions. So, rather than become cynical toward any one religion, we should acknowledge that the unsavory aspects of religious extremists result from human failings, corruption of beliefs, and feelings or perceptions of inadequacy rather than saying the religion itself is at fault.

This group of *religious fanatics* will share a common, unshakable belief that their cause is the righteous cause and that their actions are appropriate in supporting and the spreading of their religious views. Terrorist incidents, including the taking of hostages, seem to increase in a geographical region when traditional value systems of that region are threatened, attempting to change, or appear to be on the verge of total collapse. Religious fanatics will have a charismatic leader who can enthrall his followers and he will preach a form of exclusivity by which only the select few can enter heaven by following his guidance and his beliefs. As such, if you are not a member of his chosen group or sect, then you are an enemy of their beliefs. The only exception to this would be the religious loner who has no need for others to interpret his beliefs. Similar to the political extremists, the religious fanatic cannot admit any fault in their belief system and religious values. Since they are true believers in the cause, if they perceive any hostility, disbelief, or contempt toward their religion by a hostage, they may react with violence to reinforce their beliefs. When they plan an operation, their values and religious beliefs will be a part of that. Since they feel superior because their beliefs are the true beliefs and they are in the right, they may be inflexible in their pre-planned actions and have a preference for death, rather than surrender or fail in an operation. This death wish is strong in many religious fanatics.

The next category of religious fanatics is *the cult*: A cult can be described as a sect or offshoot of a religion considered to be false, unorthodox, or extremist with members living outside some society norms under the influence of a single charismatic leader without political power. A cult does not have to be based upon religion; it can be formed around any theme or belief, political, racial, looks, etc.

There are some who are religious extremists who will engage in terrorism and will seek death at the hands of someone who does not share their beliefs; they see themselves answerable only to God. People like this will behave strangely. They are often irrational and very defensive. They are very protective of their religion and their belief system and will feel threatened when someone does not understand or misascribes their leader, their beliefs, or any of the activities they do in the name of their religion. They may have the belief that to die by the hand of a non-believer is the holiest achievement possible for them and will gain them recognition in the eyes of God. Because of this belief, they may take any chance to seek death and may even be suicidal. Because of this part of their belief system, they may choose to seek a violent resolution to any situation where they have hostages by killing them, sometimes in public, without mercy in an attempt to meet the goals of their religion and attain status in the eyes of their God.

The lone religious fanatic: This type of terrorist or person is not often encountered but could present the gravest threat to a hostage. This type of belief is even more detached from reality and less rational than a person who belongs to a cult. Why? Because this type of religious fanatic will claim to be operating on direct divine orders from God; how can you talk to someone who is talking with God? Because of this mentality, he will probably be the most dangerous type of hostage taker and the least susceptible to any type of reason.

There are several more categories of hostage takers I want to talk about. They are the fleeing criminal, the criminal kidnapper, the wronged person, and the mentally disturbed person. These types of hostage takers are not members of a terrorist organization usually, but they still present a threat to you when traveling or living anywhere in the world.

The fleeing criminal: This type of hostage taker is a criminal whose attempted crime has been stopped before its completion, and the planned incident did not take place as he had originally hoped. So, the criminal then takes hostages on the spur of the moment to avoid immediate apprehension, to have a bargaining chip for his escape and because he does not know what else to do and needs time to think. This type of hostage taker usually does not want to die to achieve his goal, because he has no cause to die for. He will often settle for less than his original demand, when he recognizes he is in a no-win situation, but has a way to maintain some dignity, and not experience a sudden loss of power to his current position. A too-sudden loss of power can create agitation, despair, hopelessness, or panic, which can lead to the impulsive hurting and/or killing of a hostage. A peaceful resolution can usually take place with time. The more time that has taken place since the start of the incident, and the more the negotiators have to talk with the hostage taker, the more likely it will end peacefully.

The Criminal kidnapper: This type of crime is on the rise worldwide, and the people who commit this type of crime are motivated by money, so everyone who this type of person thinks he can get money from is a possible target. They usually will start out with an outrageous sum for the ransom demand to start of the negotiations process. During this process, they will start using political and ideological rhetoric to create fear and anxiety in those they are negotiating with. The major problem when dealing with this type of criminal is that they wish protect their identities and the locations of their operations. There is an even chance, they will negotiate in bad faith and kill their victims even if they get paid.

There is a new type of criminal kidnapping called the Express Kidnapping. This was started several years ago in Mexico and other central and South American countries. An express kidnapping is when a victim is taken and forced to withdraw money from an ATM or bank. This is usually done at just before midnight. A victim will be forced to withdraw the max cash limit available, then after midnight—when the transaction cycle is reset—they are forced to do it again. Usually, with this type of kidnapping, the victim is released after the max amount of money is taken out. It is a good idea when traveling to use a bank account with limited money in it, so if kidnappers see the withdrawal slip, they will know you do not have more to give. If you maintain a large amount in the account being used, they may keep you longer to keep withdrawing money.

The wronged person: This hostage taker wants to inform society at large of his perception of the defects in the "system" or in the "establishment" because they have had some type of disagreeable experience with the system or establishment in the past. So, this person could be seeking some form of redress for that bad experience or wants publicity of the wrong that was done to him. He tries to take justice into his own hands because he feels he has no other recourse to his dilemma. He will gain support from people outside the immediate incident because there are bound to be other people who have suffered the same type of social injustice from the same people; these people will create backing and support for the hostage taker during his incident. This type of hostage situation is very different from taking a political hostage because it is motivated by a wish for personal revenge and personal satisfaction. This type of hostage taker knows he is right and will behave in the manner of the one who is right and doing the right thing to make things better for everyone who has suffered like them. This behavior will be reinforced and compounded upon by media coverage of the incident and of sympathetic outside groups supporting the hostage taker and his mission. In his mind now that he has support and others believe like he does, he could now justify violence toward the hostages as a means of getting what he wants and knows is right. He could think that the hostages represent the "system" and are part of his problem and the hostage taker could use them to avenge those wrongs done to him, which puts the hostages in a dangerous situation.

The mentally disturbed person: There is the possibility that some hostage takers are mentally disturbed when someone is taken hostage by a mentally disturbed person: it can be either a spontaneous act or planned incident which can be surprisingly well planned in spite of the hostage taker's psychosis. The mentally ill can have intermittent periods of lucidity in their particular psychosis. It may take an extended period of observation/conversation or contact with them before their craziness is revealed in their speech or mannerisms. The particular psychosis he suffers from, whether it is delusions or hallucinations of some type, will probably not impair his ability to do what he has planned to do during the hostage-holding situation. With this type of hostage taker, building rapport will be a difficult thing to achieve and maintain throughout the incident. So, any efforts you take to build rapport with them should be consistent for the entire time of the incident. In almost all recorded cases of a mentally ill hostage taker, they have a death wish as part of their psychosis; this death wish can only be satisfied by the murder of some or all of the hostages, causing the authorities to kill him, a suicide type death that will also kill some of the hostages, or some type of combination of both. If you are a hostage of someone you feel is mentally ill, you should conduct yourself in a very relaxed, laid-back, non-aggressive, non-antagonistic manner, don't ridicule, break the hostage takers rules, etc. You should also avoid any prolonged eye contact with the hostage taker as this can be viewed by him as confrontational and a challenge. It is safest to allow him to control the situation and conversation.

Under the influence of a narcotic or alcohol: Sometimes, a hostage taker of any of these types could be under the influence of drugs or alcohol, this only complicates matters since drugs and alcohol effect different people in different ways. They could have mood swings, start making ultimatums, and start riding that emotional roller coaster. Be alert and aware of any signs that could mean a turn for the worst. Do not confront them; rather offer sympathy to them or encourage their behavior while they are under the influence.

Guidelines When Dealing with Hostage Takers

There are some general rules a person should follow if they find themselves in this type of situation; these rules or guidelines will help you determining the best course of action to ensure your survival of the incident.

Listen to what the hostage taker is saying, to others, to the negotiators, to authorities, to himself; this will help you determine what his reasons are, why this time this place, how he is feeling, etc. This is necessary in helping you learn more about the hostage taker, so that you can use that information to increase your chance of survival.

Try to determine any areas that are *touchy or sensitive topics* to the hostage taker, things like politics or religion; once you know those areas of sensitivity avoid them in any conversation you have with the hostage taker and look for signs of agitation or aggressiveness if he is discussing it with someone else. If the hostage taker picks you to vent to or confronts you about something he needs to tell someone, you need to become an active listener. Pay attention, look at him, answer in a non-confrontational way when an answer is needed, seem sympathetic to him and his reasoning. This does not mean adopting his value systems, beliefs, or reasons, but, rather, you will adapt to them in order to increase your chance of survival.

People with strong religious convictions can be very touchy and extremely defensive about their religion to others. They hate *having to justify* their religious beliefs to those who do not share them and they *hate being judged on their beliefs*. It is important if you are conversing with the religious hostage taker that you pay attention and do not make a mistake in describing his religion and characterizing its value system. After all, it would be really upsetting for this person to have been explaining this to you for 20 minutes, and he asks you a question and you cannot answer or you *mis-ascribe* the values or beliefs he just explained to you. He could think you were not paying attention or don't care—or catch on that you don't truly agree with his worldview. Never make assumptions about the hostage taker's religion or his beliefs or value system.

You must make every effort to *establish and maintain rapport* with your hostage taker or takers, this will greatly enhance your ability to survive the incident, after all they may hesitate to harm someone they see as a person and they have something in common with, but will not hesitate to cause harm to someone they do not know or know anything about; but in building this rapport, you must never attempt to assume the role of a hostage negotiator or adviser, you need to stay very far away from this role and leave it to the professionals. Rapport-building techniques will be discussed in greater detail in another chapter.

One last area that needs to be discussed is the potential use of children by your captors, as part of the guard force or support force during your captivity. Most people tend to believe that children are harmless or "just kids," etc., and can be easily swayed. This would be a mistaken assumption on your part! The youth factor and their daily living environment tend to heighten their fanaticism, making them unreceptive to any attempts to reason with them or carry on reasonable dialogue. Children in these roles also feel insulted when you try to make appeals to their morals, decency, or expressing that you fear for their safety. After all, this is the life they have chosen. They are doing something, in their mind, to better their condition, and they may even be patterning their actions after someone they hold in high regard: a hero figure, old sibling, etc. Try to avoid them when you can and limit your interaction with them; they will do what is necessary to win the approval of their elders, peers, etc., and impress them with how tough they are.

Being taken as a hostage—regardless of who, where, or why—is dangerous enough in the best circumstances, but it can safely be said that political extremist hostage takers represent the most danger because of the value of symbolic targets to the goals of gaining media attention and reaction from their enemies as a part of their political ideology.

PERSONAL CONTINGENCY PLANNING

In today's post 9/11 world, everyone should consider themselves to be potential hostage victims of one type or another, especially if traveling overseas. This can happen if for no other reason than for publicity for a cause. So, everyone needs to consider personal contingency planning as a fact of life. It is especially important before you travel and is vital if you are traveling to those areas considered medium or high risk that have an history of hostage taking incidents or criminal acts that target foreigners.

Personal affairs: You need to take certain steps to prepare yourself as a potential hostage for the rigors of any captivity; this in turn will provide you and your family some peace of mind. You need to lessen the impact and any possible trauma on both yourself and the family. The easiest way to accomplish this is to ensure your family and personal affairs are in good order before you travel. They should be kept in good order all the time since you never know when something may happen to you or another family member. You need to keep your will current with your family situation, you should also draw up powers of attorney in case they are needed by family members during an extended absence, leave your passwords to accounts, account numbers, etc., with your family so they know how to access money if it is needed, you might want to leave the information of what credit cards you are traveling with so that your family can freeze them if you are taken, denying a potential money source to the hostage takers. You should make plans and leave instructions with family just in case you are abducted or caught up in an incident where you are detained. Make up a family emergency packet with instructions for the family, cash money, credit cards, insurance policies, along with the name of who they should contact at your company, such as security manager, public relations, human resources, for assistance the company will provide. This should be left with the instruction that it not be opened unless you become a hostage or disappear.

Briefcase/personal baggage contents: You should not carry classified documents or other sensitive company information, personal information, or potentially embarrassing items in any personal baggage that you have such as a briefcase, handbag, or backpack. This includes ensuring your personal digital assistant (PDA), laptop, cell phone. Even if it is on your person, you need to ensure that it does not contain any information that the hostage taker can use. In the event you are taken hostage, you need to be prepared to explain phone numbers, itineraries, addresses, names, and other items that are being carried at the time of capture. During the time of an incident, if it is a random type kidnapping and you are being held, you should try to convince your captors that they have taken the "wrong person," and that you are of little or no value. If you are in a hostage situation, you should try to distance yourself from the hostage takers enemies and not come across as a friend or ally of the authorities that the hostage taker is fighting against. This tactic will not work if the hostage takers intent was to carry out an attack against, say, the defense attaché of a certain embassy, and one of the people taken as a hostage has documentation in in his briefcase or on his person that shows he is associated with the defense attaché or works in that office. Any type of compromising document that is found on the person taken can easily disprove the argument that a person is just an innocent, or that the terrorists have taken the wrong person. It could actually give the hostage taker an even better hostage or victim than he had planned. You should also password protect your computers, tablets, cell phones, and any documents on these devises.

Medicine: Anyone who is traveling and is a potential target of a terrorist incident should always carry a week's supply of any essential medication he needs when traveling through or is stationed in a high-risk area. If he is taken as a hostage during an incident or becomes a kidnap victim, he needs to explain the importance of his medication to those who are holding him. If it is a long duration incident, it might become necessary that he request additional medication; remember you are more valuable to the captors alive than dead, and you are much easier to care for when healthy than when sick. You should never be reluctant to accept what medication is provided. It could be a local generic brand or name, you should know this type of information for every area you travel through. Do not think they are trying to poison you or harm you intentionally. They could already do that without hiding it; so, it is more likely they want to keep you healthy and alive to serve their purpose. Only when you being killed will serve their purpose better should you begin to worry.

THE MOMENT OF CAPTURE

Resist or Surrender?

The moment of capture—probably a dynamic high-energy moment with lots of moving parts and with shock, adrenaline, and the fight or flight reflex all trying to work at once—you as the victim will have to make an instantaneous decision. Whether to resist the attackers by physical force or by fleeing the attack site or surrender to attackers. It can be very dangerous to resist the attackers, but there are circumstances in which it is more of a risk to you to be captured. The potential victim needs to be planning ahead during his movements and throughout the day. If, for example, the potential victim decides in advance that he will be attempting to escape—it is an attempt he needs to plan for it, visualize, and practice ahead of time. What this means is throughout his daily routine, he must observe possible attack sites, choke points, and points of interception. For each location, he needs to decide his best course of action for escape and have a plan; then, he must visualize these plans to resist for whatever location he is at, whether it is his home, his office, or during movement. The initial moments in the attack and capture are the most dangerous for everyone, not just the victim. The attackers are going to be very tense with their adrenaline kicking it up a notch during this period. As such, those carrying out the attack may commit unintended violence with the slightest provocation from any bystanders and the victim. Any type of normal movement or simple acts of compliance, such as reaching into a coat or purse to get identification or raising a hand to scratch or adjust your glasses, may be interpreted as an act of resistance and precipitate a violent sometimes deadly response. You as the victim may want to reassure that attackers that you are going to comply and that you will not try to escape. In most situations, it may be unrealistic to believe that during a planned operation, the selected target can escape the attack site when faced with someone who has the element of surprise and a plan. Plus, they will be determined and armed to overcome any foreseen obstacles. Many intended victims have attempted to escape the attack site and evade the hostage takers; most of these people have been killed or injured in the attempt. Other victims who resisted at the moment of capture were extremely fortunate to receive only cuts, bruises, teeth knocked loose or out, and broken glasses. This is not the best way to begin an indeterminate period of captivity: with injuries. When a victim is confronted with such overwhelming odds against him, it is important that the victim not panic or try any sudden movement that might rattle an already anxious and overly excited gunman. The victim needs to remember that the attackers have meticulously planned and executed this operation and are well prepared for it. This preparation by the attackers means the circumstances of the incident/attack favor them not the victim. The victim needs to realize that there will probably be little opportunity for escape.

The terrorists or captors who have you in their custody will use blindfolds, gags whatever is necessary to control you; this may even include the use of drugs in extreme cases, and it will happen at the time of abduction. You as the victim need to keep in mind that your attackers want you alive, if they had wanted you dead you would be, so do not be alarmed and do not resist the use of physical control measures, the more secure and comfortable the attackers feel about you once you are in their control, the safer you are. Remember they are just as worried, excited, afraid, and pumped up on adrenaline as you are. Struggling with them as they attempt to put these measures into effect will cause your attackers to react, and this will result in even more severe measures by the attackers. The terrorists may use drugs on you as a means of physical control so they don't have to have as many personnel to watch over you. They may do it to get you to sleep or to keep you quiet, and prevent from crying, causing trouble, etc. Even "truth serum" drugs, if used, have an effect similar to that of alcohol. Once again, you need to remember that YOU the Hostage have no choice in the use of drugs by your captors. So, you should not physically resist; if they want to do, it they are going to do it, and you are just likely to be beat up if you resist. The terrorists will likely use other accessories for their own security, such as blindfolds or hoods, to keep you from knowing where you are or where you are being moved too. They also help as a means to protect the identity of members in the organization that is holding you by not allowing you to identify them after your release.

As a victim, you should always stay alert to what is taking place in your surroundings; even if you are blindfolded and gagged during movement to the holding area from the attack site, you still have the ability to listen, feel, etc., what is taking place. By using your other senses to obtain information about what is taking place around, it will give you a purpose. And, since you now know you are not completely helpless, it will help control any fear and panic you may have. You can occupy your time by using your mind; try noting sounds around you or passing you, your direction of movement, the passage of time, and any conversations you can hear especially terrorist or captor conversations. This type of information will be useful later to you or to the authorities when you are released. They can try to map out what happened to you and what you might know about the terrorists, their organization, and tactics. You should also leave your full fingerprints on any surface you come into contact with, in vehicles, elevators, etc. This will assist law enforcement authorities in recovery if they find the vehicle that transported you and your fingerprints are in it. Such evidence provides them another piece of the puzzle.

STRESS

A Part of any Captivity

A simple definition of stress is the reaction of the body to any demand made upon it. You can further define it as a body condition that occurs when a person faces threatening or unfamiliar situations. Stress causes a person's energy and strength to increase temporarily to meet the new demands placed upon the body, but not all stress is bad, after all some stress is necessary for getting the best performance out of athletes, soldiers, etc., because stress causes changes in the body to take place that can help an individual overcome challenges and danger.

A person's physical condition will directly affect their ability to handle stress of any kind; their response to any stress will also depend on whether they feel that they have some control of the situation taking place. Any type of threatening or unfamiliar situation that induces fear and surprise will not cause as much stress if you can predict the incident before it takes place, overcome the stress after it takes place, or by understanding what is taking place. The ability to control your thoughts and realize your situation can help you control stress. Things are less stressful if you think you know what is happening or what is taking place.

There are ways in which you can exert control of your mind and body to influence your physiological reaction to an event and limit the *harmful stress* it can cause.

Maintain your confidence: You must keep confidence in yourself and in your ability to survive the current situation, and your ability to do this with your honor intact. You should also maintain confidence in your country's desire to end your captivity and their ability to make this come about: even though some countries have a policy of non-negation directly with terrorists. There are ways a country can exert influence on the host country to maintain your release. In a criminal hostage scenario, hostage negotiators are trained to talk to the hostage takers and resolve the situation. Maintain your faith in your family, that they are doing what is necessary for you. That they have the ability to take care of themselves until you return and in your God, regardless of what your faith, religion, or your religious values. Such things have helped people during times of stress by bringing comfort and peace of mind to them.

Maintain your physical condition: People tend to forget about maintaining their physical fitness when they are taken as a captive. If you are kidnapped and going to be there for a long or an indeterminate amount of time, you need to put a program of exercise into your daily routine. It will probably not be possible to do what you are used to, but you need to do what you CAN to keep your body fit. In line with this, you must eat and drink everything you are given no matter how strange, how bad it looks or smells, or unusual it may seem too you. It is probably exactly what your captors are eating and you need food to maintain your strength.

Take care of any family matters: Because you do not want your mind continuously going to what thing might be happening to your family while you are being held captive, you need to make sure that everything is taken care of to keep your mind at ease. If you don't, then these little things will eat away at you and can cause you worry. If you are kidnapped or taken hostage, you need to accept that your family can get along without you for a little while, that you did everything you could, and that you cannot change things now that you might have forgotten or not planned for. No sense worrying about them now.

Maintain sleep discipline: Many people when they are in captivity, lose sleep discipline; sometimes your captors will do this on purpose by not allowing you to know when it is night and day as a means of controlling your sense of time. It is important that you set a schedule for sleep and stick to it, the idea being to avoid sleeping too much which can cause you to become mentally slow, lethargic. You can lose track of time; physically you might feel tired all the time, etc. We have all seen this when we sleep too long on the weekends or on days off; this is amplified if it is allowed to continue. A good schedule of sleep will help you maintain your mental and physical abilities during your time of captivity.

Practice recreational activities: During a long time in captivity, you need some recreation to keep your mind occupied and to allow interaction with others. Once again, you are a hostage or captive, so you will need to be inventive to find things your captors will allow you to do. You can try reading, mental exercises such as building things in your mind like your dream house, writing by keeping a diary, asking to listen to the radio, or to watch TV for some parts of the day. You need to ask for interaction with others, even your captors or other hostages if there are any—even if it's just talk to each other about families, playing cards, or chess. Things done in a positive way with purpose can ease the physical and mental stress on you and any fellow captives. Anytime you are with others, there is the opportunity and time for some type of recreational activity.

Maintain a daily schedule: It is important to your mental and physical health that during a long captivity, you try to maintain a daily schedule, setting a routine and sticking to it gives you an ability to plan ahead and have some small control over your life in this situation; it allows you to regulate your sleep habits, exercise, and eating also. A familiar pattern of daily events will help take some of the fear and unknown out of life during this time, and it allows you to stay occupied and have a purpose each day.

Keep your sense of humor: Being able to laugh at some things and trying to have a sense of humor is vital to your mental health, everyone enjoys a good laugh, and it relaxes and refreshes; depending on the types of captors you have, it will be rough finding things that are humorous but you can do things like giving nicknames to your captors; joke about your situation, find humor wherever you can, laugh and joke on the inside when your captors are around; this will also help in building a bond with your fellow captives if there are any. NOTE: Prisoner of wars (POWs) in Vietnam, Korea, World War II, have said that humor was one of the things that helped them make it through.

A positive mental attitude: It is also necessary for you to maintain a positive mental attitude about your situation and your future; one of the most deadly aspects of long-term captivity is that of being mentally worn down and developing a mental lassitude (exhaustion, lethargy) after that it is not long before depression can set in creating both physical and mental problems. You need to be on guard against this not only in yourself but in fellow captives or detainees, you need to constantly, vigorously oppose it in yourself and help others to do the same.

Verbally talk yourself down: We have all been in situations where things are not going well, whether playing recreational sports or taking a test—when this happens, we talk to ourselves to build up our confidence and to help us make it through the situation we are in at the time. These situations are no different. Sometimes, if you are having a bad day or night, you can talk yourself through that bad situation. We know ourselves best so talk to yourself, go over what was done or said in a situation, and what could have been done better in that situation and how you will handle it next time.

Depressing thoughts: Do not let depressing thoughts start taking over and consume you; as soon as you start getting those thoughts, you need to stop them and start thinking about the positive aspects of what is taking place, what is being done to release you, etc. Focusing on depressing thoughts and thoughts of catastrophe will start you into a downward spiral of depression; remember, you must accent the positive as much as possible.

Religious values: Over the ages, religious values have helped many people cope with situations they did not think they could handle. Your religious values, your beliefs are things that will provide a source of strength to you through your captivity or detention, This an individual choice; all religions give strength, purpose, and help to those who value them. Practice them and maintain them in times of trouble and need.

Learn or develop methods to communicate: Communication is an important part of how we live; after all, humans are social creatures and the need to communicate or talk is strong in us. It also helps when we have others we can talk to, possibly share thoughts with, etc. During a time or situation that is outside your normal life experience, you need to communicate. When possible, talk, listen even if it is just saying hi to the person who brings your meals. Trying to engage him or her in small talk for the time they are there will help you cope with your situation. If there are other captives or people being held, you can talk to them, if the captors do not allow talking, you need to find or develop other ways to communicate with those others who are being held. If you have former members of the military captive with you, they will know and have a basic grasp of the military TAP code, which has been used extensively by former POWs to develop and maintain lines of communication with others. Just do your best to communicate with others, as *COMMUNICATING* will help you cope mentally with the new situation.

Keep faith with your fellow captives: If you are held with other hostages, captives, or detainees, it is important for you to keep the faith with them and in them during the time you are being held. These others can be a major source of strength to you, and you for them; it is important to communicate, help each other when you can and continue to nurture this faith continually throughout your captivity, to believe and help each other as much as possible. Because your fellow detainees will be such a source of strength for you, your captors may attempt to divide you and pit you against each other; he wants you as weak as possible, so it is easier to deal with you. Remember this when you are dealing with the captors and keep your faith in them, keep your strength.

MEDITATION

Another way to control the stress you may be feeling is to practice a basic form of meditation, where you can relax, think about what's happening, your situation, self-reflect, calm yourself, etc. Controlling stress is important for you during the time you are being held. So, there are four basic components to meditation necessary to bring about the effect you are looking for to help *CALM* your nerves and mind; they are:

Quiet environment: You might not have the ability to control this aspect of your captivity, so you need to find a quiet area with as few distractions as possible to allow you to concentrate and focus your thoughts.

A mental device: This is something that allows you to shift or focus your thoughts from the externally oriented thought, to the internal oriented thought. It needs to be a constant stimulus of some kind; a sound, a word, or a phrase that can be repeated silently or aloud; if this isn't working for you, you can try fixing your sight on an object to allow yourself to focus your thoughts. A major problem with people trying this is that distractions, especially distracting thoughts, tend to set the mind to wandering. Practice, practice, practice. Repetition is a way to learn to break the train of distracting thoughts and learn to focus.

A passive attitude: First off, when you try anything for the first time, it is not going to go exactly as wanted. So, when distracting thoughts occur, you need to toss them out and refocus your attention onto whatever you are using to focus your attention either the action of repetition or of gazing. Do not worry about how well you are doing the technique; the more you worry about it, the more distracted you will be and this may prevent the response we are looking for from occurring. You need to be calm, relaxed, and adapt a let-it-happen attitude; this passive attitude is perhaps the most important element in getting the desired response. Those distracting thoughts will occur; they always seem to creep in, so do not worry about them. Once again, if these thoughts start intruding on you as soon as you become aware of them, simply go back to your repetition of the mental device.

A comfortable position: To become relaxed and able to focus your mind, a comfortable position will be important, this is so you will have no undue muscular tension, cramps, pain, etc. Some people have methods that call for a sitting position, some of those will even recommend the cross-legged "lotus" position of yoga (this hurts me just thinking about it), and a lot of people, who try lying down, have a tendency to fall asleep, because of what you are trying to achieve, just remember you should be comfortable and relaxed in body as well as mind.

- To begin your meditation, find a place and then sit quietly in a comfortable position that you can maintain without discomfort, then close your eyes, and concentrate on your breathing and on your mental device.
- Now, as you are sitting and focusing on your breathing, start relaxing specific muscle groups by first tensing them and holding that tension for a slow five count and then relaxing that specific muscle group. You should follow a sequence top to bottom or bottom to top such as the following sequence: feet, ankles, lower legs, upper legs, buttocks, hands, lower arms, upper arms, shoulders, neck. During this period, if you become uncomfortable, go ahead and shift your position to one more comfortable, then continue. Finally, at the end, take some time to focus on, but not alter, your breathing.
- When you are focusing on your breathing, you need to breathe through your nose; most people don't, so you will need to concentrate on this, focusing on your breathing will also allow you to become aware of it. Sometimes, your breathing may have become quite shallow, keep taking those deep slow breaths. You should keep breathing through your nose for around 10–20 minutes. You will occasionally have to open your eyes to check the time. When you are finished, you should sit quietly for a couple of minutes with your eyes closed and, later, with your eyes open. Take your time standing up; you do not want a head-rush.

You should not worry or become unmotivated if you don't achieve your goals the first few times you attempt to achieve a deep level of relaxation. Also, don't set unrealistic goals thinking you will do it for an hour the first time; it is a gradual learning process for you and will take time to achieve. Maintain a passive attitude, don't try forcing it, and permit relaxation to occur at its own pace. Remember, when distracting thoughts occur, ignore them by not dwelling on them. If you can practice the technique once or twice daily, or right before you go to bed each night, it is better to practice and become comfortable with this technique before you need to use it in captivity. Try not to practice within two hours after a meal; the bodies digestive process seems to interfere with a person's ability to achieve the relaxation response.

Enhancing your ability to handle stress will help you out in life even if you never become a hostage; handling stress well allows you to think more clearly, to cope with new and unusual situations, and helps keep you physically well so you are not run down, lethargic, or sick. Practicing good stress management will assist you in coping in any environment you may find yourself in, and it is a skill you can use for life.

THE STOCKHOLM SYNDROME

The reason we want to be able to control stress in our lives, regardless of environment, is because the stress that is introduced into your life—should you be taken hostage or kidnapped—will have significant physical and psychological impacts. This sudden increase in stress can lead someone, who is put in this situation, to alter their behavior significantly from their normal way of behaving. One of these potential changes can occur when someone is a hostage or detainee and begins aligning himself, his opinions and beliefs, with that of the people who are holding him. This phenomenon is called the "*Stockholm syndrome*" and happens more than people realize.

The *Stockholm syndrome* first came to notice by the law enforcement community as a result of a failed bank robbery that then turned into a hostage-barricade situation in Stockholm, Sweden 23 August 1973. At 10:15 AM that Thursday, the normal daily routine of the Sveriges Kreditbank was destroyed when a submachine gun was fired to get everyone's attention, as plaster and glass fell among the 60 bank patrons and employees. One heavily armed gunman called out, "The party has just begun." This situation continued for 131 hours and ended up permanently affecting the lives of four of the younger hostages. This situation is what gave birth to a new psychological phenomenon, which was named the Stockholm syndrome. During the next 131 hours from 10:15 AM, August 23 until 9:00 PM, August 28, four employees of the bank were held hostage. This included three females, ranging in ages from 21 to 31, and one 25-year old male. The hostage taker was thief, burglar, and prison escapee named Jan-Erik Olsson; he kept them inside the 11- by 47-foot carpeted bank vault. Eventually, another person joined Olsson. This man was another criminal and former cell mate named Clark Olofsson, age 26, who was brought to the bank and joined the situation after Olsson demanded and got him released from prison. Over the next 131 hours, law enforcement personnel noticed a change in the hostages. It was discovered that, going against normal expected behavior, the victims now feared the police more than their captors. What brought this to everyone's attention was statements that they made to the media such as "The robbers are protecting us from the police," etc. After the event, an investigation was conducted as to why the hostages had changed and now felt emotionally indebted and attached to their captors; this led to the discovery and an understanding of this phenomenon.

A good characterization of the Stockholm syndrome would be: *it is an automatic, probably unconscious, emotional response to the trauma of becoming a victim.* This trauma is brought about by the physical and psychological stress the hostage or detainee is placed under and can cause the person being held to react in a manner that is totally against his normal beliefs, values, and ethics. This phenomenon brought on by the stress of the situation can affect both the *hostage taker* and *the hostage as this bond works both ways* and is produced in the high physical and emotional stress of the situation—along with the close living conditions and constant exposure to each other. This environment causes an emotional bond to form between them which then leads to the development of a new joint philosophy: "It's us against them."

When a person begins to experience a great deal of unexpected and unwanted stress, they try to find a way to handle it. But, when a person in a high-stress hostage environment experiences this stress, their mind will seek a way to enhance their chance of surviving the situation. One way to do this is the *use of defense mechanisms*, which are defined as unconscious psychological adjustments made in the presence of danger. The three most common defense mechanisms are *denial, regression, and identification.*

- *Denial* occurs when a person's mind is overloaded by a traumatic experience or event. Some people's minds will respond to these types of incidents as if they were not happening to them; they may even express such phrases as "Oh no! Not me!" "This must be a dream or I must be dreaming!" or "This is not happening to me!" One type of person may deal with the stress of the event by believing it is all a dream and that he will wake up soon and it will all be over. Sometimes, a person copes with stress by sleeping, hoping it will be over when they wake up. Examples of denial can be in response to a bad car accident or the unexpected death of close friend or loved one. Usually, most hostages begin to gradually accept their new situation and grasp the safety valve with the thought that their fate is not fixed; they will view the current situation as a temporary thing and convince themselves that the police will come to their rescue. These changes in how they cope and deal with this situation, from denial in the beginning to delusions of reprieve by outside forces, reflect a gradual growing acceptance of the facts of their current situation and environment.
- *Regression* is an adjustment in behavior and results because the unconscious mind of the victim will select a behavior that person used successfully in the past when the person was confronted with a total dependency situation. An example of this is growing

up as children we were totally dependent on someone who was our primary care giver for all our physical and mental needs, telling us when to sleep, when to get up, when to eat, etc. In this type of hostage or detainee situation, the captors take on this role of primary care giver in our mind, telling you what to do, when to do it, etc. So, the theory goes, you are regressing to a time when others basically controlled your life for you.

- *Identification*: This happens at the unconscious level of the mind, which is seeking to avoid any type of wrath or physical or mental punishment by adopting the behaviors and adapting the values of their captors. EXAMPLE: A new recruit in the military, or at a law enforcement basic training camp, will identify with his drill instructor. The recruit or cadet starts out doing it to avoid punishment and stay on the good side of the person in charge. But, eventually, he changes his beliefs and values to reflect that of the instructor's standards and values because he now wants to be like him and admires his professionalism and abilities.

People who have become victims of the syndrome share common experiences with each other about what they experienced; these include positive contact, sensing and identifying with the human qualities of their captor, and a willingness to tolerate situations far beyond what they considered their logical limits.

- *Positive contact*: These are super-reinforced feelings of gratefulness/gratitude and comes about by the lack of negative experiences. It appears through studies that the positive contact is reinforced to a greater level if the victim has had negative experiences (beatings, rapes, and murder) early in the event, which is later followed by positive contact. Example: Every day before the victim is allowed to eat, the jailer hits him several times in the face. Then, one day the jailer comes in and allows him to eat without striking him; the victim is now grateful that he wasn't beaten.
- *Sensing and identifying* with the human qualities of their captors: This happens when hostages can relate to their captors as people like themselves. Dr. Fredrick Hacker called this the "poor devil" syndrome. During the incident, the terrorists or captors may talk about their own mental and physical suffering, their perceptions of life, and of themselves being victims of circumstance rather than aggressors, humanizing themselves in the eyes of the hostages who now relate and may even feel sorry for the "poor devil." The hostages may even transfer anger from those who have taken them hostage—and are holding them—to the

society, the establishment, or the situation that created the situation that made them victims. The hostages may even feel the terrorists are entitled to their protection from authorities and care, possibly going so far as to offer their help and support.

- *Floating logical limits*: This part of the syndrome deals with a person's preconceived level of tolerance and what type of actions and treatment they will accept from others prior to the incident in which they have become victims. Usually, before this type of situation happens to someone, people will already have in their mind a limit to what they will allow and how much abuse they will accept. This line they have drawn in their mind is their logical limit of treatment they will allow before they take action. But remember, this preconceived limit is usually set when people have never experienced that type of incident or treatment so they actually have little or no experience to base their logical limit on, and because the need to survive is strong in us, when we actually become a captive, detainee, or a hostage, people and the reality of the situation sinks in. People will then make the decision to move the line of their preconceived limits far beyond what they expected, before they experienced the situation first hand.

There are several response levels that measure how a captive has become a victim of the Stockholm syndrome; these levels are measured by their responses.

MINIMAL LEVEL: This is when the hostage has now changed his perspective and is looking at the events and situation from the point of view of his captors.

MEDIUM LEVEL: The victim of the incident now shows he respects and recognizes the terrorist's captors for the gallant efforts to help others; a victim sometimes is beginning to lose his grasp of reality at this level.

HIGHEST LEVEL: This has happened when the victim actually impedes the efforts of the rescue force or the negotiators. Sometimes, the victim may think that their captors are their only protection from the rescue forces, and, in other cases, the victims have actually aligned themselves with their terrorist captors. Victims who are at this level usually suffer long-term mental and emotional problems.

The Stockholm syndrome produces a variety of responses in its victims at the minimal level; the victim sees the event through the perspective of his captors. At higher levels, the victim respects and recognizes the terrorist's gallant efforts. The victim's responses to the syndrome have ranged from hostage apathy to actual participation by the hostage in terrorist activity, losing touch with reality and impeding efforts of the rescue forces and negotiation teams.

A two-way street: While we have talked about the negative aspects of the Stockholm syndrome as it pertains to the victims, it must be pointed out that there can also be a positive aspect for the victim. Remember that this syndrome works both ways so not only is the victim effected but the hostage taker can also be affected. They can start seeing you as a person instead of a threat and can switch their perspective to your view, etc. All of this can contribute to enhancing your survivability during the incident. During an incident, the longer it goes on, the more positive contact between hostage and hostage takers begins to take place; during this time, the Stockholm syndrome also begins to take its effect on the hostage and the hostage taker.

There is one more defensive mechanism I would like to talk about that is not discussed very often. It is called the *London Syndrome*. This happens when a victim is unable to endure the stress of their new situation; in most situations, people will keep their hostile and aggressive feelings toward their captors inside. In this case, a victim will become irrational and start exhibiting erratic behavior and begin provoking and antagonizing his captors. By exhibiting this type of behavior, he is basically demanding to be executed. The London Syndrome was named because of an incident during the Iranian Embassy hostage siege in London; one of the victims refused to compromise his beliefs and continually argued with his captors. While his fellow hostages asked him to abstain from this behavior, he refused. Though he was eventually killed by his captors, his death is what triggered the assault by British rescue forces.

Everyone should become familiar with the various behaviors associated with these two syndromes. This is done so you can recognize it in yourself and fellow captives when they start to manifest. You need to understand what needs to be done to counteract them so that you can remain clear-headed and help yourself or fellow captives adapt to this new situation and recognize and counter these various responses if they manifest.

ADJUSTING TO CAPTIVITY

When you are taken as a hostage, there will be a major change in your living environment and life; depending on how long you are held, you will need to adjust to this new captivity. The best way to gauge what your living conditions may be like as a captive in a foreign country is to look at the daily living conditions of the local nations who are at the lowest level of subsistence. This will probably be your new living condition and it may even be an even lower level than that. The new existence that a hostage will have to endure will vary greatly from incident to incident. As an example, some hostages may be held for days on a bus, airliner, or train where lack of environmental controls and lack of water, food, and toilet facilities can be almost unbearable. In other hostage situations, the hostages could be locked in another room, or they may be in the same room with other hostages but are hooded or tied, gagged, and forced to face the wall away from their captors. If the incident occurs when you are at one of your primary areas when it is seized, such as an office or a residence, you will find yourself in comfortable surroundings that you are familiar with. This will serve to take some of the stress out of the incident. Those who are victims of a kidnapping, on the other hand, are usually required to live in makeshift "people's prisons" in attics or basements and sometimes in remote hideouts away from urban areas and law enforcement. Usually, the cells in these prisons are small, and, in some cases, they will not allow the hostage to stand up or move around; this places more physical stress on the hostage which then leads to mental stress. A captive or hostage's sleeping and toilet facilities will probably be scarce, consisting mainly of a cot or mattress and a bucket or tin can for body waste, and no place to bathe. In other instances, no toilet facilities will be provided, forcing the hostage to soil his living space and himself, which can be used as a tool to dehumanize you and break you down mentally.

The experience of captivity and helplessness can further be compounded by a total lack of privacy for bathing, eating, sleeping, etc., which can produce that feeling of utter helplessness and dependency on your captors for every necessity of life in your new living environment. This is exactly what they want. It can and will be hard for you the captive to maintain dignity and self-respect under such conditions, but it is very important that you do as much as possible to do so. A captive's ability to maintain his dignity and self-respect may cause the terrorist captors to empathize with him and respect him; this in turn could lessen their aggression toward him, since most people, terrorist or otherwise, lack the ability to inflict pain unless the victims are dehumanized in their eyes.

For the long-term captive or hostage, it is essential for them to maintain a good appearance and their sanitary health as much as possible under the existing conditions. So, if you do not have the ability to wash your clothes, there are things you can do to keep your appearance up, over extended periods of time. You can do this by brushing off dirt and dust off of your clothes and shoes, keep your clothing straight, keeping your shirttails tucked in, smoothing out wrinkles in clothing as much as possible to help the overall appearance of your clothing. You should also keep your hair, mustache, and, if you have one, beard combed out and well groomed and also keep your fingernails and hands clean; all these things will help your appearance, mental peace of mind and is a subtle show of strength and willpower to your captors.

Another way to keep your *dignity* and *self-respect* is *bathing* whenever possible, not only for the physical benefits but the mental as well; however, while a normal bath or shower may not be possible, you still need to keep as clean as possible, especially your hands and face since this is what people will notice when dealing with you. But, you do this not only for appearance but also for health reasons. You should ask for the chance to bath or clean up. If they do not allow this, you can still use some improvised methods: take sunbaths, use paper napkins, leaves, or sponges. You can use any cotton or wool fabric and make it into a washcloth. Use your spit, use your imagination; there are many ways to keep yourself clean in any environment and situation.

Oral hygiene is the most prevalent healthcare problem that effects those in captivity during extended periods. You need to clean your teeth and gums; if a toothbrush is not available, you can fabricate one by using a finger to wipe your teeth or, better yet, wrapping fabric around a finger or shredding (fanning) the end of a stick. You should also use toothpicks or the equivalent expedient to floss and clean between your teeth; you also need to concentrate on massaging your gums.

One of the most important things you do in helping keep hold of your dignity is to maintain a positive attitude. As a captive or hostage, whenever possible, you should mingle with and talk to other captives; the captors may not want you to talk to each other while going about daily routines but a whisper, a touch, and even a smile and wink can be a big boost to someone. Assisting other hostages who need help can serve you well in the event you need to assume the role of a leader and assign tasks to others or initiate communications, or pass on information, etc. A hostage should also maintain an optimistic attitude and try to help others do the same; this will help him to confront the problems and stress of his new living environment and situation and deal with them. Even though it sounds corny, remember smiles are contagious; as a hostage, you should wear one. It is another way to humanize yourself in the eyes of your captors and will help any other hostages cope. The reverse of the optimistic hostage is a hostage who has given up and become reclusive, has no interaction with others, and is only concerned with his own well-being. This is a reinforcing cycle and will drive other hostages away from him and will make him stand out in a negative way; this in turn can destroy morale. The pessimist or introverted type of individual will find this time of captivity more difficult, and his ability to keep his dignity and self-respect will be badly weakened.

Fear: Terrorists and any other captors you have will use it as method to control, intimidate, and wear down their hostages and the negotiators working to obtain their release. The ways they induce fear are only restricted by their imagination. Some things done in the past include loading and unloading weapons in the presence of the hostages, shooting weapons in their presence when a hostage is blindfolded, displaying excessive fits of anger, and they can resort to physical abuse, slapping, beating, kicking, and conducting mock executions. The hostages greatest time of fear is during the first few hours of captivity, when they are still confused, disoriented, and not sure of what has happened to them, but as this initial fear subsides, the victim may begin to feel he owes his life to his captor. As time passes, these feelings of fear about what is going to happen, and their situation, can be transferred from them being afraid of the terrorist, to them being afraid of the authorities trying to help them. Past experience in hostage situations has shown that more hostages die or are injured during their rescue than are killed or injured by their captors. And, while death certainly is a possibility, statistically, the odds favor a hostage being released alive.

Time: Time can be one of the hardest things to deal with while being held; no news or information from any outside source, the minutes, hours, days ticking away and you have no idea how much time has passed. Your captors will probably take your watch so that you cannot tell time and thus keep a schedule. They do this to help in your disorientation. The passage of time without rescue or release can begin depressing you, even though it works to your advantage in the long run. The issue of time is also a factor in the development of the Stockholm syndrome in captives and captors and in any rapport-building efforts by the hostage or captives. To take away from the emotional rollercoaster that goes with being a captive, you as a hostage need to avoid anticipating release dates or allowing your captor to establish these types of milestones and/or dates for you. The captors can use this tactic to keep you emotionally off balance and to cause depression, etc. An example: "You will be released Friday."

You look forward to the day, then the captors say, "No, we changed our minds." All that anticipation and emotion is now changed to disbelief and anger, etc. When you do this, you are setting yourself up for an emotional fall if these expectations of release are not met.

Improvised time telling: Can be used to help you track your time in captivity. These methods include calls to prayers, any clock or bell towers, or the activities that take place at certain times accompanied by smells, such as baking, deliveries, etc.

Boredom: This is the one constant companion you will have as a hostage in your captivity; you will need to aggressively face boredom as a challenge for you to overcome while in captivity. You can do this by engaging in creative mental and physical activities to keep yourself mentally and physically sharp. Physical activities may be limited by your captors but you can do things like isometric exercises, running in place, pushups, sit ups, crunches, etc. You need to watch your caloric intake also, since you don't want to lose too much weight, that will eventually make you weaker. Mental activities were discussed before, reread old books in your mind, play chess games, build cars and/or houses, etc. Day dreaming, fantasizing, anything that will keep your mind actively engaged in an activity.

Illness: Another possible side effect of captivity for some may be weight loss; this loss may be considerable, and depending on your caloric intake, it generally will not cause health problems. Just remember to ask for food and water whenever you feel hungry or thirsty, and it may still occur even with an adequate food supply since captives often lose their appetite from stress and worry. In other instances, captives/hostages may suffer gastrointestinal upset, including nausea, vomiting, diarrhea, and/or constipation if they are not used to the type of food being prepared or they are using a bad water supply or unsanitary food preparation conditions. These symptoms can be debilitating, but they usually are not life-threatening. Eventually, you will gain a stomach for your new diet, and since the terrorists are primarily concerned with keeping you alive and well, any hostage should not hesitate to complain and ask for medication to help treat these problems. Since the terrorist wants their captives/hostages alive. they will get you medical treatment or medicine. Do not worry about whether it is the right type of medicine or not; your captors are not likely to take chances with your health and life by providing the wrong medicine. In past instances, terrorists have been known to provide medical care for their captives who were suffering from illness and/or injury.

Rapport: When you are a captive/hostage, you need to make every attempt to establish rapport with those holding you. This rapport may be the deciding factor that saves a captives life when it comes time for the terrorists to carry out their threat of execution or punishment if their demands are not met on time. You should make eye contact when possible without being obvious; especially during casual conversation. Look at your captor while you talk to him. Attempt to engage him in small talk about weather, food, sports; small talk is better than no talk at all with your captors. If you have photographs of family members, girlfriend, etc., show them to the captors. This can build a common interest since everyone has family. If your captors want to talk about their reasons for doing what they do, you should show an interest and listen; you do not have to be sincere. However, if the conversation turns to religion or politics, you could be on dangerous ground and this type of conversation should be avoided. When listening to them explain their cause, you as the hostage should let your captors know that while you might not agree with them, you are interested in their point of view. Do not argue with them; this can be seen as disrespectful. You need to accept the hostage taker for who he is according to his beliefs, not yours; after all, this is a common courtesy. As a hostage, you should also accept the captors' culture in a gracious manner, but do not put down your own either. As a captive, you also need to disregard the political or religious differences between yourself and your captors. You do this in order to search for the common ground between you and them; finding common ground is a step toward building rapport. One of the best ways to show an acceptance of another's culture is to learn their language and history. To start, a hostage should learn short phrases in his captors' language: greetings, please, and thank you. During this time, you should also work on other cultural idiosyncrasies that may reinforce the feeling that you accept their culture. This includes not refusing or otherwise making fun of their food. It is disrespectful and by rejecting it, you are saying it's not good enough for you. Avoid doing anything that is disrespectful to your captors; eat and drink everything they give you.

Isolation: More than likely at some point, you will be placed in what those in jail would call solitary confinement, but in actuality, you are being placed in social *isolation*. This is when the hostage/captive is completely denied interpersonal contact, no talking, seeing, observing others. An even more intense way to manipulate a captive is for your terrorist captors to use *perceptual isolation*; this is when they deny the hostage outside stimuli. They do this by using headphones, white noise, blindfolds, and tents or small enclosures to accomplish this goal. When this tactic is used by the captors, the captive must rely completely on mental activities to adjust to his captivity and try to overcome each type of act being used when he is placed in isolation. During time in isolation, the hostage will have fewer opportunities to build rapport with his captor, since he has no contact with them. So, he must use the chances he does have for interaction to their fullest in his efforts to know and build rapport with his captors. Rapport building will be discussed in more detail later.

INCIDENT RESOLUTION

Now, after having adjusted to captivity, the hostage has new challenges he will be faced with such as the end of the event or incident resolution. Remember, people are taken as captives/hostages so that the terrorists can establish a bargaining position, where they didn't have one before. Sooner or later, this will lead to rescue. If there is no hope of reaching a deal or release, when a deal is reached to the terrorists satisfaction, these resolution methods include armed recovery, unconditional release, negotiated release, ransom payment, escape, and worst- case scenario, death.

Armed Recovery: The rescue will be very dynamic, loud, and hopefully a surprise. Usually, the rescue will begin when the first hostage is executed. That act will serve as a green light for rescue forces that have been standing by and planning. You as a hostage must know the general acts of a rescue and be prepared to do certain things during rescue attempts. As the hostage, you are in significant danger. *NOTE: 79 percent of all dead hostages are killed in the rescue.* It is very important that as a hostage that you are alert to what is taking place around you, cautious, and obedient to any instructions from rescue forces when the rescue is occurring.

A sequence of events takes place when an armed response is being planned and beginning. First will be some type of surveillance, so those planning the mission will know how many terrorists, their location, and any threats to the hostages; second will be to take away the terrorist's ability to know what is going. Usually, snipers will shoot any exterior guards or lookouts; third will be a breaching entry, which means doors will be knocked in or windows broken out. They might use explosives depending on how the terrorists have barricaded the area; next will be flash bangs. These are small grenade-type devices that give off a loud bang and blinding light; they are used to blind and disorient people in an enclosed space so they cannot resist or fire on rescuers; then, they will begin clearing the building/rooms of all threats. This is the battle; finally, they will search each room and take control of all people until they can be escorted out and their identity authenticated. When the rescue begins, there are things that you need to do to enhance your survival. The first thing you need to do is to drop immediately to the floor, stay as low as possible, and avoid any sudden movement, especially with his hands. Remember they are trained to point their weapons toward sudden movement, especially the hands, and at this time, they do not know you are not a threat. *NOTE: During a rescue operation at Entebbe, a female hostage threw her hands up to praise the Lord as the commandos came bursting in, and she was shot by the commandos. Sudden movement also caused the deaths of two hostages in the South Moluccan train incident when Dutch commandos assaulted the train.* Find cover on the floor and start shouting your location, names, etc., so that the rescue forces can find and secure you faster. SHOW YOUR EMPTY HANDS SLOWLY and always keep them in the site of the rescue forces until you are secured by them. Do not attempt to run. You may be mistaken for a terrorist trying to flee. Do not pick up a gun and attempt to assist the rescue forces, even if you feel you have the training. The rescue forces will not know WHO you are or what you are trying to do; all they see is an unknown person with a gun, and you may be mistaken for a terrorist.

After the rescue forces gain control of the area, the hostage will probably be handled roughly. This is standard operating procedures for rescue forces; they must separate the true hostages from terrorists who may have thrown away their weapons and masks in an attempt to disguise themselves as hostages. *NOTE: This occurred during the May 1980 rescue operation at the Iranian Embassy in London. British Special Air Service (SAS) discovered terrorists hiding among the hostages after the initial assault.* Comply with all demands by rescue forces and do everything they tell you. DO NOT ARGUE. As soon as your identify is authenticated, you will be unbound and aid will be given. They are doing this for YOUR protection as well as theirs; not complying will get you roughed up and, in the extreme, could result in death.

Armed recovery on airplanes: This is a unique environment for the rescue forces to work in and for you to be in, so there are some differences to what you should do to enhance your survival of a rescue attempt on an airplane. First, know where the exits are and how to open them. Usually, the first indication of an rescue attempt will be an explosion. You should be prepared to do the following: assume the crash position, head in lap hands over your head, this gives you a low profile; pick your feet up off the floor, remember the flash bangs, and possible grenade use, the force of these explosions will follow the path of least resistance, which means under the seats of an airplane, by raising your feet you are protecting your feet, ankles, and lower legs from being damaged and possible broken; keep your eyes open to what is taking place around you, know if you need to move; in several instances, fires have broken out on planes during rescue attempts and people did not move to get out, or terrorists started firing into the civilians to kill as many as they could before they died. Get to the exit and get out. Once outside the aircraft, raise your hands and do whatever you are told; avoid any sudden movement, such as standing up, popping your head up, or jerking your hands (unless there is an incident like just described); do not help unless directed to by rescue forces, they may need you to help carry the wounded, help others off the plane, etc. But wait until they direct you to do this, as any action you take could seem hostile to them before that. Never touch any firearms if they are laying around. If you have a concealed weapon on you, tell the first rescuer you come in contact with and identify yourself. Do not move your hand toward it to show or expose it; they will secure you and take the weapon. Once out, run away from the plane with your hands up shouting "don't shoot, I am a hostage" until someone takes control of you. Comply with everything you are told to do. Remember that they have to verify your identity to confirm that you are not a threat.

The release: Most people never realize it, but the moment of their release from captivity is like the moment of initial capture, a dangerous circumstance. For the terrorists, they are giving away the one thing of value they have and are losing their bargaining chip. For those who are hostages, during this time, they may feel threatened by the change in established routine and some may even panic from the disruption of their normal daily activities. The terrorists will probably not tell the hostage anything so while the hostages will know something is happening, they will not know it is their release. *NOTE: The hostages of TWA Flight 847 were herded at night into a school yard. They did not know they were being released until they were turned over to representatives from Syria, who told them.* During this time of tension, there are rules the hostage needs to follow: they need to pay close attention to the instructions the terrorists are giving them when the release is taking place, after all the terrorists are in a high-stress situation again, outside their area of protection and exposed. Do not argue or question them and do not panic or attempt to run. You might cause the terrorist to take some type of action such as shoot you to stop you, etc. Remember, they are now outside of their comfort zone where they had total control, so don't cause them to panic by your actions at this time.

THE AFTERMATH OF A HOSTAGE SITUATION

Just as you prepared yourself mentally for being a hostage, now you must begin to prepare for the aftermath of your hostage ordeal. *The media* will probably be the first challenge encountered after you are released or rescued. The now former hostage should ask for a media spokesperson, if there is one available from his company or place of employment, or if the site where he was taken hostage such as a bank or airline has as a public affairs officer or other spokesperson available that you can get advice from and possibly act as a buffer between the former hostage and the media until he can get his bearings and get used to his change in status.

If the former hostage is confronted by the media and chooses to respond, then he should say or imply nothing that could be harmful to his fellow hostages if any who are still in captivity. You should keep comments as short as possible not discussing anything in detail and limit them to statements such as "I am thankful to be home" or "… alive" or "… out of captivity." You should never say anything or give any comment that is sympathetic to the terrorists' cause which might endanger hostages still in captivity or encourage them in future endeavors. The media will be all over you and your family because you are now NEWS; seek advice and avoid them when you can. It will help the incident pass much quicker.

The now former hostage should be mentally prepared to be *debriefed* by those in authority, the government, law enforcement, and military personnel. Once you get released from captivity, you should write down everything you can remember about the incident as soon as possible to aid in the debriefing process that will follow: things of interest to the authorities will be the location of guards, the description and placement of weapons and explosives, and any other information that might be of value to help those still being held or to help those in authority learn the terrorist tactics, techniques, and procedures. The former hostage needs to remember that although the information he is providing the authorities might seem insignificant to him, it could be the final piece in a puzzle that will aid them in the release or rescue of other hostages who remain in the captivity of the terrorist group that held him; or, it may assist in apprehending the captors and bringing them to trial.

Some former hostages may emerge from these ordeals with *hostile feelings* toward those in authority, the government, sometimes even family, etc. Most of these feelings of hostility are from the fact that they feel that these people, organizations didn't do enough to help them during their hostage ordeal, and that they should have been more active in their attempts at gaining their release.

And finaly, many former hostages, after having undergone their ordeal, will experience *feelings of guilt* for the way they acted during their captivity; this is especially true if not everyone is released or other hostages die during the incident. Any person during their time in captivity as a hostage may suffer some defeats; everyone has a breaking point, there should be no shame in this, but once released, these feelings will gnaw at them and will be constantly on their mind. Some former hostages may need professional help that will enable them to sort through their feelings and emotions about what happened during their captivity. If this assistance is available, the hostage should use it. If this type of counseling is not offered, then the former hostage should ask for help for himself and his family if it is necessary. Many times, people forget the families' fears and emotions during this time are just as rocky as those the former hostage, counseling, and assistance will help them.

CHAPTER 5

Rapport-Building Techniques

There have been times in all our lives when we have expressed prejudgment against others. We have or we know someone who has expressed a prejudice against an individual or group of people without ever having had any real dealings with them. Have you done it yourself?

Then, later, after you actually get to spend time with those you have prejudged, gotten to know them, you changed your mind about them. You found that you had to alter your preconceived perceptions, ideas, and prejudices. Whether you realized it or not, some rapport had been established between you and the people you had previously not dealt with and had known only from a distance. The process of establishing rapport not only enhances the communication process, but also has, in fact, been responsible for saving lives during hostage situations. Rapport building is a necessary extension of hostage survival training and techniques and can be used effectively to enhance survival. An example of how the power of rapport building was used as a lifesaving mechanism is during the skyjacking of Air France Flight 139 in July 1976. This incident culminated in a remarkable, successful rescue attempt by Israeli commandos in Entebbe, Uganda. While the hostages were being held on the ground, one of the terrorists had been given the specific instructions while guarding the hostages, he was to immediately kill them in any rescue attempt. During the incident over time, he had engaged in lengthy conversations with some of the hostages, learning about them, their beliefs, families, etc. During the rescue by the commandos, this terrorist who had interacted with the hostages decided to fire on the commandos, instead of killing the helpless hostages.

DOI: 10.4324/9781003292647-5

RAPPORT

What is rapport? The Oxford Dictionary of English Etymology defines rapport as a "*harmonious or sympathetic relationship*" and identifies its roots in the Latin word "*opportare*," which means to carry something back. Later on, we outline how carrying or reflecting something back to another person is a basic principle of rapport building.

You will also soon discover the techniques of rapport building are simple. As they are presented, and you begin to practice and use them in your daily communications with others, they will soon become a comfortable part of both your passive and active communication styles. Then, as you become more comfortable and confident in using these techniques, the uses for them in everyday life for all people you deal with will become more apparent; these techniques will enhance your ability to communicate with them, as the professional and social uses of rapport building are virtually unlimited.

Who can you establish rapport with; in other words, what sorts of people have instant rapport with each other? Who do you have rapport with? Usually, friends, family, and co-workers have good rapport with one another, because these people have many things in common in their beliefs and values. Once again consider for a moment your friends and people you like a lot, are their beliefs and values the same as yours? Now, consider the people you dislike; do they have the same beliefs and values, or are those different? Remember that old phrase "Birds of a feather flock together"; well, in reality, it is really true; we tend to seek out others with the same beliefs and values as ourselves. Other factors such as your occupation, economic situation, cultural background, and educational levels and experience all contribute to forming a person's beliefs and value systems. If you think back over your life, you might remember someone you started to behave like or act like, because people tend to become like the people they associate with the most.

Over our lives, each of us at some time has attempted to establish rapport with someone else for business or social reasons. Can you recall or imagine for a moment one of those past experiences? What did you do, and how did you build rapport with the person? If you successfully established rapport, you probably started by learning about the person's beliefs, background, and values and adopted some of them, or at least pretended to in order to give you something in common so that you had a base to build upon. Now, remember back to when someone you didn't know wanted something from you and was trying to build rapport with you. Would it be best for them to try and force their beliefs and values on you to get what they wanted or would it be better for them to pretend to adopt yours? So, as a starting point in rapport building, we will say that to set a foundation that rapport can be established between two people who have things in common by sharing the same beliefs and having a similar system of values.

NEUROLINGUISTIC PROGRAMMING

I will be discussing specific techniques for building deep rapport, very quickly, at the unconscious level of the person you are trying to develop rapport with. The techniques used are based on neurolinguistic programming (NLP) and are very effective. NLP was first discovered through psychotherapy as a means for doctors to develop rapport with patients, so they could be treated more effectively. Since then, these techniques have been taught to general officers, lawyers, high-level executives, and salesmen who use them on a daily basis.

One of the major elements of NLP and why it works is the belief that people do not operate on *objective reality*, people operate or function based on their interpretations of reality or what is called *subjective reality*. Although we do use some objective reality in our daily lives as individuals, we are forced to operate on our perceptions of reality. In our living and working environments when perceiving reality, we distort it. There are many reasons why; in some cases, it is because of our physical limitations. As an example, there are certain frequencies of sound and light that humans cannot detect even though they still exist. When we perceive smells, tastes, and feelings, they must possess certain intensity or relative intensity for us to notice. When we have any type of physical handicap—hearing loss or loss of eyesight—these can reduce our limited abilities even further.

We also distort our reality because it helps us function in the world because we are constantly being bombarded with sensory input in our daily lives. Because if we tried to pay equal attention and give equal importance to every sight, sound, smell, taste, and feeling, we would be overwhelmed to the point of being incapacitated. To allow us to handle the flood of information that bombards us, we unconsciously generalize, delete, and distort the input to a level we can use to function. As we generalize, we observe the patterns in our objective reality and then conveniently place things into broad categories to help us handle the input. Deletion of information is an ability that our brain has developed to analyze and screen out information that is unimportant to us. Distortion is when we change reality because of our physical or mental perspectives so that it fits us individually.

So, basically, NLP is the study of how individuals perceive and understand the world, or it can be called the study of subjective reality.

NLP was recognized in the early 1970s by Richard Bandler and John Grinder as a result of their studying three very successful therapists: the Gestalt therapist, Fritz Perls; the family therapist, Virginia Satir; and the world's foremost medical hypnotist, Milton Erickson, M.D. Through their observations of these three in action, Bandler and Grinder soon discovered that each one reacted in very specific ways to the verbal and nonverbal communications of their clients. In most cases, this resulted in an immediate and deep rapport that greatly facilitated the therapist's desired outcome. Bandler and Grinder were then able to break down these unconscious techniques so that they could be used consciously and intentionally and then incorporated into a person's behavior and communications. NLP gives you the ability to communicate below a person's level of awareness, which is what the three therapists were doing without knowing it.

When talking about mental perspectives, we are talking about our beliefs and values systems. We need to realize and understand that every person in the world is totally unique with their own "*map of the world*." *Map of the world* is an NLP term that refers to each person's total perception of reality around them. The map is built upon a person's unique experiences in their life, each book read, each movie watched, every experience good or bad that they have had in their life goes into making their own map and it's this map that allows him to function in the world and is totally unique to the individual. As an individual, we do not easily accept information that does not fit into our individual *map of the world*.

In our lives, everything that every person says and does is affected and influenced by their own personal beliefs and system of values. When dealing with others, you can either accept this and then use it to your advantage in building rapport, or you can ignore this and disregard its uses and, potentially, allow it to become an obstacle.

WHAT IS COMMUNICATION?

For you to be able to put into use what has been discussed up to this point, you need to first understand that everyone is continually communicating both verbally and nonverbally. Another thing to realize is that, according to research, approximately 85 percent of all communication between people is done through nonverbal communications. During the initial 5 minutes of meeting a blind date, a job interview, an interrogation, or even first contact with a terrorist hostage taker, that person will base almost 100 percent of his impressions of you on the nonverbal behavior you exhibit.

SYMBOLIC AND BEHAVIORAL COMMUNICATIONS

Symbolic communication is that which is expressed by the use of the spoken language and writing. In this type of communication, meaning has been assigned to the sounds that we speak and to shapes and characters we draw to symbolize things that exist in our environment and objective reality. This type of communication has distinct advantages along with certain disadvantages. Advantages are that symbolic communication is a highly formalized way to communicate, it is very precise, and can be transmitted in many ways. Some people believe that symbolic communication is the basis for civilization and that our civilization would probably not exist without language. But, symbolic communication or language has some drawbacks, since words can tend to generalize a person's experience and their emotions. A good example to illustrate the point is think of a chair; everyone knows what a chair is, but this particular word can be used to refer to any type of chair, and the one you pictured is probably not what the person next to you thought of, each was different based on their map of the world. We should also remember that many things in reality do not have names or names that people recognize because they are not a common experience in everyone's life. Think about when you have carried on a conversation with someone from a different part of the country, or another country, and they used a word you had no clue what they were talking about. Another difficulty with the use of symbolic communication is that we tend to give our own interpretations to certain words regardless of who uses them, after all *Love* could mean something completely different to two different people even if they are in the same conversation. So too could *hate*, *terrorism*, *criminal*, etc. We interpret these words differently based on our beliefs, values, and map of the world, so sometimes, there is some miscommunication between two people. Finally, the use of symbolic communication or language can be used to convey false information, to tell lies, to mislead others; after all, you have to take symbolic communication at its face value.

Behavioral communication is the information we provide through how we act and our behavior; it can be referred to as body language; it can include anything from a person's body position to their breathing rate and skin color. In all animals, including humans, our behavior and how our body acts is a direct manifestation of our neurological processes. What this means is that physical changes in our outward appearance accompany an internal process, and these physical changes are manifested in ways others can see. These physical changes in our body are behavioral manifestations of our internal responses. People are usually unaware of these manifestations and behaviors when they are occurring, so this type of behavioral communication can provide unbiased information to a trained observer. Examples of this can be seen in everyday life, when a person's body language doesn't match with what they are saying, we do this best with people we know well such as wives, girlfriends, close friends, or family. Recall a conversation you've had in which a person tells you something, but what they are saying doesn't match their body language? Did someone ever cook food for you, asked how you liked it and, even though you replied that it was great, you can tell that they didn't quite believe you? When you are having a fight, and a friend says it's okay, but you can tell it's not. When you can tell when someone is lying about things, such as they like your shirt or outfit, your new car, your new boyfriend or girlfriend. When someone says they are okay, but you can see they are not feeling well, or when they say they want to go see that terrible movie you like, but you can tell they don't really want to go to it. These are all examples of you knowing what cues people close to you give off and you can tell how they really feel; with a little insight and training, you can learn these types of cues from other people as well. *In order to be a more effective communicator, you have to be able to read and understand both kinds of communication and then use them to achieve your goals when building rapport.*

Reflective Pacing

The things that we will discuss next are some of the best tools available for rapport building. Remember the three therapists Perls, Satir, and Erickson? These are the techniques they used when they were reacting to their clients' verbal and nonverbal communication. Again, initially they did so at the unconscious level, but we will discuss how you can use these techniques on the conscious level and adapt them to your own communication style.

Pacing is probably the best rapport-building technique you can master for use in communicating. It is basically the act of demonstrating to the persons "unconscious" mind you are trying to build rapport with that you have things in common and your map of the world is very similar to his (remember, we are attracted to people that are similar to ourselves). This can be accomplished by reflecting the person's unconscious verbal and nonverbal behaviors while you are trying to build rapport. This will cause his mind to assume you have similar feelings, attitudes, beliefs, values, etc. He sees you unconsciously as having the same perceptions of reality that he has (map of the world), this will result in a rapid, deep building of rapport.

The idea behind this technique is based around theory that the brain is constantly processing information; we take in approximately 2,000 bits of information per second, we couldn't possibly handle all that information, so it is filtered through our map of the world. What this does is takes our life experiences and deletes things that are not relevant, distorts things and generalize things, so we can use the information we take in, since each of us is different, our filters delete, distort, and generalize different things. Even though this is done continuously on unconscious levels, remember that all sensory input that the brain receives must be filtered in some way so that we can deal with it. Usually, the majority of the information is logged into a portion of the mind that we are not aware of consciously and is brought into our consciousness to satisfy a need or purpose. So, in theory, when we use pacing techniques, we are working on the unconscious portion of the mind of the person we are trying to build rapport with; his mind will unconsciously recognize patterns, movements, gestures, behavior similar to his; once you can start communicating on the unconscious level, everything else gets easier.

Nonverbal Pacing

This is when you simply copy the persons behavior that you are trying to build rapport with, such as his posture, how they sit, tilt of head, how they are holding their arms, etc. Three areas are covered in nonverbal pacing. These are body position, breathing, and gestures. When doing nonverbal pacing, it must be done covertly, respectfully, and with grace. Because your actions must never come to the conscious attention of your subject, he might think you are mocking him or making fun of him which could lead to any number of problems. Nonverbal pacing is not limited to that discussed above, it can be anything; remember, any behavior that can be observed can be paced and used by you in attempting to build rapport. You are studying the person you want to build rapport with and looking for his body language and behaviors some he might not even know he does himself; any systematic or stylistic behavior or use of the body should be used to pace your rapport subject; all nonverbal pacing is accomplished using two techniques *matching* or by *mirroring*.

When pacing your target of building rapport, you do not have to be directly in front of him, but you must be in his vision in some way; his unconscious mind has to see you pacing. This technique does not require that you copy the person's behaviors and movements exactly; also, you do not need to perform pacing simultaneously with your target subject's movements. When your target subject makes changes in his body position, wait a short period of time just enough to be discreet and then change your body position to match his. When using the pacing technique, you need to pace your subject as much as possible, changing your body language to match his and as long as possible during your time together without the target subject noticing that you are doing this.

MATCHING

This technique is used when you are facing the same direction as your target subject. When performing the matching technique, you adopt the same posture as your target subject. What this means is basically if he tilts his head, you tilt your head to match, etc. You must try to match as many of his body language or behavioral aspects as possible; following are some examples:

Target subject body position: You will need to adopt the same body position as your rapport subject; you do this by matching either his upper or lower body position at first; then, over a period of time, you match his entire body position. When matching the *head position* and movements of the target subject, remember most people hold their heads a certain way and do so without knowing it, they keep it level, tilted either left or right, centered, chin up, chin down; sometimes, they have a small shake or twitch to their head, nod their head to emphasis points or during speaking breaks, etc. Their *upper body or shoulder position* is like their posture, they might sit shoulders back, level, slumped forward, hunched in, they also might be sitting in such a way that they lean back or lean forward. Overall *muscle tone or body tension* is most observable in the neck, head, and hands; observe if their muscles are tight like they are clenching, or are they lose, and relaxed. You will also need to match any *habitual or stylistic hand or body gestures* they make, facial expressions or nervous habits; if your target subject taps a finger, you do it with the same finger; if they cross their arms, legs, you do it; if they place their hand on the side of the face, start rubbing their shoulder, etc., you do exactly what they do over time. Anything they are doing can be paced by you, even when it comes to drinking or eating; if the subject holds a glass a certain way and puts it down a certain way, you do it; if they eat a certain way, you do too. You also need to make a close observation of how he stresses or emphasizes points they are trying to make, so you can use the same method when emphasizing points you want to make. This can cause the target subject to believe you more readily when you are speaking. If he is using certain gestures or expressions when expressing doubt, you use the same ones when you want to express doubt. One area often overlooked when attempting to build rapport is matching the *breathing pattern* of the target subject; this is a very powerful aspect of pacing, because it is a basic bodily function, you adopt the breathing temp and type, such as mouth, nose, deep, shallow, etc.

MIRRORING

Is a form of pacing used when you are facing your target subject; you still pace the exact same aspects of his behavior that you did when you were matching him, except now, you do exactly the opposite movement, like you are looking into a mirror. If the target subject crosses his legs, you cross yours to create a mirror image of the target subject, the same if he tilts his head, crosses his arms, leans to the left or right.

Verbal Pacing

This is their speech, *voice tone, and tempo*; you will need to try to match their speaking tone and speed or tempo of their speaking voice. You can also pace any habitual or stylistic use of your target subject's speech and speech patterns. After all verbal pacing is matching, in your own speech, those unconscious aspects of your subject's verbal communication. What this means is you will pace his tone of voice, tempo, vocabulary, and predicates, as well as any habitual or stylistic use of his voice, any pet phrases, idioms used can also be paced. So, if the target subject raises the pitch of his voice when making a point, raise your voice when making a point. Any noise the target subject makes, either intentional or habitual, can be paced either fully or partially. Just like using nonverbal pacing, when you use verbal pacing, it must be done respectfully and gracefully and must never come to the conscious attention of your target subject. You must remember you are pacing the form, not the content of his communication. When pacing his vocabulary, you are using similar vocabulary, including repetitive phrases.

Matching the target subject's use of *predicates* (verbs, adverbs, and adjectives) can be another powerful rapport-building tool; the one drawback to this is he must be using a language you understand, and you both need to speak it well. Verbal pacing is a great way to establish rapport because it is a bridge into the target subject's mind and can allow us know how his mind works; to do this, you must first understand the concept of primary representational systems. One of the basic principles of NLP is that all functions of the human mind, including how we see things, speak, etc., are conducted within the context of the primary sensory representational systems, which include the *visual*, *auditory*, *kinesthetic*, *olfactory*, and *gustatory* systems. For most people, their conscious and unconscious functions are accomplished within the visual, auditory, and kinesthetic modalities. When we "think" of something, we accomplish this by recalling or constructing *visual images*; sounds, such as voices or internal dialogue, *auditory*; or feelings, either tactile or visceral, *kinesthetic*. While we are thinking and speaking, we are continually accessing cues, physical movements, or positions that are helping us tune into one representational system more strongly than others; this is the one representational system we are more comfortable with and use the most in our map of the world; many of these accessing cues are generic and universal while others will be unique to an individual.

EXAMPLES of accessing cues in head/eye movement: When someone is recalling visual images, their eyes will usually move up and to the right as you are looking at him (or to the left, depending on whether he is right- or left-handed). When they are constructing visual images that they have not seen before or they are putting separate images together in a manner not seen before, his eyes will move up and to the left. Someone who is having an internal conversation or dialogue (talking to themselves) will move their eyes down and to the right, and someone who is experiencing feelings of any type will move their eyes down and to the left.

The predicates you use, just like the nonverbal accessing cues you use, help indicate what system your target subject is using while he is thinking, writing, and talking. These predicates can tell you whether he is using visual images, internal dialogue, or feelings to understand different things, express things during conversations with the target subject. If during your conversation with the target subject, he has constructed a visual image of the situation with his words, when you reply or speak with the target subject, it would be better received by him if your reply was made in visual terms rather than in auditory or kinesthetic terms.

EXAMPLES of PREDICATES:

- Visual-system is used by approximately 70 percent of all people: see, look, view, appear, show, bright, hazy, dim, picture, clear, envision, imagine hazy, focused, illuminate; predicate phrase—an eyeful, dim view, in light of, get a perspective on, paint a picture, showing off, short sighted, tunnel vision, narrow view, mental picture, etc. "You don't paint a very clear picture." "I can't see where you are going."
- Auditory-system is used by approximately 25–30 percent of all people: say, hear, loud, ring, sound, quiet, silence, deaf, question, tune in, tune out, listen, all ears, etc. Predicate phrases—afterthought, clear as a bell, call on, loud and clear, pay attention, tattle-tale, unheard of, well informed, earful, inquire into, etc. "That comes through loud and clear." "Doesn't ring a bell."
- Kinesthetic-system is used least by people; touch, feel, hard, soft, catch on, throw out, concrete, get a handle, solid, grasp, slip through, catch on, tap into, flat, rough, smooth, cold, warm, etc. Predicate phrases—all washed up, boils down to, hold on, hot head, control yourself, get a handle on, hang in there, heated

argument, keep your shirt on, pain in the neck, stiff upper lip, stuffed shirt, pull some strings, smooth operator, come to grips with, etc. "I don't feel we have a handle on that."

Things to remember when verbally pacing; you need to respond to your subject in the system that he most commonly uses; this means if the target subject is operating in the visual-system, you need to verbally pace him using visual terms. Now, if your target subject is using more than one system, which many people do, you will need to verbally pace him using the last system he used when speaking. As an example, say your boss is your target subject and you are trying to convince to do something. He replies to your presentation, "I see what you are saying, but the whole idea leaves me a little cold." He has used all the three systems in his statement to you, but you need to reply using the last one his mind was focused on, so your reply needs to be in the kinesthetic and could something like "I expected you to be a little cool toward the project initially, but the plan is solid and I feel once I've explained how to implement it, you will warm up to it."

The use of verbally pacing someone's use of predicates can be difficult to master, mostly because we are usually more concerned with the content of the conversation that we don't listen for form. Like all techniques, you need to practice, one way to do this is to analyze conversations that you are not taking part in, in a bar, restaurant, or by watching TV, reading a book or newspaper, just practice learning to recognize the representational system people use.

When using any of the pacing techniques I have discussed, if you feel that pacing the target subject in a particular way will result in you being compromised—or feel he is starting to notice—you need to stop pacing temporarily. After a few minutes, when you feel the danger or threat of recognizing you are using such techniques dissipated, start back using either a partial or crossover pacing technique.

Partial Pacing

It is something that can be done if doing the exact same thing the subject is doing would raise suspicion; all you do is substitute a partial movement or posture for the full movement or posture that the target subject is using. Examples: If the target subject keeps putting both hands or arms on a table, you put just one; if he is frequently crossing and uncrossing his legs, you partially pace him by crossing and uncrossing your ankles; if he is tapping his fingers on the table, tap on your leg; or he might have an obvious nervous mannerism that you cannot pace exactly like a facial tic, you can partially pace him by slightly tensing and relaxing the same facial muscles.

Crossover Pacing

It is pacing a specific aspect of his behavior with a different aspect of your behavior. An example is tapping your fingers to pace his facial tic, or crossing and uncrossing your arms to pace his crossing and uncrossing his legs. With crossover pacing, you must always use the same aspect of your behavior to pace a specific behavior on his part.

After a period of time at attempting to build rapport with a target subject and you feel that rapport has been established, you can test and confirm it by changing your pace, body position, or any aspect of your own behavior. After you do this, you need to observe the target subject to see if he now follows you; this technique is called *leading*. If the target subject follows your lead within three or four minutes, either fully or partially, you have now established rapport below his level of awareness; if he doesn't, then resume the pacing techniques. Once you have achieved nonverbal rapport, you should do the following things: engage the target subject in conversation, so you can now pace him verbally and continue to pace him both nonverbally and verbally to deepen and maintain the rapport you have built.

REMEMBER the existence of even a little rapport between you and your captor can mean the difference between life and death. It can result in the terrorist selecting someone else for execution, causing a split-second hesitation on the part of the terrorist in carrying out his orders to kill hostages, allowing rescue forces to kill him, causing the terrorist to let his guard down just long enough for you to kill him and escape, or otherwise allowing for a peaceful resolution of the entire situation.

CROSS-CULTURAL COMMUNICATION

It is hard for most people to believe but the United States does not set the world standard for communicating, things that are fine to do in the states, sometimes do not go over very well in other countries and in dealing with other cultures. The following are some very general actions to avoid, when dealing with people from different cultures:

- Conversing with your hands in your pockets.
- Pointing your foot at another person.
- Showing the bottom of your foot.
- Eating or passing objects with your left hand.
- Patting children on their heads.
- Backslapping.
- Pointing, particularly with one finger.
- Yawning in public or during conversation.

- Time, this is managed or interpreted differently in other cultures; when working overseas, you need to expect the pace of life to be slower. It won't matter whether you are closing a business deal or are being held for an extended period of captivity, the time frames will be looser. This is important because you may find it frustrating; you don't want to get angry or upset. You need to relax and accept the fact that things, especially those concerning time, will be different and you will not be able to operate like you would in the United States, this will help lessen your frustration.
- *Work-social mix*: Many people overseas still depend on "survival networks" of family connections to the point that they are more likely to emphasize personal and family relations over their job or country. This is often different than how most Americans feel, where a job or their work is the more important equation in their life. "Getting down to business" for people overseas will more than likely include chitchat and small talk before, during, and after formal business sessions. What Americans tend to perceive as simple chitchat and a waste of valuable time is business to them. When dealing with people like this, use indirect and more tactful approaches; American directness may be misinterpreted as a careless or rude attitude toward them and their culture.
- *First names*: For many cultures outside the United States, using first names often signals the start of a deep friendship with many lifetime obligations. Many Americans do not feel comfortable with using titles instead of first names; you should not encourage the use of first names to make yourself feel more comfortable. You might inadvertently lead the people you are dealing with to believe you are indiscriminate about friendships, and they may begin to believe that you have betrayed them, or belittled them if you do not follow through with obligations associated with a relationship that uses first names. You might not even be aware of these obligations, but it does not mean they do not exist or that others won't judge you by your actions.
- *Status*: Many cultures outside the United States, the people are much more formal and respectful of status than Americans tend to be. Once again, Americans tend to try and be as informal as possible to make themselves more comfortable. You must keep reminding yourself to be more formal in your associations with those of other cultures, especially in their country. This will help you avoid having people believe that you do not respect them, their beliefs, or their way of life. Just remember: "When in doubt, overdo it."

- *Indirectness*: People in many other cultures and places outside the United States do not separate themselves from their work as we do. Because of this reason, direct criticism about their job performance, even though you may consider it being truthful and constructive in nature, may be regarded as a personal affront. Also, you need to avoid criticizing people in the presence of others, this can damage the person's credibility with his "survival network" connections that he needs for business. Keep an open mind and attempt to become attuned to the cultural peculiarities in your new working and living environment. You might find that there are ways acceptable to the locals so that you can make the same point without alienating anyone and without appearing to be disrespectful to others or their culture.
- *Distance*: People in the United States tend to stand at arm's length from others when we converse or in other things we do. When two Americans get on an elevator, they will each stand on the opposite side for distance; in other countries, the people will stand right next to you, even if the elevator is empty. Most other cultures consider this type of behavior to be standoffish and cold. People from other cultures are more touchy feely, and they tend to stand much closer, especially people of the same sex. Don't become rude, nervous, or show how uncomfortable you are, you could insult someone by accident.
- *Touching*: In most countries and cultures outside the United States, you are more than likely going to find people in those areas touch more, especially same sex touching such as friends holding hands. There are exceptions in certain Far Eastern countries where people touch less than in the United States, so it is all culturally relative and something to be attuned to and aware of. One of the things that makes Americans uncomfortable in these cultures is the amount of touching that takes place between the sexes, there is likely to be hugging, holding hands (even among males), and kissing when greeting and parting, and more touching than is normal in American society this is to signal friendship, not sex. You need to be aware that when encountering a touching society or culture like this, a reluctance to touch on your part is likely to signal that you do not like the person. Between sexes though, these rules of conduct will usually be much more stringent than in the culture of the United States. There are things you will need to do to avoid sending the wrong signal to those you are working and/or socializing within these cultures; women from the United States would be well advised to maintain a more formal attitude and to stay cooler toward relationships, especially casual relationships and friendships than they normally

would. Men from the United States also have to look out for certain things; overseas, when you shake hands, a softer handshake is used; if you try to crush the guy's hand in greeting, you can be considered rude and offensive, showing off, etc. Starting any relationship this way is not advisable. The thing to remember and take with you is to learn about the area and cultural dos or don'ts *BEFORE* you go.

- *Eye contact*: In the United States, we use eye contact intermittently during conversations to ensure that the listener is still paying attention and to gauge his response to what is said. However, eye contact is never held for long periods since this indicates a challenge and a violation of personal space. The amount of eye contact varies greatly in other societies and cultures. In some countries and societies, such as those in the Middle East, they view a break in eye contact as inattention and disinterest on the part of the listener and consider it insulting. On the other hand, in societies and cultures in the Far East, like Japan, any eye contact at all makes the person you are talking to feel uncomfortable.
- *Language*: When traveling, many people do not speak the native language of the area they are visiting; you will find that local nationals will appreciate you more if you speak English slowly and softly. You must try to avoid the natural American tendency to raise your voice in an intimidating fashion when speaking to someone of a different culture; loudness and rudeness do not increase an understanding of the English language, and when acting this way, more often than not, if someone does speak a little English, they will not admit it or help. If you are learning another language, you should attempt to understand idiomatic expressions and unconventional aspects of the language (slang); if you can master them, they can open new doors in communication and, in most cases, make communication easier and more effective. If you are in captivity, the ability to speak the language of the captors can be used to your benefit in establishing rapport. Of course, this can be a disadvantage as well, because your captors may feel threatened by your ability to know and understand what is taking place around you. Just remember that every situation is different and demands your resourcefulness.

OTHER RAPPORT-BUILDING TECHNIQUES

There are other rapport-building techniques that have been used successfully in the past. These were designed primarily to make the hostage taker view the hostage as a human being rather than an object to be used to further their agenda. Studies of past hostage incidents showed that the longer a hostage is held, the chances of his survival increase; this is due in a large part to the additional time the hostage has to establish rapport with his captors.

- Keeping photographs of your family or religious articles on you and showing them to your captors can help establish rapport and may stimulate conversation with your captors. The conversations should center on areas of common interest, such as family, children, belief that are not likely to elicit negative feelings from your subjects. If you are not married, have no kids, carry pictures of your parents, other family members, etc. Do not leave the generic pictures that came with your wallet and claim them as your own, your captors might have the same wallet.
- Active listening is another technique that will help you establish rapport; you need to let your subject know that you understand him and his point of view, even though you may not agree with it. When using active listening, attempt to rephrase your target subject's statements in a way that that lets him know you sympathize with him. EXAMPLES: "I understand how angry you must be at the people who did that to you," or "I know I would feel the same way if it was me." When using this technique, continue to pace verbally and nonverbally. Remember, it is generally better to identify and emphasize areas of common agreement with your target subject rather than focusing on the differences.
- *Be knowledgeable*: Before you leave to visit or work in another area, take the time to study the politics, the history, and the religion in your area of assignment, even if you don't think you will have any contact with local nationals. If going to Latin America, many terrorist groups are communist or nationalist. You should know the history of U.S. involvement in the region. You should also know enough about communism to discuss it intelligently in both fact and theory. You do not want to talk about these voluntarily if a captive, but there is a chance you can win your captor's respect with an honest, sincere defense of your values. If traveling to the Middle East, you should know about regional terrorist philosophies and the history of the United States in the region. There is a lot of history to study; you have the Palestinian cause and Shia fundamentalism, and its difference from Sunni's. If religious issues are brought up in discussion, it would be beneficial to emphasize the similarities between Islam and Christianity.

CHAPTER 6

Detecting Terrorist Surveillance

No matter where we are, or what we are doing, early detection of surveillance against us by criminal elements or terrorists is important to our safety and security. It gives an intended victim a chance to decide if he will become a victim of some type of attack and change behavior or their security profile as necessary. Surveillance is the *VISIBLE* hand of the threat as they start planning operations against their intended victims. The threat needs to get outside their controlled environment to gather information that they need to plan a successful attack against their intended victims. So, now they can be seen and detected; this is an opportunity that can be a warning to you that you are now considered a target. There are numerous stories of how potential victims have discouraged an attack by being unpredictable in the daily lives, making them more difficult to target. Your ability to understand what surveillance is, how it is conducted, and what type of information the threat needs is essential to knowing how to detect any type of criminal or terrorist surveillance. You must remember, except in very few cases of being in the wrong place at the wrong time and becoming a victim, every criminal and terrorist operation or attack is preceded by some type of surveillance.

DEFINE SURVEILLANCE

So, what is surveillance? It is basically the monitoring of behavior. As a matter of fact, the word *surveillance* is French and means to "watching over." Another definition of surveillance is the "continuous or periodic act of observing, usually by surreptitious means, a person, a place, or an object for the purpose of obtaining information otherwise unavailable or impractical to obtain." But with all of this, you can just basically say that surveillance is spying or stalking.

DOI: 10.4324/9781003292647-6

SURVEILLANCE TECHNIQUES

There are many techniques used by the threat, all are similar; after all, there are only so many ways to spy on or stalk someone. Many techniques that are used, especially when they are new are pioneered by law enforcement or the military, are then copied by the threat for their own purposes. Let's talk about some common tactics.

Most attacks or incidents take place where the victim is the *MOST PREDICTABLE*. For many people, this is of course the area near where they live. This is because people have taken years building a daily routine, and after so long, it is not easy to change because it has become habit—especially if you have a family and a set work schedule. Since people are more predictable in the morning, they are more vulnerable at this time, especially when departing for work. There is probably a set time to be at the office, or at work; also, our minds are not focused on security but about what is going to take place at work or throughout the day; what you didn't do previously and what you need to do when you get there—or perhaps on any morning family issues that came up. Evening times are less predictable for departing work or other primary areas because there is not a set time or schedule you must adhere to for employment. You could work overtime, have a late meeting, etc.

Stationary or Fixed Surveillance

The technique used most by any type of threat is *stationary or fixed surveillance*. It is the most common because it is the easiest to employ for them and the hardest for the target victim to detect, ensuring they are not compromised and alerting the victim. The threat surveillance personnel will see a place/location that will permit them to observe the target without being seen themselves and without becoming suspicious to outside observers. Initially, surveillance will start at your home or your work since they KNOW that eventually you will be there and they can start observing and taking notes. It is important to remember that for the threat surveillance to work, they have to be able to SEE and OBSERVE the TARGET VICTIM. If they cannot see the target, they cannot observe you, so there is no surveillance or gathering of information.

There are several common places that the threat can set up surveillance in a static location, which include—but are not limited to—the following: hotel/motel rooms, apartments, houses, offices, or other businesses; remember, whatever the location is, it MUST provide a view of the area to be watched and the TARGET. Sometimes, a good fixed site location is hard to find for the threat, especially in the community or neighborhood where the target victim lives, or in the area where he works since space is at a premium in business districts. When getting a good fixed site location, there is usually a paper trail left for law enforcement or security agencies to follow. The threat will still do everything in their power to acquire these sites because it is their best technique against detection by the target victim, law enforcement, or security agencies.

In some areas like the intended victim's neighborhood, and in some downtown areas, or business areas, the threat might not be able to get a physical location, so they will use other ways to find a means of staying in one place long enough to conduct surveillance activities. They do this by using vans, utility vehicles, and automobiles as stationary or static surveillance locations. This is easier for them in some instances, such as being able to park in a parking lot or garage that allows them to observe the intended target. This can include parking on the street in front of a neighbor's house, or in the drive way of a vacant house or in the parking lot of a small neighborhood business. The vehicle preferred for this is usually some type of van, the windows that allow outside observation make good surveillance platforms, and they can be tinted so people cannot see in. Many times, when vehicles are used for surveillance activities, they have some type of business or official logo attached to provide a plausible reason for them to be in that location. If a truck or car is used for surveillance operations, the threat will in some instances be parked facing away from the target they are observing, this allows them to use the vehicle's mirrors for surveillance without raising suspicion about what they are doing.

Whenever the threat is conducting surveillance from a fixed or stationary position, they MUST have a PLAUSIBLE reason for being there, an unknown car parked in front of your house would raise suspicion, a cable truck, utility truck, or a lawn care service truck wouldn't. Whatever ruse or cover for action they use is limited only by their imagination and their knowledge of the area of operation. Some commonly used ruses include posing as a person having automobile problems, bicycle problems, a sales or pollster person, a religious figure such as a priest, some type of law enforcement officer, a woman with a baby carriage, a person conducting utility or construction work, someone walking a dog.

As far as who will be conducting surveillance against you, many times not only men, but women, children, and any combination of these are often used by the threat to give the greater appearance of innocence, since most people never consider women, children or women with children a threat.

Moving Surveillance or Enroute Surveillance

The next type of surveillance technique that is used is called *moving surveillance or enroute surveillance*. This type of surveillance is much more difficult to conduct. The threat will need vehicles, communications, training, and experience to do it well; if they are using moving surveillance against you, odds are you are now a target because of the resources being used to gather information against you. Like all surveillance, it only works if the people doing the surveillance can see their target victim; so for the threat to accomplish this, they must place individuals or vehicles close to the target so that he can be observed while he is moving. There are two ways to conduct moving surveillance, by foot or by vehicle.

Foot Surveillance

Foot surveillance can be done by one person or by many; the people doing the surveillance must remain very close to the target so they can see everything he does; remember, they are looking for routines and predictability in the victim's routine. Because they have to stay where they can see the victim, the victim can see them, this is what makes one person foot surveillance easy to detect. When conducting surveillance with more than one person, it gets more complicated and detection is harder to accomplish; it does provide much greater flexibility to the surveillance team but requires planning and much more training for the surveillants. The best makeup of a foot team will be mixed men and women and usually requires at least three personnel, never more than eight personnel because then it gets too complicated. The ideal surveillance team is usually made up of five or six experienced operators.

Vehicle Surveillance

Vehicle surveillance is what is used against people from the United States most often, and it is especially effective since Americans are so used to driving everywhere we go in the United States. Most people take some type of vehicle transportation when visiting, living, or working in other countries, instead of walking. Like foot surveillance, vehicle surveillance can be by one or more vehicles. Conducting vehicle surveillance takes high degree of training, since there are many more moving parts, and other vehicle traffic to deal with. If they are conducting one person surveillance in a vehicle, they will have a tape recorder in order to keep track of the target's movements. If two or more vehicles are being used, they can still conduct the surveillance with one person in each vehicle but that means the driver will need to have a recorder and be working the radio for coordination. With other vehicles, this can be difficult to do for one person since driving, recording, talking on the radio and giving directions is hard to do especially if you are trying to do it so no one notices you. Two people in each vehicle is the best option, that way the driver just concentrates on driving, keeping the target in sight, and the second man records the targets movements and coordinates on the radio with the rest of the threat surveillance team. Like foot surveillance, a good mix of vehicles and vehicle drivers is necessary to avoid being detected by the target; usually, four to six vehicles are the normal surveillance team make up, with two or more people in each vehicle. The vehicles used for this will be common to the area and will have nothing that stands out or catches your attention. When you are conducting surveillance operations, the vehicle will normally have four doors, windows may be tinted, and if more than one vehicle is involved in the surveillance on you, one of the people in the vehicle, probably the passenger, will be talking on a radio or cell whenever you pass by a decision point to let the rest of the team know which road and what direction you are going.

There are several techniques used by the threat to conduct surveillance operations during enroute surveillance, to limit their exposure to you without limiting their ability to gather the information they need to conduct an operation against you.

Leading Surveillance

When conducting leading surveillance, the surveillants travel in front of the subject, while watching the target subject for any turns or stops he makes. When the target makes that turn, a note is made, and surveillance breaks off, the next time the surveillance team still in front will make a turn where the subject did the day before, they are still in front watching for the target's next turn or stops. This continues until the threat surveillance has the entire route from start to finish on the subject, including each place they stopped along that route. This type of surveillance is only possible if the target only uses one route to and from his home to his primary areas; it is difficult to detect.

Progressive Surveillance

There are actually two ways to conduct progressive surveillance. The first way is to put people at each decision point along the route of travel from the target subject's starting area (decision point is any place along a route that a person can change streets and direction); these people will be waiting, when the subject makes a turn, it is noted for the next day. Then, the surveillance team is moved along all the decision points along that new road, when he makes a turn, it is noted and they move again the next day, eventually the threat surveillance will know the entire route of the targeted subject. This is the most secure method but it is very time consuming for the threat and it is very manpower intensive, so they may not have the resources to use it. The second way to conduct progressive surveillance is more commonly used by the threat; it is still secure and takes less people. The threat surveillance will follow the target subject in a vehicle, when the target turns, it is noted and the surveillance breaks off. The next day the surveillance vehicle is waiting on the street the subject turned on the day before, the surveillance then follows him from that point until the next turn, breaking off and starting along that street on the next day. Just like leading surveillance, eventually the surveillance team will learn the target's entire route with a minimal chance of being detected by their intended victim.

The above methods only work if the intended victim is predictable and uses the same route every time they leave for work or to go to one of their other primary areas. Being predictable will ensure that they are targeted.

TECHNOLOGY

In our world today, there have been many advances in technology, especially in electronics and security devices, most of these devices can also be used for surveillance. So, now the threat be it criminal or terrorist have readily available to them all kinds of gizmos and gadgets to help them conduct surveillance on individuals they want to target. They have all kinds of cameras available, still and video, many very concealable, heck most cell phones can take still and video pictures. There are also tracking devices for individuals and vehicles that anyone can buy off the Internet now; while they are normally used to keep track of people's kids, they can be used to keep track of anyone. There are now devices that let you listen and record other people's conversations, including wireless microphones that can be bought off the Internet and placed in a vehicle, office, purse, or backpack (how many people every clean or check every compartment in a bag they carry on a regular basis); there are personal digital assistants (PDAs), Blackberrys, Smart Phones and of course computers. All of these devices can be used to help a threat identify a prospective target. They conduct surveillance operations on them, tracking and recording their movements can help assess any security procedures that are around the target or his office to help them in determining whether this perspective target is reachable or if he needs to be bypassed.

In any type of high-threat or high-risk environment, you can expect the criminals and the terrorists to have a combination off all the tactics and techniques we have just discussed available to them, and they will use them against you.

Objectives of Terrorist Surveillance

So, why do terrorists or other threats, such as criminals, carry out surveillance against the intended victim or target? They do it because they need information, as much as possible about the intended target so they can decide whether the person is a target they can attack with the resources they have available. Then, all the information they have gathered will be assimilated into a precise plan of action; the more information they have on the intended victim, the more the likelihood of a successful operation.

GENERAL ITEMS OF INFORMATION REQUIRED BY THE THREAT

Information on the *target subject's residence, worksite, and other primary areas*: A look at past attacks and incidents show that most occur near the residence or the work site, the two places a person is most predictable. When I talk about a residence, I also mean temporary residences such as hotels, motels, or guest houses; like a permanent residence or home, it is very difficult to be unpredictable near these locations. Around the locations where the target is most predictable, the threat must become intimately familiar with the living, working environment, traffic patterns, basically the personality of the possible attack site. Their operations planning will need to be specific and unique for each area so the planning will be quite different if the subject resides in a rural area rather than in an urban area. For each potential attack site, an unlimited number of variables needs to be examined by the threat. They are not only looking for the predictability of the intended victim, but they need to look at the area around the site for cover and concealment, avenues of approach, possible chokepoints, location and reaction time of security forces along with other things that will have an impact on their tactical planning.

They will need to know how the potential victim gets around, *what type of transportation does he uses*. The majority of attacks directed against Americans occur during movement, so they must attack their vehicle to get to their target. So, it is essential that surveillants obtain as much information as possible about a subject's mode of transportation, armored, unarmored, etc. Also, if the potential victim is using his privately owned vehicle, or vehicles from a work car pool, chauffeured vehicles, or public transportation, this is all very important for the threat's planning. It will definitely have different effects on the threat's tactical planning operations.

The threat will need to know the subject's *routes to and from work, also routes and locations to any other primary areas* he goes to. This in-depth knowledge of the routes the subject uses to travel to and from work or to other static locations that the subject frequents on a recurring basis is very helpful to the threat for planning purposes. The threat has to take everything into account for operational planning purposes; there will be big differences if the subject travels on rural or isolated routes rather than on major thoroughfares in urban areas. The types of roads used will have an influence on the threat planning; one-way streets, traffic circles, and narrow bridges all will have different considerations that the threat will have to cope with and use.

Information on the target subject's *routine behavior* is very important to the threat; it's where they learn how the intended victim is most predictable. This means that the target subject's everyday routine will have the strongest impact on whether or not the subject will become their target. *IT IS A FACT*: the more predictable the target subject is, the easier it will be for the terrorists to accomplish their operation.

Next, they will need as much information as possible on the target subject's *general security awareness*. This is very important to any potential threat or terrorist and is a major consideration for them when looking at potential victims. If the potential victim is unaware of any threat or does not believe a threat exists, the threat planning will be that much simpler. If, on the other hand, he has a good security profile, is security aware, or has security assigned to him, the threat will need to decide if the intended victim is worth the resources it would require to overcome the potential victim's security.

NOTE: Many people only consider the routine of the victim; REMEMBER security elements can build noticeable routines also; security elements can become PREDICTABLE, if your security is predictable. YOU are predictable also.

Places the *target subject frequents (primary areas)*. This type of information can be very important to determine any routines the potential victim may have inside, also the threat can develop sources inside these facilities to gather information on the target subject such as the date and time of a golf game, next lunch or dinner reservation, scheduled court dates for racket ball, etc. Knowing where the target is going to be at any given time will help in the operational planning development for the threat.

NOTE: Many times, people with children overlook school and sporting events when conducting the threat assessment for security purposes.

ANY time the threat knows where the potential target will be, when he will leave, and what routes he takes MAKES HIM PREDICTIABLE, even if it is a school carnival, play or basketball game for his kids. Most schools post event calendars online, open to the public.

Types of *protective measures employed*. This type of information is critical to the threats planning of the operation; this type of information includes any security systems employed at the potential victim's residence, including a temporary residence, at his work, at any of his primary areas. They also need to know about guard forces, roving patrols, alarms, closed circuit TV systems, guard dogs, etc.

Security forces in the area of the operation. This type of information will include those forces not employed by the target subject, that is local law enforcement, military, or other security forces in the areas. They will need to know their exact location, their response time after notification, type of vehicles, type of weapons, and type of training. This information is vital for contingency planning for the operation and knowing how much time they will have at the attack site before any potential help can arrive to render assistance to the potential victim.

The Phases of Terrorist Surveillance

Target selection/assessment phase: It is during this phase that the threat will have a list of potential targets based upon what their objective is and their capabilities. They must now determine who is the softer target, with the lowest risk to themselves; in other words, who is the most vulnerable to an attack. To help them determine this, they will conduct surveillance on everyone on their list, looking for the information we just discussed. This initial surveillance effort could involve a large number of people conducting surveillance depending on how many people they have on the list of potential victims. Since most terrorist organizations and groups are not large and have a small core of permanent cadre, they will have to resort to outside help from their supporting elements and may even have to pay non-members to help accomplish this initial surveillance effort to obtain the information needed to make their final target selection list. This initial phase of terrorist or criminal surveillances is the weakest link in their operational planning cycle, because of the total amount of information that they need to do a good assessment of the potential targets. Since they need to focus on routines and predictability, the surveillance will need to continue for a good period of time to allow them to collect this type of information. There is also a risk of discovery of surveillance personnel at this phase because the terrorist organization needs to go outside their trained and trusted cadre for help in obtaining the information; for the organization, this will mean newer, less experienced, or inexperienced surveillance personnel, with little or no training who are usually selected for the willingness to do this work and their ability to pass a cursory police or security inspection. *This is the best time for the potential target* to detect surveillance since at this stage they are using those untrained personnel who are much easier to spot with a surveillance detection program.

Operational/attack phase: This phase begins after they have collected the necessary information and done a selection of the target that meets their requirements, based on the information collected during the selection/assessment phase. At this time, the surveillance will be reduced and will be conducted by better trained more experienced members of the organization. They do not need the same constant daily surveillance they had during the first phase, because now they already know the target's routines, patterns, where he is most predictable. During this phase, surveillance detection becomes very difficult, since they are using the more experienced, better trained personnel and less surveillance is being conducted; detecting surveillance during this phase in itself will more than likely have no influence on whether they continue the operation against you, unless you change your routines, patterns, and your security profile after detection.

TECHNIQUES THAT CAN BE USED TO DETECT SURVEILLANCE

One of our first lines of protection should be the ability to detect surveillance; this means having a plan and following it for the entire time you are in an environment where you are at risk, since you never know when you may become a target. Whenever you are attempting to detect surveillance personnel from either a fixed or a stationary location, the threat surveillance personnel will be doing everything they can possibly do to blend into that environment and routines in order to keep from being detected. If you are new to the area, then they being natives or local nationals will be much more familiar with the working and living environment than you are, so you might need to bring in trusted locals to help you start your surveillance detection plan until you can learn the new environment and who does or doesn't belong.

The first thing you must do to detect surveillance being conducted from a fixed or a stationary location is you need to become intimately familiar with what is normal in your area so that you can recognize anything that may be out of the ordinary. In other words, you must know the daily environment, routines, personalities, and the profiles of your surroundings. A good way to assist you in becoming familiar with your surroundings is when you first arrive to conduct and maintain a neighborhood behavioral pattern analysis, for your living, work areas, and for any other primary areas you visit. A behavioral pattern analysis is nothing more than a sketch map of the area with details such as:

- Neighbors' vehicle types, how many they have, any family members that visit on a regular basis;
- Where do your neighbors park, what times do they normally park, leave for work, arrive home at night, etc.;
- You also need to know about vehicle license plates, park permits, etc., indigenous to these areas, just like in the United States, there are license plates for each state; most countries have either a numerical or an alphabetical system to differentiate between cities, provinces, etc.
- Service vehicles, electric, water, gas when they take readings, cable, trash pickup lawn services, any service type personnel normally in your neighborhood and at what times they are usually present.
- Locations of manhole covers, telephone, power mains and how they can be accessed and by whom.
- The regular times and locations of vendors, street carts selling food, newspaper stands, ice cream trucks, etc.
- Any other information that will help you in becoming familiar with your surroundings.

To be able to detect enroute or moving surveillance, it will be necessary to increase your awareness of the environment to the point where attention to details becomes integrated into your normal daily activities. You will also need to get the popular mythologies of surveillance fostered by television and the movies out of your mind. Regardless of what you see on the news or read, terrorism is not only the male gender, nor are criminals or terrorists recognizable by any features that only they have, or by country of origin, accent, etc. You should never assume that your surveillants are just going to be men; they could just as easily be women or children. They could be any age, have any skin color, be from any country or nationality. Do not get locked into untrue popular myths or stereotypes about the threat. You should also never assume that the surveillance will only be behind you. Remember, as long as they can see you, then they can be anywhere. They could be in front of or across from you, or above you using windows or rooftops, and they could be stationary someone you drive or walk by, buy a paper from. Hostile surveillance can be *ANYONE, ANYWHERE* that you can be observed.

One thing you are doing, when performing actions to detect surveillance is you want to force (trick) anybody attempting to keep you under surveillance to make a physical statement, this will help confirm surveillance or not. What it means to force someone to "make a statement" is that you want to cause them to react in a way that you can observe them and their response to things you are doing. If their actions key off of things you do, or are correlated to yours and you can observe this, they are identifying themselves as surveillants. Surveillance personnel trained or untrained, having no experience or being very experienced have a fear of being detected by the person they are trying to do surveillance on, it is a natural fear that you can use to your advantage.

You want to do things that will cause the surveillance to react in that certain way you can observe; you do this by employing passive surveillance detection maneuvers.

Passive Maneuvers

These are techniques that are normal activities that do not draw attention to you, but these simple maneuvers allow you to confirm, or get an indication, that someone may be watching you without you having to blatantly confronting them. You need to consider that someone conducting surveillance against you that is compromised may commit a hostile act against you; after all, they are terrorists and criminals.

Passive Maneuvers on Foot

When moving by foot, you can *retrace your course* (often called a reverse or a 180). This allows you to observe people around you, especially those behind you, it also forces them to now come up with a reason to reverse or change their direction. Look at the heads: sometimes, surveillants will turn their head away or have that deer in the headlight look when you look directly at them. This technique needs to be done naturally so when in a mall, store, or other building, use the stairs, since many times they pass back over each other from floor-to-floor or escalators which do the same thing. Shopping in a mall can allow you to do the same thing; you always want to shop from the rear of the stores you go in to the front, that way you are working your way back toward the door and any surveillance will now be in front of you instead of behind. When you have done this a few times, going in and out of stores or using stairs, you might begin to spot the same people, indicating that you are probably under surveillance.

When moving by or through areas with lots of windows such a hotel lobbies, restaurants, shopping areas, business districts, etc., *use those reflective surfaces*, windows, mirrors, etc., to observe the actions of people around you.

You can *change your pace* or speed of movement. This is a very simple thing to do but is highly effective in helping you to detect surveillance. We all normally walk at our own pace, but if you start to alternate your pace, walk normal, speed up then slow down, then walk your normal pace again, you are forcing anyone conducting surveillance to adjust his or her pace to match yours. When you are altering your pace, discreetly try to observe who else around you is altering their pace. If you sped up and someone was matching your speed, but then slowed down, then that person should have passed you, why didn't he? You need to be subtle; you do not want to alert the surveillants that you are suspicious or to the tactics you are using. Stopping is also changing your pace; if you are walking and stop to watch the news on a television in a store window, or stop to look at the price sticker on a car, to read a subway map, to mail a letter in a post box, etc., then anyone following you now has to have a plausible reason to stop also and then start moving again when you do.

You need to remember that you are trying to force the surveillants to make a statement. When performing the actions we talked about or others, you must be watching for people who look surprised, react inappropriately to your action, suddenly change their direction, will not look at you, who look at you and then turn away suddenly, etc.

NOTE: It is hard for people to overcome the fear of being detected. It is something we have had since we were children. Some examples are remember watching someone you really liked, girl or boy and they suddenly turn to look at you, you looked away, turned red, felt guilty about being caught? Now, that you are older, if you've ever watched someone you don't know doing something, a woman putting on lipstick, a man fixing his hair, then they notice you looking at them, you may still immediately look away, embarrassed. These feelings are amplified when conducting surveillance; *NO ONE* wants to get caught.

Passive Maneuvers while Driving

Changing speed: Just as in walking people usually try to maintain the speed limit or stay with the pack when driving. If you alternate going slower, then going faster, then driving the speed limit, you will be forcing surveillance vehicles to do this also. If you go faster than the posted limit and then slow down to under the speed limit, most vehicles will pass you to maintain the higher speed. If one doesn't pass you, then that vehicle is potentially surveillance. Remember, you know why you are changing speeds; you have a reason so anyone who keeps the same distance behind you only has ONE reason, and that is he must stay behind you.

Signal for turns and then continue straight ahead: By signaling a turn, getting in the turn lane, and preparing to turn you force any surveillance vehicles to do the same thing, when you don't make that turn, observe and see if any vehicle that was preparing to turn also does not make the turn, that is possible surveillance.

Make a U-turn: U-turns are the same as doing a reverse or a 180 on foot, you need to do it where it is safe to do so, when possible, you want to use a good natural reverse when driving so any surveillance does not think you are trying to bust them out. Examples of a good natural U-turn are when you have to make one to turn into a store or parking lot on the opposite side of the street, traffic circles, turning against traffic when leaving a parking area, make one at a stop light to move back down the street to a gas station or other reason to stop, etc.

Stop on the shoulder of the road just beyond a curve or a hilltop: Surveillance vehicles will try to keep as much distance between you and themselves as possible; the closer they are, the easier they are to spot. When going over a hill, or going around a blind curve, when possible, you can pull over to the side as soon as you are out of sight of any vehicles, then get out, act like you are using the rest room, looking at the engine, etc. Pay attention to vehicles now coming around the blind spot. Any surveillants will have some type of reaction, hit the brakes, deer in the headlight look, etc. If you cannot pull over in one of these areas, you can speed up as you enter the turn or start going up the hill. Once you are in the blind spot, slow down, don't stop, and watch the reactions of the vehicles that come up behind you. If they come around speeding, they should continue on to pass you. If they stop or slow down, they are possible surveillance.

Circle a block using a series of right-hand only or left-hand only turns: If you know where you are going or the area, find an area where you can make a series of same direction turns to get to your location. It should not be a route most people use. If the same vehicle follows you through at least three turns, it is probably surveillance, since most people would take a more direct route. *NOTE ON TURNS: The rule for surveillance detection is anyone who follows you for three turns is surveillance since the statistical odds that you would be following that exact same route to a location at the exact same time are almost nil. I don't like using turns for this. I prefer using the term decision points instead of turns for most places. They are just as effective. Since someone following you through three decisions points either on foot or in a vehicle, going the exact direction you are going at the exact time, should also make you suspicious.*

Drive throughs: This is when you pass through housing areas that have little or no traffic throughout the day, usually higher-class neighborhoods, so any vehicles that look out of place for that area should look suspicious to you. Driving through different types of areas that the threat might not have planned for when developing their cover will also make the personnel uncomfortable in what they are doing and this will heighten the chance of them making a mistake. Don't make this a habit or routine or they will get used to it and be prepared for it.

Parking lots: These are great for doing natural reverses and for identifying potential surveillance, since most lanes are one way just drive up and down like you are looking for a certain parking spot, anyone who passes up any empty spots you pass by and continues following you is possible surveillance.

Traffic circles (ROUDABOUTS): These are normally interesting places anyway since most people don't know how to use them, but when you add the element of someone trying to follow you without being noticed, it gets really interesting. A car can just drive completely around the traffic circle before exiting in their exit, since most people exit when they come upon their turn. This will make anyone who follows you around the traffic circle and then takes the same exit really stand out, because they didn't take that exit the first time they passed. Any surveillance team will have to follow them around the entire circle unless they already know what exit the target will take, that's why it's important to have more than one route and to alternate use of these routes to avoid predictability.

Traffic lights: Can be used just like in the movies, last minute changes of lanes to move into a turning lane will require the surveillance to attempt the same thing before they get to the light. In countries that actually have traffic laws and police, you can slow down or delay going through a traffic light until right before it turns yellow and then go through before it turns red, look for anyone who tries to run the light after you.

CUL-DE-SACS: These are basically dead-end streets that don't have an outlet, so driving down one of these streets to the end and turning around will allow you to drive by anyone who had been following behind. This can really make a surveillant uncomfortable and allows you to actually look into their vehicles and possibly take pictures. This only works if the surveillance does not know it is a CUL-DE-SAC; if they do, they may just stop and wait for you to come back out or send in someone on foot or on a bicycle to see which house you visit.

Country roads: These are tricky for a surveillance team because there are few places to blend in; they are usually long with few obstructions and some only lead to one destination. Since you already know where you are going and why, the surveillance team will need to make adjustments and attempt to have a purpose for being there at the final destination. There are several things you can do. Just pull over for a rest break. If any cars behind don't pass you but stop, slow down, or pull over that would be very abnormal. Varying your speed as discussed earlier really works well on country roads. If you have any blind curves or elevated positions you must pass that will block you from the view of anyone behind, you can speed way up, get a lot of distance, then slow down. If someone behind you speeds up once they see what you have done, then slows down so as not too pass, they are probably back there for a reason.

Route Surveys

You should become very familiar with all the routes that you will travel; you should have three different routes to and from all primary locations. A great way to help you in becoming familiar with your various routes is to conduct a thorough route survey for each route. A route survey is nothing more than a written document that helps you collect and analyze information; it should include the following information, but can be changed to adapt to your working environment:

Route description: This will make note of the starting point of the route, the end point, general direction, and total distance traveled with length of time noted for each time of day it is used. Also, a route for these purposes is only ONE direction, so you need the same route information coming from a point as you do going to that same point.

Road surface composition: Make a note of the type of road surface on this route, is it asphalt, concrete, gravel, dirt, etc. Also, make a note of where it changes from one type of surface to another if it does.

Weather effects: You need to know how the weather or changes in weather will affect the road surface on the routes, because this will affect your driving and may alter your driving time. *NOTE: Some people build a pattern by only taking certain roads during bad weather, snow, etc. because those roads are better cared for by maintenance crews during bad weather. DON'T BE PREDICTABLE.*

Temporary construction: Write down the location start and end points of any construction, how far it is from your start point, how far from the end point, when the construction started, type of construction, etc. When construction starts on a route, you should call the city street department and check for permits, etc., also make note of the construction vehicles, government workers, or private contractors; call and check up on them also.

Traffic patterns: You need to take notes on the traffic patterns for each route at the different times of the day you may be driving it, density of foot and vehicle traffic, vendors, schools letting out, etc.

Critical navigation: Areas such as any traffic control points are places that force you to slow down, channelize your direction, or cause you to stop; they include *toll booths, toll roads*; these control points force you to stop and pay a fee unless you have an electronic means of driving through and paying; they also channelize you into lanes for movement until you pass through and merge back into traffic on the other side; *Peak traffic times, and areas*, in some cities during peak traffic times, because of the volume of traffic heading one particular direction at certain times of the day, such as the end of the work day, some streets may convert to one way traffic to help avoid traffic congestion and avoid delays. Traffic police may be put out at high traffic areas to control traffic, vehicle congestion could slow down movement or cause it to stop, traffic lights may change faster, etc., for places; some areas with large businesses that have shift work may let out at certain times, causing a large influx of vehicles and people onto the street at the same time, the same is true for schools, public transportation, etc.; *one-way streets* can become very congested at certain times both with vehicles and with pedestrians; also in some cities, one-ways streets turn into two-way streets at certain times to ease congestion. *Traffic circles* are tricky enough anyway, but during certain times, they can be very hard to navigate. So, at such times, it may be better to avoid them; *narrow bridges or roads* can prevent you from performing any type of evasive maneuvers such as turning or backing up; also, they are much easier to block for an attack so it is easier for the threat to control your vehicle movement; *entrance and exit ramps*: to use these, you have to slow down the speed of the vehicle, they are narrow so they are easily blocked and they can channelize you, many exit ramps also have stop signs or yield signs controlling your movements even more. The entrance ramps are the same; while they allow you to build speed to merge in traffic, they also have yield signs to slow you; no city or site is ever exactly the same, so you need to make sure you list any other traffic areas, conditions, or critical navigation points *where you cannot predict what traffic* will be like at the time you will be traveling along that route.

You should also know where all the potential danger areas are located along each route. These areas include places like *parks or town squares*, or other public gathering areas where large groups of people or demonstrators can gather. These types of gatherings can lead to riots or disruptions. That can stop traffic, alter traffic patterns, and increase the chances of security forces needing to get involved. It is best to avoid these areas or at least keep abreast of local news or advertised events and know when these types of gatherings are planned and avoid them during those times. Universities, colleges, and local technical schools are all places where demonstrations and events can take place that can be dangerous to you as a non-native. You need to know where the choke points are. Choke points are locations YOU HAVE TO PASS THROUGH, where there is no other way around or a way to bypass the area. You want to limit these on the routes you take since the threat will know you have to pass through that location once you are on it. The locations of political party headquarters should be noted along your routes, even if you are just passing by a building that only has a small office in it for one of these organizations. These places can be lightning rods for political dissent in the population that can draw violence or protests. Areas of poverty or low income can often have a propensity toward crime, such as muggings, carjacking, etc. They also usually have little or no law enforcement protection, so it is best to avoid these areas, especially since these are the types of areas and people that terrorist organizations appeal to to get support and recruit from. Every city and country is different insofar as what could be a potential danger to you, and you will need to identify a list of what you consider to be potentially dangerous along your routes.

Along with knowing where the danger areas are along the routes you choose to travel on, you need to know those places and areas that will offer you some type of protection or safety in case of any incident that you feel is threatening, dangerous, or an unforeseen/unexpected event. You should have several *safe areas* along your routes and know how to access them. These locations include but are not limited to:

United States or other friendly diplomatic facilities, embassies, *etc.*: These types of facilities not only have a military presence from their own country but usually the security for the outside of the facility is the responsibility of the host nation. So, there are not only military, but police on the outside and probably a quick reaction force in the event of any incidents. Driving through this area may put off attackers or surveillance; entering an embassy will give you some excellent protection.

Police/fire stations: Criminals along with terrorists want to avoid any involvement with law enforcement or security forces. They will not follow you near locations like this and will certainly not attack near them; fire stations may not have weapons but they have radios that are more than likely directly linked to law enforcement.

Hospitals: They usually have their own security. Around the emergency room, there are normally some law enforcement officers there because of accidents, or incidents, plus hospitals normally have direct radio contact with law enforcement dispatchers.

Military facilities: This includes anywhere there are military personnel; they can include security checkpoints, outposts, stations, etc.

Mosques, churches, temples, or other sites of worship: While these used to be considered sacrosanct from doing others harm, and the terrorists may not be members of that particular religion, they still may not wish to violate the sanctity of the location and bring condemnation from their own religious leaders for an attack on a holy site. And, they do not want to erode or run off any popular support they have by attacking someone in a place many of the locals consider sacred.

Banks: Banks or other money institutions will always have security, a means to contact police, or other security, guns, video, etc., so they are excellent places to go since most criminals and terrorists will avoid them;

Jewelry stores: Jewelry stores or shops that sell similarly high-value items will, like banks, have security, guns, a means to contact police, etc.

NOTE: While many of these sites in permissive or semi-permissive environments will afford you some protection or the means to get help, in a non-permissive environment, zone of conflict, war zone, etc., they might not. That's why you should do research and check each route to make sure safe areas are available and are something that YOU can use.

Some surveillance indicators along your route could be:

- Any vehicles that remain parked in the exact same place for extended periods of time, regardless of time of day, for no visible reason.
- Vehicles that start and stop at the same time you do; this includes any vehicles that are keying off of your movements, when you pull away from a curb, they pull away, when you park, they park, etc.
- Vehicles that pass you and pull over to park, this is the same as starting and stopping at the same time; remember, surveillance does not have to be behind you, as long as they can find a parking place in front of you where you can be observed they can do their job, watch for this and watch for them pulling out right before you do, then drive slower to see what direction you go, or watch for them pulling out after you do and following you.
- Vehicles that are keying off of you during movement: This means that other vehicles that are driving too fast or too slow for traffic conditions in attempt to stay behind you should be looked at as possible surveillance.
- Any vehicles that travel at the same speed as you and maintain the same distance from you, regardless of traffic or you speeding up or slowing down.
- Vehicles that pause in a traffic circle until you pass them or chose which street you are going to exit, then they speed up to follow you.
- Vehicles that appear broken down, especially in locations where they can observe you at one of your primary areas, decision points you pass through or any critical navigation areas and choke points. How long they are there, how often are vehicles broken down in these areas, etc.
- Any vehicles with altered license plates or those that for some reason have their license plates obstructed in some way so that they cannot be seen, clearly. What can make this really suspicious

are little things like using mud to obscure the plate but the rest of the vehicle is clean.

- People who are inappropriately dressed for the area they are in, such as suits and ties in a warehouse area, or torn jeans and tee shirts in a business's district; every district has their own personality because of those that work and live there or near there. Learn what they are and look for those people who are not fitting in. Also, consider the time of year, wearing long coats during the summer, when everyone else is in shorts, wearing hats that obscure the face on cloudy days, etc.
- Any type of work crews or vehicles, emergency crews or vehicles near your critical navigation areas, choke points, and danger areas.

There are going to be many vehicles moving around you, so you are going to need other ways to help you separate innocent vehicles from possible terrorist surveillance vehicles, besides their movement behavior, etc., so you should also consider the following:

Use cameras, both still or video if you can. By videotaping the routes you take each day and reviewing them or have someone else like security review them, you will notice changes in the daily environment, they provide positive descriptions of any suspicious people or vehicles, and you can provide photographic evidence to back up your suspicions to law enforcement or security.

Take the time to write down all observations, suspicions, and descriptions in a daily log or a route pattern analysis sheet for each route traveled. This just means that you will record anything that seems out of the ordinary or suspicious along your route, and then at the end of each day, transcribe this daily record onto a route pattern analysis sheet to determine if there are any reoccurring people, vehicles, or situations along different routes that might necessitate further investigation or things that might make you consider raising your security profile.

OBSERVATION AND DESCRIPTION

All this talk of remembering details and writing down suspicious person, vehicles, and/or events means that we need to work on our observation skills and especially our ability to describe what we see to others, such as security or law enforcement so THEY will now have usable information they can act on.

Observation is "*The complete awareness by an individual of his surroundings, achieved through maximum employment of the senses.*" So those who are experienced and practice good observation skills will increase/enhance their ability to recognize and recall any object or situation accurately, fully, and clearly, with a minimum of distortion.

Remember when we talked about our "Map of the World" and how it filters everything in our environment so that we only see, hear, feel, smell, etc., those things our mind perceives as important. This causes many things to happen when we allow our unconscious to filter out things because in observation—"*One sees only those things one observes; however, one observes only those things already in mind.*" What this means to us is our ability to perceive depends upon our innate ability, experience, and training in relation to our environment, for to *perceive* means to *see and understand.*

EXAMPLE: You don't know anything about cars, and you never notice them or pay attention, until you buy a new one. Now, that you own a new car, you start to notice other cars of the same make and model as yours as you travel around. License plates: you probably don't notice them too often, until you travel, then you start noticing those from the state where you live; you can also say this about expensive clothes, watches, electronics such as cell phones, etc. WHY? Because before it was not part of your i believe it should say part of your map of the world, whereas after you buy it, now you are aware that you are unconsciously looking for them.

Any accurate observation requires the mental effort necessary to recognize, analyze, and relate all of the different parts of our surroundings and to interpret those patterns and any relationships that are present. The problem with us being able to accomplish this is that we usually perceive or comprehend only those things which interests us, or we are capable of understanding with the least amount of effort.

Having an extensive vocabulary is also very important and is usually built upon knowledge and life experience; this in turn gives a clear conception of the object to which a term is applied. So, a person with a good vocabulary and who understands descriptive terms usually comprehends more than the person with an inadequate vocabulary, because basically their "map of the world" is larger.

People with experience or training in observation will usually perceive another person as a whole and not as a grouping of their particular physical characteristics. In our daily lives, we meet people every day, but these meetings do not enlarge our ability to describe the features of those persons. We remember what we need to and toss the rest away. The way to get good at observation and giving descriptions is by training ourselves to make accurate observations. To do this, you must:

- Begin by replacing our casual observation of the generalities in our surroundings with study and observation of details.
- You need to train yourself to estimate accurately the passage of time, especially while you are doing something, to gauge the speed of moving objects, and distances.

- Become more familiar with descriptive terms pertaining to colors and shades of colors, makes and models of vehicles, and terms that describe clothing and physical characteristics of people indigenous to the area. There is actually a marked difference between men and women when it comes to this. For example, women know every shade of the different colors because a woman has an interest in color, based on its importance to personal appearance, including hair, make up, and clothes. So, many women frequently learn as much as possible of the various shades of colors and the vocabulary necessary to describe them. Men on the other hand normally have a similar in-depth knowledge about cars or trucks because they are of interest to them. But for dresses and clothes, a man usually observes the basic color only because that is all he needs to know. We just need to expand our knowledge into all these areas to give us the ability to describe more accurately what we have seen.
- You also need to be able to visualize people, vehicles, things, and especially things that happen in our presence. Usually, we only remember what our priority is, and never pay attention to other things taking place around us. We just need to practice expanding our awareness to include more of our environment, in order to expand our observation and retention skills.

When we talk about training in visual observation skills, this does not require that we attempt to observe and remember every face, every detail, and every scene. Instead, we should be training to recognize those details that affect us, our security and safety, and concentrate on retaining that information for possible future use. But, our ability to retain information that could be important to us, security forces, and law enforcement means nothing if we cannot describe that information effectively to someone else or present it in a format where someone who wasn't there will understand what we are trying to describe to them. *Description* is "*the technique of factually reporting one's own observations of an experience*" to someone else. The purpose of giving a description of a person, place, thing, or event to someone is so you can *paint an accurate word picture* so the person you are describing it too will understand. We want to be descriptive enough so that we can create in the mind of another an accurate picture of the incident, person, etc., for them.

Also, we need to remember and keep reminding ourselves that describing something with great accuracy, but not being able to give a complete description, is much better for security or law enforcement than giving a complete description with inaccuracies in it. We have a tendency to talk about things that we think are correct when we are not sure. Any descriptions given should be as complete as possible so that they can be used by others who have never seen the subject of the description. The time and circumstances of the incident or event do not always permit completing the "long form" description; in other words, giving you enough time to remember everything accurately. So, a format should be used to help you when visualizing the event, forming a picture in your mind and then describing it to someone else:

Distinguishing characteristics: Almost every person possesses some distinguishing or outstanding physical characteristics, something that catches the eye. This type of characteristic is then the most important part of a person's description, because if it stood out enough for you to notice, others will notice it also. Examples of features that could be considered distinguishing are:

- Body scars and marks such as tattoos that are visible
- How someone walks or their gait, how they swing their arms; believe it or not, everyone walks differently—and gait analysis is a legitimate forensic discipline
- Their voice, everyone also has a unique voice, their volume, tone, and how they speak
- How they dress; most people have a certain style as to how they present themselves

General characteristics: Six general characteristics are used in the description of individuals. They are:

- Sex
- Race, this is tricky; remember, we talked before about being accurate with what you describe. If you don't know the subject's race, give a skin tone or color; if you say a person is Mexican, then that's who security forces will be looking for: a Mexican. Meanwhile, the person might be from Spain or Central or South America. If you say Hispanic, then they will look at all who might fit that type of heritage
- Age
- Height, use objects around a person to help you determine this, how much of him you could see over the top of a car, and how much space was there between his head and the top of a door or window, etc.
- Weight
- Build

Changeable characteristics: Changeable characteristics are those aspects of a person's appearance that can be readily changed or modified to affect a disguise, such as

- Hair style/color, taking off or putting on a wig
- Glasses/eye color, putting on or taking off glasses or changing the style of the glasses; contacts can also change eye color
- Clothes, putting on or taking of jackets, hats, or changing shirts, etc. One thing people have a tendency not to change is their shoes, especially men
- Props: This includes things like walking sticks, umbrellas, briefcases, backpacks, shopping bags, etc. These can be used by either picking something up or discarding it in an attempt to change their general appearance

For vehicles, it is basically the same thing as for people, so when describing a vehicle, use the same basic format.

- Distinguishing characteristics such as dents, scratches in the body, or bumpers, special antennas, cracked windshield with stickers in the window, etc.
- General characteristics (make of vehicle [Audi, Chevy, Ford], type of vehicle [pickup]); remember, if don't know for sure the manufacture, give a good description of the characteristics you do know for sure
- Changeable characteristics such as license number or plate type, special wheels, hub caps, bumper stickers, things in the window, etc.
- Permanent details, four-door, two-door, hatchback, or convertible, etc.

CHAPTER 7

Individual Protective Measures

> If someone can kill an American soldier, it is better than wasting his energy on other matters.
>
> —*Osama Bin Ladin*

There are many different attitudes in today's society both here in the United States and around the world in how we feel about the many threats against us for the terrorist threat it is "If a terrorist really wants to get me, then there is nothing I can do to stop him." For the criminal threat it is, "why do anything, the chances of me being robbed, attacked, carjacked, raped, etc. are almost non-existent, those types of things only happen to other people." These types of attitudes about threats against us are very typical of many members of society today, and, yes, it is almost impossible to prevent a threat from successfully attacking someone or something if they really want it. But, there are ways that we can make ourselves undesirable as targets for any threat. The threat needs to succeed and not get caught, so we are lucky that any threat be it terrorist or criminal is influenced by the idea that "When you are hungry, it is foolish to hunt a tiger when there are plenty of sheep to be had." Individual protective measures (IPM) is designed to show you ways, attitudes, techniques, and precautions you can take that are designed to teach you how to be a tiger and avoided, instead of a sheep. The attitude and drive to make yourself undesirable as a target is an individual responsibility. Nobody can make you do it, and the extent you will go to make yourself undesirable as a target depends on how much you value your life and the lives of your loved ones.

> To be prepared beforehand for any contingency is the greatest of all virtues.
>
> —*Ho Yen-His, Chinese Scholar*

DOI: 10.4324/9781003292647-7

To do this, you will have to learn to evaluate the threats for the areas you live, work in and any direct threats against you. You do not and cannot be in 100 percent defensive security mode all the time; it will wear you and your family out and waste resources. Time and effort that you can direct in a more efficient manner once you know and understand the threat. What you basically need to do is strike a balance between PRUDENCE AND PARANOIA; this balance will be based upon the threat leveled against you, the environment you are working and living in, and the procedures you can take to ensure your security. A good security plan is more than just the physical aspects of protection, it is being able to understand why you might be a target and taking the precautions necessary. It is objective evaluation of you and your life to find the weaknesses that may be exploited by a threat; it is taking the time to look at and understanding your working, living environment so that you can lower your profile and become less of a potential target, and it is the attitude that "If they want me they can get, there is nothing I can do to stop them, but I am not going to make it easy for them!"

HOW TO DETERMINE THE THREAT IN AN AREA

Let's suppose that you just got word that you have to move and live in a new area—or that there has been an increase in incidents, criminal attacks, terrorist crimes, etc., in the area you currently live and work. You will need to determine the threats for the area you are going to or, in the case of the latter, reassess the changing threats where you are currently living in. You need to gather as much information as possible on terrorists and terrorist activity, gang activity and criminal tactics and statistics in the area from libraries, embassies if going overseas, and newspapers not just American newspapers, but those for the country/city where you are traveling to. U.S. news tends to concentrate on what is important to the United States, and the newspaper, not on criminal, gang, drug, terrorist-related violence in other countries. Go online and start reading English language version newspapers for the areas you are going to, magazines, books, people who have been or are now in that area, law enforcement, etc. For traveling overseas, you can go to the Department of State website; they keep good information posted on current threats to Americans traveling/living abroad; once you get in the country, continue to obtain information from the U.S. Embassy, local law enforcement, people you are working with, the Internet, etc.

You need to determine which gangs, group/groups may pose a threat to you and learn all you can about these groups' beliefs, ideologies, and their goals. By doing this, you may be able to lower your profile, change your public image, take other precautions, etc., to lessen your value as a target to them. Many times, the history of an organization will provide some insight into a group's patterns of how they select targets and show types of attacks they have conducted on victims or key dates that show increase in their activities such as the anniversary dates of the group's formation, successes, defeats, death of members, holidays. For criminals, it could be events such as concerts, sporting events (crime went up dramatically at the Olympics in Atlanta and in Salt Lake City, and usually, at the cities hosting the Super Bowl or World Series), etc.

You also need to learn the nationalities and race of the victims being targeted in the area. Some criminals, gangs, domestic terrorists only target people not of their race or nationality; others will target anyone regardless of race or nationality. Also, terrorist groups have published manifestos stating who their targets will be, such as Al-Qaeda saying it will kill Americans. And let's not forget in June 2000, Osama Bin Laden published a manifesto indicating Americans are the targets of choice for all organizations to strike at. So, knowing this type of information can allow you to change your plans or at least raise your security awareness.

You also need to determine the potential for violence of the threats in the area; some gangs, criminals, and terrorists are more violent than others. Look at some gangs and the rise of violence in major cities; this is not only in the United States but in many countries around the world. Most countries never advertise there are criminal-, gang-, or terrorist-related problems in their cities because they don't want to scare away the money that tourism brings in. Drug-related gangs and crimes also usually turn violent when there are shoot outs over territory, etc.

When doing your research, you need to figure out what the present activity level is for all the threats in that area. General crime up or down, gang crime and violence, drug crime, are there any terrorist groups in the area that are active, or are they in an organizing phase. When was the last major event? Who was the target? Why? Are law enforcement and security operations up in the area? All this information will help you determine what is taking place now in the area you are in or going to visit. If it is bad, you might want to postpone your trip or move it to another location, but, since this is not always an option, at least you can prepare yourself to meet the demands of the current environment.

In your research, you need to find out how sophisticated the gangs, criminal element, or terrorist groups are. If they are well organized, equipped, and supported, this will help you plan to decide the levels of security you might need. Are they a young organization that has not yet reached a sophisticated level of development? Once again, this tells you the levels of security and layers you might need to plan for, since organizations that are less organized, equipped, etc. have to resort to violence more often to obtain their goals. But, this doesn't mean that those better organized groups or gangs are less of a threat. It just means they are better at controlled violence, planning and gathering intelligence, and hitting specific targets; so, they generally pose the greater threat.

The next thing you need to do is try to determine how much popular support the threat has in the area. Many times, gangs, extremist groups, and criminal organizations have some degree of popular support because of family members who may belong, they might be providing protection for certain neighborhoods, help out those who need it, etc. Many terrorist groups have popular support for the same reason: they have family members or friends that are members, they believe in the cause the group is promoting, and want to help them achieve their goal. Usually, when they commit their criminal acts, they do so out of the area where they have popular support, and they do not attack or commit acts against locals. Other groups and organizations do not have any popular support because these groups usually are operating in areas where people disagree with them, do not like their cause, or believe them to be nothing but criminals who prey on them. Some of these groups or gangs may use intimidation or coercion on the local populace and force them into providing the support they need to function. This happens with gangs in cities, major criminal organizations and terrorist organizations such as The New People's Army (NPA) of the Philippines. They still carry out assassinations of village and town officials in an effort to control the local government, thereby controlling the people. But remember, it does not matter how these different organizations and terrorists have gained their support; the fact is they have it, so it may not be wise to venture into certain areas that are supportive of terrorists or other threats.

You need to find out what methods of operation the terrorists and other threats are using currently and what they have used in the past. This will give you an insight into possible attacks and methods that will be used against you, allowing you to prepare yourself to meet the threat. This works because when a method of operation is successful for a terrorist group, they will continue to reuse the method in other operations, since they have now trained, experience at using it, and more importantly confidence that it will work. Other groups, once they see how successful this method is, will copy it and use it in their operations as well. There are numerous examples of operations that have been repeated by terrorist groups and criminal organizations all over the world. A few are the overrun techniques in an ambush, drive-by shootings, victim initiated improvised explosive devices (IEDs), secondary IED devices, and using vehicle-borne improvised explosive devices (VBIED) to drive into a building or checkpoint, suicide bombings, etc. The list is endless.

While you are researching what methods of operations the threat is targeting, you may also need to learn what tactics the terrorists use and are currently employing when they conduct these operations. There are many manuals that terrorists and now criminal organizations get their tactics from; they include *Special Forces Operational Techniques*, the *Ranger Handbook*, Carlos Marighella's *Minimanual of the Urban Guerrilla*, and *Guerrilla Warfare* by Che Guevara. Al-Qaeda also published its own manual on tactics, as did the Revolutionary Armed Forces of Colombia (FARC) in Columbia. Your research will also help you determine various types of attacks terrorists are using which is another benefit to you since it can help you focus and inform your security on those areas where they are strongest.

Many threat groups are not capable of performing certain acts because of a lack of resources, training, or the security environment they have to work in, while others favor only one or two acts for their symbolism to the people they are trying to influence. Sometimes, terrorists will publish manifestos stating who their targets will be, and why they are targets: what they hope to accomplish. You should also check with the U.S. Government and local governments law enforcement and military to find out what their policy on dealing with terrorists is. This can be very important to you and your security since it can narrow the focus of what a threat may attempt against you. For instance, U.S. Government, including military personnel, do not make good kidnap victims, because of U.S. policy in dealing with terrorism, which is they do not negotiate with terrorist organizations. So, for you, if a threat to you is primarily using the two techniques, kidnapping and assassination, then you need to concern yourself more with assassination techniques—such as bombings or ambushes—and strengthen your security profile and individual protective measures (IPM) against this type of attack.

When you have completed all your research and have determined the threats against you, you now need to apply the appropriate IPM to your and/or your family's daily activities. You also need to continually reevaluate your threat level on conditions in your area of operations and should raise and lower your levels of IPM according to these changing conditions so you can be better prepared to meet the threat as it changes and evolves. NOTE: Threat conditions are not only assigned by the U.S. Government, the embassy, or the local government; you need to do your own evaluation based upon the ones you assign to your daily activities such as movement to and from work, checkpoints while traveling, etc. Threat levels issued by the government are based upon the threat against them and general assessments and, on the whole, not against the INDIVIDUAL.

WHY WE ARE TARGETS? HOW WE BECOME VICTIMS?

Many people are targeted worldwide by terrorists or criminal organizations and it seems that people not native to the areas where the attacks occur draw the most media attention, which is what the threat wants, publicity. But, there are other reasons that we as Americans are sought after as targets; The world has gotten smaller. Travel between countries and continents are normal now and easy for just about everyone. That means that as American citizens, we can travel even to places we shouldn't and without the protections that most government workers enjoy. This increased presence throughout the world means there is a greater chance of becoming a target to those elements that wish to gain publicity by harming foreigners, or more specifically Americans. Let us not forget also that as Americans we have a greater symbolic value than people from other nations. Most countries and peoples around the world have the perception that all Americans are rich, work for the government. America is perceived as interfering in other countries' business. Some propaganda is even put out in many countries that blame the countries' poor economy and corrupt government on the United States. Striking a blow against the United States would be a great symbolic victory for the threat. As Americans when we travel, we usually have a high visibility rating to the threat. And, most Americans are not used to travel or foreign cultures. For better or worse, many Americans travel in large groups, don't speak the language, and are proud to be an American—so they advertise it with American flags, t-shirts, etc. Since we are so used to having excellent police and law enforcement protection in the states, we feel that other countries are the same, which is not always the case. As Americans, we usually have very poor security practices when we travel, this makes us easier targets for the threat. Finally, there are the negative, sometimes superior, attitudes most Americans travel with: for example, that they are smarter than the locals, cleaner, deserve to be helped first, our problems take priority over theirs, etc.

There are other ways to become a victim of any type of attack or incident which include: by location, which is nothing more than being at a certain location when an attack occurs. You were not the specific target of the attack, you were just in the wrong place at the wrong time, which would make you a victim of circumstance. We can be a victim by associating with a person who has been selected as a target by the threat. You are now a target also if the attack takes place while you are with him. If surveillance on him identifies you as a potential target because you know or work with him, then you can be placed on a target list yourself; this is called Victim by Association. You can also become a victim by presenting yourself as a soft or easy target, thereby allowing the terrorists to capitalize on the opportunity you present to them when you are traveling with no security, no situational awareness, or otherwise not understanding the threat; you are now a target of opportunity for them.

In today's high-risk world, things are not getting safer. Increasingly, U.S. citizens are becoming the popular terrorist target as they travel and conduct business throughout the world on a daily basis.

IDENTIFICATION AND SELECTION OF TARGETS

One of the primary ways that potential targets are identified is based on belief of importance as perceived by both the individual and the terrorists. In other words, it's not how important you think you are, it's how important THEY think you are. Now, this does not mean you are important or not important. But how someone who has never seen you before and is outside "the fence" looking in thinks you are; this is based on the Threats PERCEPTION of your importance.

So, who are important people? Advisers, official representatives of an organization or government, business partners, etc. Anyone who may get special treatment by the host government or business as very important persons (VIPs) out of respect, gratefulness, or in an attempt to impress. People who are VIPs are generally given high-profile red-carpet treatment; sometimes, they are met plane side, be escorted through the airport, have people with signs waiting to meet them, have limousines or motorcades waiting to transport them. All these types of things raise your profile, especially at an airport; if possible, tactfully discourage VIP treatment and maintain a low profile.

U.S. Embassy personnel, people working with the host nation, business executives, and any other people who use staff vehicles or official cars are perceived to be important. If you have no choice in the matter, you must try to limit the use of staff cars. The best bet is do not use them at all. If it is a requirement for the work you are doing or for security reasons, and you must use one, make sure the vehicle blends in as much as possible with the vehicles used by the local population. Remember also your level of importance is about perception; if you catch a ride with a VIP for an event and you are seen getting into one of these vehicles, the surveillance who saw you doesn't know you are catching a ride. All he knows is you must be important to ride in that type of vehicle!

How these vehicles are marked is also important. A vehicle with diplomatic plates, any other type of plate that has some special meaning or gives some type of benefit for having it on your vehicle, clearly suggests the presence of an important person. Avoid using this type of license plate whenever possible. You or whoever you are working for should try obtaining a license plate that is indigenous to that country and the same as natives of that country get. Some countries give foreigners license plates that identify them as being foreign and the plates are also marked as to what their country of origin is.

Depending on what you do for work, sometimes DECALS are required by the military base or embassy and some businesses require them for access to parking, schools, gyms, and country clubs. These can identify you as someone of importance, if your sticker allows you access to VIP parking or into an exclusive club. Whenever possible, these should not be permanently affixed to your vehicle. Instead, place the stickers on a device that can be easily and quickly observed when entering a facility or parking area, for example, a piece of cardboard or a 3 × 5 card. When leaving you can then remove the sticker from the window and place it in an unobservable position such as under your seat or in your glove box, removing it from the sight of both casual observation and any surveillance. Any type of decals that give title or rank should also be kept out of view since you can become a target just because of your rank or title.

Anyone who is using chauffeurs or has drivers are considered some type of important person. When you can do your own driving, if because of your unfamiliarity with the streets or local driving laws, you must have a chauffeur, use him until you become familiar with the area and the routes, and then decline his services. If your job, position, or local security concerns requires that you have a permanent chauffeur/driver, you can still decide which routes to use, what speed to use, pickup times, etc., and you should still try to use a low-profile vehicle and not use a driver or chauffeur wearing a uniform.

Another double-edged sword is the use of a bodyguard. Only a VIP, or someone who believes they are important, will have a bodyguard. The more important the person is, or believes he is, the more bodyguards he will have. Why is this a double-edged sword? Because now the threat is going to want to know why you need bodyguards, why you think you are a target, and what makes you important. If you were not on their radar before, you will be now, so you need to keep the number of bodyguards to an absolute minimum and make sure that both you and your bodyguards blend in with the local population with your physical appearance, including what you wear and how you act. Any bodyguards you have should not be obvious, which means they should blend in, also having bodyguards does not give you special privileges in most instances. Your bodyguards shouldn't be pushing people, threatening people, trying to get you special treatment for security reasons; it just makes you stand out. In past attacks and incidents, there have been occasions where armed bodyguards have engaged attackers who just wanted to kidnap their ward, and by firing the first shot, they have forced would-be kidnappers into becoming assassins, since they couldn't complete their original plan. In many other cases, bodyguards have wounded or killed the people they were supposed to protect during firefights. If you must have and use bodyguards, remember that should blend in as much as possible, as this hampers the threats ability to gain knowledge of their strength, weapons, and deployment practices. If they cannot get that information, then they cannot plan on ways to defeat your bodyguards; be low profile, be unpredictable.

Expensive cars are also a no-go, many people—especially in countries outside the United States—believe that anyone driving an expensive privately owned vehicle has to be important. In those societies and cultures, RICH equals important; it is also the same in the United States. To reduce your vulnerability to this perception, you need to use the type of vehicle commonly found in the area you will be operating in. Another added benefit to doing this is that it will also make it difficult for any surveillance by the threat to identify your vehicle since it won't stand out. Once again, don't forget outside PERCEPTION, getting an upgrade to an expensive rental means that any surveillance criminal or terrorist that sees you driving around in it is going to think you have money and are important. They don't know you may just have traded in travel points!

People who have special designated parking spaces, either because of who they are or the position they hold, highlights who the important people are since it once again places them above the normal person in that environment. This type of perk also endangers you as well as family members and friends who might park in those spaces; since it is a known location for you as a potential target, an attack or incident could take place there. You should never accept a designated space, and you should come up with a plan to rotate your parking space often and randomly. One way to do this is if your office or facility has allocated spaces, and they are all in a certain area, take off the position designation, such as Commanding Officer or CEO and number them, then establish a system/raffle to randomly choose spaces daily or weekly. That way, no one can predict what location you will be at in the morning when you arrive or the evening when you leave.

What we carry and how we use these props such as a briefcase, pager, cell phone, tablet, or laptop can characterize you as important depending on where you are. Contrary to popular belief, not everyone has a laptop, tablet, blackberry, cell phone, etc., and they are not constantly using them. You can tell the difference between work and play when you see people who are sitting in a park or at the airport conducting business, chatting with friends, or playing games. If you can tell the difference, so can any potential threat. If you are constantly on the phone, taking notes, using both phone and computer in public places, it could be assumed that you must be very important since you cannot even take a lunch break without having to conduct business. It should be noted that many people currently have lost their ability to speak softly when on the phone; with ear buds and microphones, many times you can hear a conversation from 10 feet away as people speak. Understand that this lets people know the gist of your conversation and probably gives them a good idea of what you are doing, business or family, when speaking. When you are traveling or in public, limit the amount of time you use these devices, not only can they make you stand out, but they distract you from observing those around you and lower your situational awareness. So, place any work-related papers, books, tablets, phones, and computers in a gym bag or in another type of inconspicuous holder. If you absolutely have to use a briefcase, select an inexpensive one that won't stand out, not an expensive leather one with gold initials, etc. When you are driving, you should place items like briefcases, backpacks, parcels, etc., in the trunk of your vehicle. Not only does this put it out of sight of any surveillance looking for potential targets, but it stops the criminal element from doing smash and grabs on them. Many people can be identified as rich or important because of the make of cell phone they use, so make sure you keep your cell phones, personal digital assistants (PDAs), etc., concealed to avoid being obvious. I know keeping something like that in the pocket isn't as cool as carrying it in a belt holster, but doing it keeps you from being a victim of grab and runs by street criminals.

The type of identification you use can make you stand out as someone different or important. Things like using an official or diplomatic passport indicates an important status, since not everyone has one. If possible whenever you travel, you should display and use your tourist passport. If you must use your official passport to enter an area, keep it out of sight until you are required to show it and always get both your official and tourist passport stamped. The same goes with any ID badges that you have to carry for the work you may be doing. We have all seen people who display their badges when they are outside of their office or facility, buying coffee, eating lunch. In some cases, people hang them on their car mirrors so they won't forget them when going into work. This just highlights you even more to those people looking for potential targets. Always keep badges, ID cards, etc., out of sight until you need them; you must APPEAR TO BE A NORMAL person at all times to any surveillance by a threat and NOT an important person.

IDENTIFICATION BY NAME

Another method used to select people as either potential targets or confirmed targets is identification by name. In some cases, the use of names and titles cannot be avoided; however, you should always try to limit the use of names in news press releases and on social media, especially since a person's name, title, etc., can be obtained in many open-source ways:

Loading manifests: These are a requirement on all flights both for the airline, the country they are leaving, and the one they are flying into, and in some cases, they are required for trains and buses. They contain information such as seat number and full name and may even say how the ticket was purchased. This holds true for military flights also; the military manifest also contains the sending unit, the receiving unit, and the departing or landing air facilities. It is an easy way for someone who works at the arriving airport to find out who is on board a certain flight.

You also have bills of lading if you are doing a move to your new location. These are the labels placed on household goods, hold baggage, or privately owned vehicle (POV) shipments, basically anything you are having shipped to your new work or living area. It is supposed to be the responsibility of the arrival area security manager to ensure that these documents are properly controlled and disposed of; it may be better instead of sending it to your name, address, etc., to send it in care of the company you are going to work for; this limits the exposure of your name.

The immigration and customs records that you are required to fill out when entering another country and when you return to the United States. All of these forms contain names, addresses, and additional information, such as where you are going to stay, passport number, your nationality, why you are there, business, tourist, etc., but there is no guarantee that these records and forms will be properly controlled. I am not advocating lying on these forms; they are legal documents. But, can you use a post office (PO) box instead of a physical address for you home of record? Do you have to stay at the hotel you put down, etc.? It would be very easy for the threat to gain access to these records and know where you will be staying, your name, and when you are leaving. Not everyone who works in airport industry or for any government is completely trustworthy; it only takes one breach of security for this information to get out.

Social rosters for businesses, parent contact rosters for schools, emergency recall rosters, military unit rosters. All of these types of documents or rosters provide names, home and business phone numbers, cell phone numbers, sometimes email addresses. If it is a social roster, it will have the name of the spouse, number of children and their names, and additional information that can be used by the threat to gain intelligence against any potential victims.

These types of documents and rosters are usually given to everyone in the section with all the rosters being kept in one place such as a security desk, operator station, etc. For any military or government rosters, they are given to commanders, noncommissioned officers in charge, charges of quarters (duty watch standers), the various staff sections, and of course to the wives so they can plan any social events. Getting your hands on a roster like this is not a difficult task for anyone, let alone a determined person. After all, what happens when a new roster is made? Who is responsible for making sure the old ones, especially the ones kept at homes or in briefcases, are destroyed properly and not thrown in the trash? Usually, no one. Many times, these types of rosters can be found just by going through a trash can; these types of rosters should be considered sensitive in nature and controlled and disposed of properly to ensure that the threat does not gain access to it.

Different types of manning boards are used by companies, sections, and most military units; they are usually maintained by a secretary, receptionist, security desk, or by the Non-Commissioned Officer In Charge (NCOIC) or the commander. While these boards are set up differently, they all contain information that could be useful to the threat, such as an individual's name, duty title, where they work, who their boss is, current status (leave, vacation, work trip, etc.) for the military; they can contain squad, company, or platoon information. They are usually located in such a way that the person who is responsible for maintaining it can see it clearly during work hours, which means anyone who is in that office area can see it during the day. This allows easy/fast recognition of personnel manning by the person maintaining it. In some cases, manning boards include a picture of each individual, along with other information. If your company, business unit, uses a manning board to keep track of its people, then it needs to be kept in a limited access area, in restricted office space, and they should be covered or placed in such a way that they cannot be seen by casual observation. The threat—just from taking a picture of an organization's manning board—would have the breakdown of the whole business, section, facility, or unit, including who is in charge (the important people), by name, location, when they are in or out of the office, when they left or are returning, etc. These types of items are great for the threat when they can obtain the information off of them.

Telephone books or directories are an excellent source from which to obtain the names of persons overseas regardless of country and in the continental United States (CONUS). Sometimes, organizations such as military installations or large businesses and/or government compounds publish their own telephone directories. In most of these directories, in addition to the individual's name and phone number, they may also list the individual's title, rank, spouse's name and their home address, or if it is a work directory, their office location, room number, or address.

When getting a phone, you should request an unlisted telephone number, and that you be kept out of any telephone directories since some areas will still put your name and address in. You may have to pay to do this but it is worth the money. Another benefit is that it usually keeps your name, address, and phone number out of online search engines and people locator services.

Year books, alumni books, Who's Who books, an Army Green book, and a navy or marine float book can be used to obtain personal and professional information about a person. Many of these types of publications contain photographs of individuals and short biographies, what your profession is, home of record, family info, where you are working, and contact information. You need to avoid being listed in any of these publications since anyone can get their hands on them.

Many universities, colleges, trade schools, and even some military units now have alumni web pages or websites for current and former members, students, etc. These pages list the same information we just talked about: who you are, where you are, what you are doing, family and contact information, and everything they publish or put up on the web about you comes from the information that YOU SEND THEM.

Individual/personnel data files. Many companies, businesses, social organizations, schools, military units, gyms, etc., purge old personal data files containing names, addresses, etc. whenever you move, drop a membership, or graduate. Ideally, they should be shredded or in some other way destroyed. You could stop by and ask for these files yourself and destroy them, making sure it is done right. But, these organizations usually like to maintain them in their records for a certain amount of time, then they are supposed to be destroyed by the person responsible for them. If you cannot make sure all outdated files are destroyed or collected when you are no longer working there, or using that business, stop by the office with a permanent black marker and mark through things like address, where you are moving to, any account information that is no longer needed by that organization which should be everything but your name. NOTE: A lot of identity theft can be traced back to the thief dumpster diving at businesses and homes to get all the information needed to steal your life. You never want this information to fall into someone's hands, especially the threats; do not trust others to be as careful with your information as you should be.

Discarded mail. Most people and organizations have a tendency to overlook the potential intelligence that can be gained from old or discarded mail, even junk mail. It can be used to identify the person who received the mail, the person who sent it, and the city from which it was mailed. People also throw out letters that may have information the threat can use, postcards about vacation locales and return dates, membership information in organizations, school literature that identifies what schools children attend, what church you attend, etc. This information could be used when starting a file on someone and that could be used later when planning an operation against that person or his family. It could help to obtain information that could be used against a victim if they should become a hostage or kidnap victim. You need to safeguard all of your mail by using a PO box if one is available. Never use a home address. When sending mail, take it to a drop box at the post office, don't leave it in your mail box at your house. Someone could come take it, open it, take the information they need, then reseal it, and mail it later. Always remove address labels from magazines. How many times have you seen magazines in a waiting room and it has someone's home address listed? Mail of any type should be shredded when you are through with it, and magazines need to have mailing labels cut out before being discarded or donated.

Office correspondence is another way for the threat to gain valuable information about a person or an organization. Discarded office correspondence, such as leave requests, call rosters, new letters, and event fliers for office get togethers, birthday party announcements, memos that talk about people's achievements or promotions, or to announce when a system like a security system or the air conditioning will be down for repair, or when a secure parking area is going to be closed one day for repainting, and other types of memorandums all have the potential to provide valuable information to threat groups. Many times, these items are printed en masse and placed in distribution, in a person's mail box, on their desk. People look at them and just toss them in the trash without considering the information they contain. All hard copy office correspondence should be destroyed when it is no longer needed, or used by shredding or burning; a good office policy is to have a hard copy destruction plan and all paper used in your office or organization should be shredded or burned. REMEMBER, once you have printed or typed something to give to someone else, YOU HAVE LOST ALL CONTROL OF WHERE THAT DOCUMENT and its information GOES when it leaves your hand; be careful who you give it to and what's on it. When talking about office correspondence, we also need to talk about electronic distribution via email. Many times, we forward office or work correspondence to our home emails or to friends that can contain information a threat might need, such as a person's name and job title. I have received forwarded emails three pages long that had several peoples, names, titles, phone numbers, business address, etc., along with it. If you are going to forward items like this, take the time to remove everyone else's information before sending it on, just like in hard copy distribution. Once you have hit the send button, YOU have lost all CONTROL over that email; you NEVER know where it will end up; once again, be careful who you send it to and what's in it.

Name plates on your desk or office doors can make it especially easy to find you or your office for the threat when they are looking for you. It is best to not use this type of identification and there should be no need. After all, everyone in your office should know who you are; name plates should be for identifying you to someone who doesn't. Also, marking rooms in your facility or office can give the threat the ability to know exactly which offices belong to important people and where they are located, making it easy to target them from inside or out. I have seen some office buildings where you could stand in a lobby or hallway and note the exact location of the security office, CEOs office, accounting, cashier, mail room, administrative, etc., because each door was marked and visible. This gives the threat all the information he needs to mount either an attack inside the facility or from the outside, since he now knows which windows belong to which staff position.

The media is not your friend insofar as protecting your identity or privacy. Just one news article could cause a terrorist organization, criminal gang, or some other threat to take an interest in you as a target. Many people like doing interviews or having their picture taken for articles about them or their company. But, you should avoid interviews if possible and do not allow yourself to be photographed for news articles. I found out who the senior enlisted special operations sailor was at the embassy in Greece through an article in a skydiving magazine. The piece listed his name, where he worked, who he was awarding a pin too, along with a picture! In a house magazine, I got the entire layout of the house, the grounds, the location, etc., for a CEO of a fortune 500 company. All this type of information is invaluable to someone looking for a target. If your job requires you to be interviewed or photographed as part of your duties with that company—or you are doing it to support a good cause or event—you should play down your importance, give as little personal information as possible, and do not say or do anything that will antagonize or challenge a hostile force.

What you carry in your wallet or purse? We always carry miscellaneous articles, such as company ID cards, business cards, membership cards, insurance cards, military identification cards, driver's licenses, and credit cards, etc. This type of information can furnish a large amount of information to someone who either steals or finds an individual's wallet or purse. Even if you get your wallet or purse back with everything in it after it is lost or stolen, you have no way of knowing what was copied, or what information was compromised while it was not in your possession. Make sure your wallet is concealed and placed where it would be difficult for someone to steal it; the same with your purse and don't carry everything with you all the time. Just carry what you know you need to go about your daily activities.

Store, credit and ATM cards receipts. Credit cards and debit cards provide your name and sometimes partial account number information on the receipt and on the carbon copy when one is used. It also tells the date, time, and location of where you used it; many times, these receipts are thrown away in the trash, left around a desk or in a car. This information can tell the threat where you like to shop, which ATMs you use to withdraw money on a regular basis, etc. So, they will help in establishing a pattern of movement for you, making you predictable. Whenever possible, use hard currency, and if you are overseas, use local currency. Use the money exchange at the airport or a bank to get some. However, if you must use credit cards, do not let them swipe the card more than once. And if they do not have electronic confirmation, which they don't have in some countries or venues, ask for the carbons from the receipt. When you are using an ATM, be sure to protect your pin number from people in the immediate area and from any cameras that might have been placed above the keypad. Never allow someone to get too close, or start talking to you to distract you, etc. You should also memorize your pin number; don't keep it in your wallet, checkbook, or purse. Have a generic face on your credit or debit card for use; these days you can get these cards with any emblem or symbol on it. If you are trying to stay low profile, it is better not to have SWAT, law enforcement, Military, FBI, or other organization symbols that stand out on your cards. If you do become a kidnapping victim or hostage—and are telling your captors you are a nobody—having an identifying symbol on the card or a Platinum visa card—does not fit with the story you want your captors to believe. You will be in trouble.

What's in your vehicle? This refers to all the items and papers that people keep in their vehicles that can identify you, your organization, club affiliations, schools, military service, etc., and those items that list your home of record, contact information, etc. Many of us treat our vehicles as basically mobile homes, and we carry all kinds of things in them that we feel might need throughout the day. This includes mail we have received or need to send, laptop computers, business or personnel papers such as airline reservation or hotel reservation printouts, invitations to events, checkbooks, travel itineraries, etc., and everyone usually carries vehicle registration and insurance information in their glove box. This type of information can provide the last piece in a puzzle that the threat might need to finish planning an operation against you. So, you should keep it all organized in a binder and out of sight either in the trunk or in a locked compartment in the main cab of the vehicle. All high-value items such as cameras, laptops, briefcases, purses, jackets, coats, etc., should be kept in the trunk so that you will not become a victim of a smash and grab. Don't forget not to hang those ID badges on your review mirror; they can be read or photographed through the windshield.

Please remember to keep your garage door or living area gate remote out of sight in your vehicle. If your vehicle is unlocked or someone gets into it and the glove box, they now have a way to get into your house via the garage door and your address. Do not make it easy for them.

Remember it is not how IMPORTANT we actually are or we know we are. Becoming a target is about how people who don't know us and are standing outside the fence looking in PERCEIVE us to be. If they think or assume we are an important person, for all practical purposes we are!

PERSONAL RECOGNITION

In many overseas areas and countries, foreigners are issued different colored license plates than those of those native to that particular country, or they are given a certain number or letter on the plate to indicate they are from another country and what the country is. Rental cars in many places have specific plates that identify them as rental vehicles (tourists and not local vehicles), this can cause you problems. You need to get a set of local/native plates for your vehicles. It is not impossible, but it may be difficult or cost extra but the added security is worth it. NOTE: In some locations where there are military bases, such as in Germany, you must have the plate that has the U.S. identification on it to buy gas at the on base gas stations, which usually sell at lower than the local rate. This is to prevent soldiers from filling up their friends' vehicles on post. You can still get gas there with orders and an ID card.

Avoid bumper stickers and window stickers that identify schools (military or civilian), nationality, government, or targeted business affiliation, etc. When overseas, displaying an American flag or a personalized license plate with this type of information will easily identify you as an American and a potential victim. We also tend to decorate out vehicles with bumper stickers, baseball hats, etc., when the threat, especially terrorists, are looking for someone to target; remember, they are looking for people that are good symbolic targets. So having ball caps in your rear window with state department logos, United States Marine Corps (USMC), or other branch of service logos, American flags, etc., when traveling and living in these overseas areas, is probably not a good idea. This brings up another point, putting foreign country flags on your vehicles in the United States. This can make you a target for supremist groups, racially motivated gang violence, etc. There is nothing wrong with being proud of your country, or a country that's part of your heritage, but be AWARE of the environment you are living and working in. Be careful with stickers placed on your vehicle. These stickers can tell the threat married or single, how many kids, pets/dogs that could provide protection, what schools your kids go to, where you work, what clubs you belong to, etc. This type of information is invaluable to the threat in gathering intelligence on their victims.

Many of us put our names, contact information, home of record, our destination address, or company name on bag identification tags when we travel. Some people even use paint or permanent markers and stencil this information onto cloth bags they travel with. Some government agencies and the military stencil personnel information, including Social Security Numbers, on bags of its members so that they can track them during training. There are things like decals of origin on your luggage, city names, country flags that can help identify you, as a foreigner or tourist. And don't forget about school decals, service decals, business or organization decals, etc. All of these are a no-no. Also, traveling with expensive luggage can make you stand out also.

The sequence of events for this is a terrorist or member of a criminal gang waits to see who picks up what luggage. If they are looking for someone by name, then that person or persons will examine all the name tags on the luggage as it comes down the pickup carousel, returning it to the line waiting to see who picks it up. Now, they not only have a name but know what you look like, and then they can follow that person. The threat now has everything that they need: the individual's name, his location of origin, and possibly his home address and phone number and what he looks like to start working on him as a target. For the criminal element, it is likely that they will pick out people with expensive luggage, tourists, etc., and wait and see which hotel shuttle or which hotel phone they use. Now, they know where you are going or staying, and they can pick up surveillance on you there. People who have cars meet them and drivers with signs are also potential targets for any threat. If a car is going to meet you, the driver needs to be dressed casually and know what you look like, by being sent a picture if necessary. That way, they don't have to stand out there with your name on a sign identifying who you are.

Clothing. Many times, our clothing and how we dress sets us apart from the locals—especially when we wear loud clothes and shirts with civilian or military sayings on them, country of origin flags, rude or obscene sayings or gestures, etc. The style of clothes we wear can make us stand out as either United States in origin or will tell what kind of work we do. If you have traveled through an airport in Jordan, Kuwait, etc., and seen people wearing 511 shirts and pants or royal Robbins' slacks, with expensive sunglasses and desert combat boots, you can pretty much guess they are security contractors on their way to work somewhere. You don't need to dress down, but you should dress as generic as possible, white-collared shirt, tan slacks, etc. You don't need to purchase the same kinds of clothing and footwear the locals wear, but you can dress neutral enough that someone observing the airport will not be able to pick you out as coming from the United States. NOTE: There are not many countries where people wear baseball hats, cowboy hats, etc. You need to look around and see how what other people are doing when you get to the airport; if no one else is wearing a baseball hat, then you shouldn't be either.

How we act and our behavior can make us stand out. If you have ever traveled through an airport outside the United States, how hard was it to pick out the Americans? On the whole and speaking as a citizen myself, Americans, when traveling, have the tendency to be loud, rude, and obnoxious—when dealing with others including those trying to help them. Thus, they draw attention to themselves. When we travel, we don't want to be the typical "ugly American." We want to be as neutral as possible with people not knowing our country of origin. We want to keep a low profile and try to blend in as much as possible with the other travelers around you. Remember the 50 percent rule; if you are doing or acting like 50 percent of the people around you, you won't stand out as different. You may never be able to pass as one of the locals, but you may pass as a traveler from another country. Remember the 50 percent rule!

Tattoos are another way to draw attention to yourself when traveling. The majority of people in the world do not have tattoos. Those that do usually have little ones in areas they are not normally seen such as shoulder blades, ankles, or lower back for women, etc. People with tattoo sleeves down there whole arm or on their necks and face will stand out. Many members of the militaries around the world have tattoos with military sayings, unit identification, etc. Some people have civilian slogans or logos on different areas about their body. If you have tattoos, you should cover them. You should be aware of the attention they can and will probably draw, especially in foreign countries. So, when you go out, you can wear types of clothing such as a long-sleeve shirt or jacket that will keep them from casual view. NOTE: For many areas of the world, people with tattoos are those who have been to prison, belong to gangs or members of the Armed Forces, and people will treat you the way they treat people from their own country with these affiliations.

In some areas, there will be bus stops that take people especially tourist to shopping areas, the beach, or will be set up to return tourists to the hotels in which they are staying. Bus stops like this catering to non-locals are not difficult for the threat to figure out the people using them are a majority of foreigners. If you have to use one of these bus stops when you are traveling, there are some ways to make yourself safer since these sites have been attacked before. One is that you should not stand at the bus stop itself, but stay a distance away from it at a vendor or off by an area that can provide some cover until the bus has arrived and stopped. You should wait until most of the riders have boarded, and there is a little or no line before going over and boarding the bus as quickly as possible. You want to avoid being in the immediate area around these types of bus stops and especially avoid large groups of people while waiting at the stops since they make excellent targets for any threat.

You should avoid using U.S. currency when you arrive in country either for shopping or tipping; it increases your vulnerability of being identified by terrorists and thieves as a possible rich target. Most international airports have money exchanges, so you should exchange some of your money for local currency there when possible. The exchange rate at your hotel or the embassy will probably be better, so exchange a nominal amount and get it all in small denominations. This way, when tipping or paying for a taxi, you have enough to get you at least to the hotel where you can exchange more money as necessary. NOTE: Be careful if using non-local currency to purchase things on the street or exchanging money on the street. In many countries, the law requires you to do this at banks or money exchange offices only, and it is illegal to use non-local currency in transactions in some countries. So, find out what the law is, you don't want to be arrested for breaking the law just to save a few dollars.

Target selection also takes into other considerations that are of vital importance to the threat such as RISK VS SUCCESS. Basically, they will want as little risk as possible and the highest probability of success possible for each operation; they do this by looking for all the factors that will increase these odds for them. They do this by looking for those SOFT targets that will involve little risk to them with a high probability of success. The threat will avoid selecting targets that involve high risk with little or no chance of a successful operation, UNLESS the proposed target is such a high value to them either symbolically or tactically that they would consider it a good trade off.

So, what is the major difference between a soft and hard target when we are taking about profiles of potential victims? During the process of selecting their targets, the threat will evaluate all of the potential victims in terms of softness or hardness. How we conduct ourselves at all times, how strictly we maintain a good security profile and adhere to IPM procedures will determine whether a threat classifies us as either a hard target or a soft target.

SOFT TARGETS

These are some of the criteria for being considered a soft target:

- Unarmed, the potential victim is not armed or has weapons but simply displays a lack of willingness to use them or practice with them. Does not allow his bodyguards or security to carry weapons.
- There is a minimal chance of confrontation with law enforcement or security forces for the threat because the potential victim's travel patterns or routines do not take him near police or fire stations, hospitals, friendly embassies, or other safe haven locations.
- The potential victim is easy to approach because of his not being aware of his surroundings, this makes him Accessible. He will be easy to get to because he works or lives in an area with minimum security, he travels to high-risk areas by himself, he does not consider security measures necessary or the threat as a major concern for him.
- The potential victim is predictable in all or part of his daily routines; he follows a set pattern or does the same thing every day. Uses the same route, etc., never altering from his established pattern of behavior or movement.

- The targeted individual is unaware of the threat to himself, so he is complacent in his security awareness or he has no security conscious. He follows no IPM or basic security precautions using nothing to mitigate any threat against himself.

HARD TARGETS

Criteria for what the threat would consider a hard target:

- The target is armed with a weapon that is in good working condition; it is readily accessible, and he is proficient in the use of the weapon and will not hesitate to use it.
- The potential target has a hardened vehicle which is equipped with armor, bullet-resistant glass, alarms, communications, and the driver has been trained and will not hesitate to use the vehicle as a weapon, if necessary.
- The target has a hardened residence; it has a layered defense. This could mean that the potential target's security includes armed guards, roving patrols, neighborhood watch, high walls, fences, anti-intrusion devices, lights, watchdogs, etc.
- Good communications, the potential victim not only has a cell phone that gets good coverage, but he has two-way radios in his vehicles, work, and at his house. If he as a security element they will also have the same means of communication available for their use. The target keeps some type of communications with him at all times. NOTE: Many people feel that radios are not necessary in today's world of cell phones, but radios have better range, will work in places cell phones won't, and usually are a direct communications link to security.
- During vehicle movement and foot movement, the target has a security escort vehicle that accompanies him with a trained driver and detail. The detail should be alert and quick to react to any perceived threat and can be used as a visual deterrent; sometimes, this alone may deter a terrorist attack.
- The target has a heightened state of awareness so he is continually using good security practices, adjusting his level of IPM and does not become complaent; the target, his family, workers, security detail are in a constant state of alertness at all times.
- Unpredictable. The potential target is unpredictable in his movements and actions and will ensure this is reflected in his daily schedule. He will use a system that allows him to avoid developing routines and help him determine his daily routes, times of

departure and return, and dining establishments. Being unpredictable makes it almost impossible to plan an attack, so this alone can cause a terrorist to perceive the target as a hard target.

Another part of the selection process for the threat is the concept of EASE VS VALUE. In other words, they are looking for how easy a target you would be to hit compared to your value to them as a victim. So, they will look at how easy you are to get to and strike, but measured against the value you have to them and the statement they are trying to make. After all, killing or kidnapping a clerk does not send the same statement as killing or kidnapping a CEO or two-star general. Does anything you do in your daily activities make it easy for the terrorists? A terrorist will not attack a hard target unless he has been ordered specifically to do so. In the majority of cases, the terrorist will simply pick the easier target, which has some value that they can use in furthering their agenda; the terrorists like soft, easy targets.

One of the ways we can become that soft easy target is by having obvious routines in our lives that the threat can exploit and use to cause us harm. When we have these routines, it allows a threat to plan an operation on the intended target KNOWING he will be at a certain location at a specific time. Knowing these two things about a person will greatly enhance a threat's ability to plan an attack against them and it reduces their chance of getting caught during the planning and the operation time itself by reducing their exposure time to the victim, law enforcement, or security forces, which makes them less vulnerable to discovery. It's important to remember that there will always be routines in our life, no one can live routine free and that generally most routines are OK when the threat against you is low, but as the threat increases, you need to vary your schedule and your routines as much as possible. By doing this, you are keeping the terrorist's attempt to gather intelligence on you off balance and more difficult for them; this makes you a much harder target. So, how many places does a normal person have routines that can be exploited by a threat?

Routines at home are something everyone develops to help them get started in the morning, wind down in the evening, or to simply make it easier for the family; some of these are:

- Picking up the newspaper first thing in the morning or meeting the paperboy in the morning to get it
- Walking out to put out your outgoing mail in the mail box, or walking out to meet the mail man and give him your outgoing mail while receiving your incoming mail
- Taking care of pets such as walking the dog in the mornings before you leave for work and in the evenings before you go to bed and feeding and watering the dog if it is kept outside

- Also, going outside and starting your car to warm it up in the winter and melt the ice so you don't have to scrape it off
- Turning lights on or off as you leave or enter your residence or when you get up in the mornings or are going to bed
- Food delivery nights, having pizza or other type of food delivered on certain nights of the week such as family nights, or having it delivered when you work past a certain time
- House or yard maintenance, watering the grass, cutting the lawn, trimming bushes, cleaning the swimming pool, etc.
- Setting out trash for pickup and moving the trash cans back to their normal place and having a trash pickup service that comes the same time and day each week
- Walking or taking your children to the school bus or the school bus stop
- Birthday parties, especially for children, having large parties with lots of guests at the house or at a restaurant that caters to children

Basically, any routine around the house that would allow the threat to know when you are going to do something, be somewhere, etc. This would allow them to plan their attack around the time you are most predictable at your residence and the most vulnerable. NOTE: Don't forget routines at home include your FAMILY!

We also develop routines at work to make our days go as we planned; we have schedules to keep, places we have to be, etc. These types of routines can include the following:

- Using the same route to and from work, or using certain routes when the weather is good and certain routes in bad weather
- Always arriving at work at the same time, leaving at the same time, or on certain days, you leave at set times for family commitments
- Eating at the same place for lunch, getting coffee from the same place in the morning on the way in, using a lunch wagon, coffee cart, newspaper stand for breaks, even if you take your lunch eating it in the same location like a bench or by a fountain in the park, etc.
- Holding meetings on the same day at the same time each week, or having company get together on the same day and time each month
- Dining room, dining cart, gut truck things like this that are always there at the same time, open at the same time
- For military, holding formations at the same time, same location everyday

- Using the same airline for business travel, calling the same taxi or car service for runs around the city, using the same caterer for business functions

There are other routines that we tend to develop in our lives and some that are in place and developed for us; these deal with most things outside of the residence or work:

- We as Americans, when working or traveling overseas, like to frequent places that remind us of home such as certain restaurants, bars, and clubs that serve American-style food or that have inexpensive prices
- In some places, people will go to an establishment because other Americans go there. Some businesses, government offices, Embassies have places that everyone goes to after work or on the weekends
- Sports teams participation, we like to participate in sports, softball, golf, volley ball, etc., and they have set schedules or even leagues that post names, locations, and schedules in the newspapers or on accessible bulletin boards
- Hobbies, such as antique hunting, yard sales, racing radio-controlled cars, planes, or boats, etc., are all things that usually require you to frequent specialty shops and other specific locations for that hobby; this also includes things like wine tasting, art shows
- Which brings us to being patrons of the arts, going to the opera, plays, museum show openings, etc. This type of information is in the society pages of the newspapers or local media, usually with who will be attending, times, locations, etc.
- Shopping at the same stores, drug stores, farmers markets, always going shopping on the same day, etc.
- Using the same shop for car maintenance, filling up with gas on the same day at the same place, washing the vehicle at the same place, same day or time, etc.
- Using the gym, same time each day, running or biking the same route every day at the same time, using the pool, etc.

Being in the military or in law enforcement also tends to form routines for standardization in many areas:

- Physical fitness training, having a mandatory time and places to work out or following the same routes to run, walk, etc.
- Accountability formations, always held at the same time and in the exact same place

- Military bus stops, both on and off post, usually run on a set schedule which is posted at the bus stop shelter

Other things people do not consider routines but can make you predictable are those character traits we exhibit. Such as wanting to help someone in need, so we stop to render aid at a roadside emergency; as a matter of fact in some countries, it's the law if you see an accident that passersby stop and render assistance. Just be sure it is a real accident, if you didn't see it take place, or there is no blood and fire, then instead of stopping how about just calling emergency services. Also, some of us always want to help that person who is stranded. Picking up a hitchhiker, offering a ride to someone whose car has broken down, or is standing in the rain. Look at the circumstances before offering this type of aide, if other cars have passed her/him and offered help, why didn't she/he go with them? Were they waiting on someone in particular? Why did they not get on the bus that was just there, etc. You never know who you may pick up when doing this.

The terrorists are going to consider your VALUE as a victim, exactly what and how much value can they expect to gain from the act they are planning? To measure this, they will consider:

- Importance of the victim, how important are you to others as a victim, what publicity can be generated with you as the victim, and what will the terrorists gain for their cause?
- How much terror will be generated as a result of the act itself? How much more with you as the victim? Making people afraid can affect an entire city, region, or country. By committing those acts that generate the most terror because of what the act was and its victims' terrorists can manipulate, the population, security forces, and the government. Remember Mao and this thoughts on this "Kill 10, scare 10,000," the terrorists believe the same thing.
- Is it possible to receive a ransom for you? As most people know, the U.S. Government and most governments around the world will not deal or pay terrorists because they don't want to encourage or finance them. But, that doesn't mean the company you are working for won't: your church, family, friends, or good Samaritan, etc. They don't care where the money comes from; just that they get it from someone who is willing to pay it for you.
- Many times a demand from the terrorists will be to free comrades, either people from their own organization that have been captured or people from other organizations that have the same goals as themselves. If you are the victim and the terrorists take you hostage, will the demands for the release of their comrades be met?

- If you are being held hostage or kidnapped, are you worth safe passage for them? During an operation, if all else fails, or in addition to their other demands, the terrorists will more than likely demand safe passage to an area of their choice for their own safety and escape.

Whether you become a victim of a terrorist act or a target of a terrorist is largely up to you, by how you act and conduct yourself. What the threats perception of you as either a hard target or a soft target is entirely up to you also, so you can make it easy for the terrorists, or you can become that hard target they want to avoid. To do this, you have to create an amount of risk to them and work effort so high, that their chances of success are so low, that the terrorists will leave you alone and select another easier softer target.

PROTECTION MEASURES FOR MOVEMENT

We are always the most vulnerable while we are traveling; during this time, we are taken out of the environment where we have total control and placed into an environment where we have little or no control of the events, acts, people that are now moving around us. It is during this time of movement, we should be the most aware, careful, and PROACTIVE, by planning our movements to keep us as safe as possible for the circumstances.

When you are planning your routes, think about the things we have discussed previously. You should consider possible safe areas (police and fire stations) for each route you are looking at; you also need to consider the possible trouble areas (radical universities or bad neighborhoods). You need to then analyze the areas that you HAVE to pass through, places you cannot avoid (choke points), and find the closest safe area to them. Then, you need to look for danger areas or areas that can mask the threat during surveillance and during an incident; remember they have specific guidelines they need to look for in an attack site, find those areas and avoid them. Once you have your routes planned out, you need to plan simple courses of action that can be implemented quickly in a potential crisis, such as what direction to turn or drive at each intersection to get to a safe area the fastest. Having a plan of action already in place, along with a higher state of awareness at the trouble spots, enables you to react much faster to an incident and increases your chances of surviving a terrorist attack. You should write down your routes and plans of action but you need to identify your plans and routes to those responsible for your well-being, your spouse, office security, etc.; this way if you are involved in an incident, kidnapped, etc., they will know the route you were taking.

But, allow no one else access to these arrangements; you never know what people will say or talk about. You should always avoid traveling alone when either walking or driving and whenever possible, travel on busy streets and well-traveled thoroughfares with a large flow of pedestrian or vehicle traffic. If you do not speak the language, you should practice, learn, or keep a cheat sheet of key phrases that will enable you to ask for help, ask for directions in the local language. You should also find out how to use the local telephone system. Practice and know what numbers to call for assistance and always carry change for the telephone.

Before you leave, you need to get detailed information on the countries, regions, cities you plan to visit, including the ones you are just going to lay over in or pass through during travel. You never know when a plane will break down or a flight be canceled, so having information about the city will be a big help. You can get information from the Internet, travel pages, Department of State website, the countries embassy, etc. The type of information you are looking for needs to include threat, safe havens, best routes, areas to avoid, and anything else that may impact you during your business or recreation visit. Many travel sites even tell you how much to pay a taxi for the ride from the airport. Make sure you check newspapers and other media about crime rates, statistics, attacks against foreigners, etc. NO ONE likes to put out about how dangerous their city or area is, but local newspapers will have this information; if you don't speak the language, don't worry, many online newspapers now have an English-language version.

You should also make a list of people, addresses, and phone numbers of people in each city or area you will be passing through that you can contact in case you need assistance. You should also make a list like this of emergency contacts for use along any routes you use and for use at your destination.

Never carry any sensitive business information, personal materials, or other classified material while you are traveling, especially commercial travel; whenever possible, have it shipped by a trusted courier or delivery service. If you work for the government or military, use an official courier system. If none of this is possible and you will be carrying sensitive business information or classified material with you, as a civilian you need to make sure it is wrapped and packed properly and you need to put it out of sight. If the information is on a computer, thumb drive, or other electronic device, you should make sure the information is encrypted and password protected. If working for the government or the military, you will need to consult Department of Defense (DOD) policy on the handling and transportation of classified materials; there are specific guidelines and procedures that must be followed.

Make sure and keep someone informed of where you are during travel. If it is work related, you should keep your supervisor informed.

If it is recreational travel, you should keep a family member or friend informed. You also need to develop the habit of "checking in" before departing your primary embarkation point, and at each location, you stop over and then later start your trip again and you should immediately call upon arrival at your final location. This checking in serves a purpose of knowing your whereabouts at certain points of time. This way, if you are attacked or kidnapped, the people who you check in with can then give the authorities a last known location to start looking for you. They will be better able to locate the place where the attack has taken place and respond much faster than if they had to go over your entire route of travel from start to finish.

MOVING ON FOOT

We need to remember how vulnerable we are to assaults when we move by foot with other pedestrians whether it is a criminal attack, mugging, or a terrorist incident. When moving by foot, we have no protection, no 360 degree coverage, so we cannot see what is taking place behind us, or around the corner from us, and we have no layers of protection, like you do with a vehicle, you are moving through an environment of which you have no control, except over yourself. When we move by foot as with other types of travel, you need to plan your movement, avoid any routines, and have more than one route available for use; also, you should never walk alone if at all possible, DO NOT GET COMPLACENT!

When walking, you need to stay on the main thoroughfares and the normal flow of pedestrian traffic, and you need to stay alert to the events occurring around you at all times. If you are new to the city or area and not familiar with it, you should not wander off of the main thoroughfares until you become more familiar with the environment in the area. You should never go down avenues—dark streets, alleys, etc., especially if locals avoid these areas. Remember, STAY with the NORMAL FLOW OF PEDESTRIAN TRAFFIC; if locals avoid certain routes, even short cuts, there is a reason.

You need to train yourself to walk facing traffic and make it a habit; there are a several reasons why this will make you safer. First, if a threat tries to attack you by vehicle, they will have to be approaching you from where you can see them. Prepare yourself. When they stop the vehicle, you are already moving away from them and they will have difficulty backing up to move closer to you or chase you because of the vehicle traffic behind them. If they start their attack on the other side of the street with traffic passing between you and them, you can start moving in the direction they have driven from. Once again, this causes them to back up into traffic and the attackers have to move through traffic to get to your location, which should draw your notice and allow you to react. NOTE: When moving (running) away from a threat in a vehicle, you always want to run in the opposite direction it is moving. This means the vehicle will have to back up to pursue you or won't be able to pursue because of traffic. If you run in the direction it is moving, it can continue the chase with no problems.

When you are walking along a sidewalk, you also need to make a habit of walking in the center of the sidewalk. Staying toward the center makes it more difficult for someone to either push you toward traffic, a waiting vehicle, or to push into an alley or doorway—because they will have to go through or around other pedestrians to accomplish this. Walking in the center also gives you a better view for spotting someone hiding behind trucks, between cars, in deep doorways, around corners, or waiting in an alley. This is because it gives you a better angle of view on these areas. If you walk too close to the buildings or to parked cars or traffic, your angle of view is cut short or is non-existent for looking around these obstacles until you are right up on them—and this can be too late to take protective actions.

You need to maintain a cautious attitude and not get complacent. Cautious does not mean paranoid. It just means you are aware of your surroundings and take measures to make yourself that hard target. When you approach a crosswalk and the light is red, instead of waiting in the group of people, position yourself with your back to a wall. When the light turns, you cross with everyone else. When you cross an intersection or street, you need to cross with other people or in groups. This way you are not out there as a solitary target. Whenever you cross the street, you must be very alert to approaching vehicles and the people in them. Are they staring at you? Did the vehicle speed up when you started crossing? Stay off the cell phone or reading a PDA/tablet when walking as it distracts you and lessens your ability to observe your surroundings.

You need to use the surveillance detection methods previously discussed when walking, especially in potentially hostile environments, and apply this. Walking in the middle of the sidewalk will give you a wider angle of view, so you can use reflective surfaces such as windows, mirrors, vehicle windshields, vehicle bodies with high gloss paint. You can also look through windows that take up two sides of a corner to see persons who may be following you: speeding up and slowing down to see who is actively trying to ignore the normal flow of pedestrian traffic and stay behind you; using a route that goes from a high-density pedestrian population to a low-density pedestrian population will also aid you in identifying surveillance. You can easily spot a person who moves with you from a high-density area to a low-density area. Your best defense is to maintain a keen sense of awareness of your surroundings, DO NOT GET COMPLACENT.

You also need to think about and develop a crisis response plan for each route you travel on. Your crisis response plan should include safe areas and possible hostile areas along your routes of travel and what you will do if you are attacked. Your plan should be something you physically do like running to a safe haven while yelling, pulling an air horn out and starting to blast it, etc. If your plan is to yell for assistance, consider what is called the "New Yorker syndrome." To explain, other people are not likely to stop and help if you cry, "Help! Terrorists! Help, MUGGER," etc. Instead, you need to yell something that will make people look and get involved, like "Fire!" But, drawing attention should only be part of your plan. Don't forget to MOVE also, never stay in the area of the attack. By having a preplanned crisis response and visualizing what you will do at different sites, and for different incidents, you will react faster when an incident happens—instead of standing there with your "deer in a headlight look" and thinking about what to do. This faster reaction to the threat could cause confusion in them and throw of their plan, which will help you in getting away to safety.

When planning your walking route plan for day, night, and bad weather, you should always have a route that is well lit. You need to walk in those well-lighted areas, and you need to stay with the normal flow of pedestrian traffic even at night or in bad weather.

You also need to make sure you know of those areas with high volume noise such as train stations, construction sites, or temporary construction areas. These loud volume noises will drown out your cries for assistance if that is part of your crisis response plan. You want people to be able to hear you, and these noises can drown out gun shots, squealing tires, and other noises associated with attacks.

You need to make sure you walk in areas where there are other pedestrians and a steady flow of pedestrian traffic, but you need to avoid crowds of people, demonstrators, and large groups of people who are walking together. They could be a hostile demonstration focused toward Americans/foreigners. You will be able to tell the difference between a crowded street in a highly dense population area and a crowd of people moving together. If you encounter those large groups or demonstrators, you may have to alter your route, cross over to another street, or even enter a building or business until the crowd has passed. No matter what you do, you need to make sure you FOLLOW and STAY WITH THE NORMAL FLOW OF PEDESTRIAN TRAFFIC.

MOVING IN A VEHICLE

When traveling by automobile, make yourself a harder target, you have a layer of protection between yourself and others, you have a means of escape, you can also use your vehicle as a weapon if necessary, but there are also other measures you can use to present yourself as too difficult of a target for the threat to attempt.

Your vehicle.

The vehicle you drive needs to be an innocuous vehicle, one that will blend in, not stand out. Driving a vehicle that is hard to pick out, or one that people do not notice, makes it difficult for terrorists to identify you as an American, VIP, rich or as a foreigner. Using this type of vehicles also makes it more difficult for any surveillance personnel or teams to locate and follow your vehicle. If it blends in really well, surveillance will have to get very close to it to ensure they do not lose it in traffic. The closer surveillance has to get, the easier they are for you to detect. They will be jumpier and more prone to mistakes, which is something you can use to your advantage during surveillance detection.

You need to use vehicles that are not associated with status in the society you are now moving in, so you must avoid vehicles that are obvious symbols of wealth. These can be vehicles such as JEEPS, Cadillac's, Pick-ups, Mercedes, Rolls Royce, etc. These can give off perceptions of wealth or privilege, so you will need to avoid them all when possible and sanitize your vehicle. There should be nothing inside that can be seen through the windows, no flags, country club stickers, embassy markings, rental tags, etc. These can all make you a target of just not terrorists but criminals also.

You need to outfit and equip any vehicle that you own, and will use on a continual basis, so that it will handle an attack or other crisis situation long enough for you to get out of the attack zone and reach a safe area, which is not possible to do with rentals.

Vehicle armor, depending on the type of vehicle, a fully armored car from a manufacturing firm that specialized in it, can cost between $100,000 and $300,000. These fully armored cars are capable of sustaining an attack from large-caliber rifles and heavy weapons for only 30 seconds to a minute, but hopefully enough time to keep you safe from the initial attack and get you away from the kill zone and your attackers. Many of these armored vehicles cannot survive an IED or mine blast depending on the type of charge used. If you don't have that kind of money to spend, there are several ways you can equip your vehicle with 200 pounds of armor for approximately $10,000 or less. This type of expedient armor will not stop large-caliber weapons or explosives, but it will provide considerable protection from handguns and small explosives. You should armor your vehicle based upon the capabilities of the threat against you, and DO NOT advertise that you have an armored vehicle. If it is a known factor, the threat can plan for ways to defeat it.

Tires: Many people when they upgrade a vehicle will tend to forget about upgrading their tires. These are an important, yet often neglected, item. When selecting your new tires, you should choose a radial tire instead of a bias ply. They last longer and can take more punishment. The choice of steel, fiberglass, or Kevlar will probably be based on what is available in the area you are now working in, rather than on what you prefer. You don't want to have to order tires because you might not be able to keep enough of the specific kind you want on hand. You need to choose a tire that can sustain high temperatures and that will maintain excellent traction in the area and the different climates that you will be traveling in.

Tires that are not rated for the higher temperatures, or that are worn, may "blow out" in as little as three minutes at speeds of 100 miles per hour or more. On an extremely hot surface, the speeds at which tires fail will be lower. There is a system of rating tire quality that uses different letters for different things: temperature is A, B, or C. The rating is a measure of how well the tire dissipates heat and how well it handles the buildup of heat. The temperature grade applies to a properly inflated tire that is not overloaded. Under-inflation, overloading, or excessive speed can lead to more heat buildup. The tire traction is rated AA, A, B, or C; for straight-line braking on a wet surface, AA is the best for traction. This rating is based on the tire's ability to stop a car on wet concrete and asphalt. It does not indicate the tire's cornering ability; the only acceptable rating is A. The speed ratings are designated in the laboratory using tires that are in perfect condition on excellent road conditions, with the correct inflation and no wear and tear. The higher the speed rating, the better handling and maneuverability compared to the lower speed rated tires. M is the lowest rating at 81 MPH; it goes higher: M, N, P, Q, R, S, T, U, H, V, W, and Y which is rated at 186 MPH.

Make sure you get the tire that best meets all your needs, daily movement, inclement weather, and security driving when necessary. High-performance or high-speed tires are not very good in some environments because of the tread pattern. Do your research and get the right ones for your situation. Never assume that just because they came with the vehicle, they will do just fine. Also, remember that rubber is a luxury during an incident. If you have to, you can drive forever on the rims, and that's what you should do in a crisis situation if necessary. Other important items to consider are tread life, run flats, self-sealing capabilities, and the terrain that they will be required to function on.

Vehicle mirrors are important since "the more you see the safer you will be." You need to install oversized outside mirrors on both sides of the vehicle, along with fish eye mirrors attached in the corner of the larger mirrors to widen your view. You also need to get an oversized rearview mirror inside to allow you to see everything possible behind you. You can consider getting mirrors on your sun visors as well so that your passenger can also view what is taking place behind you. In some instances, I have seen people mount a review mirror in the back seat so that those passengers can see behind also.

Radios are also important, and you need to install a two-way communication system in the vehicle or vehicles used, with a base station that is monitored by someone during any movement you are making. I know in the time of cell phones people are asking why use radio? Because cell coverage doesn't work everywhere, especially in high-density urban areas or rural areas where you may be traveling. Sometimes, bad weather can effect cell phone coverage; a good radio will work in these conditions and will be able to transmit farther than a cell phone.

Interior trunk latch for opening the trunk lid from the inside needs to be installed and with as low a physical profile as possible. Many newer vehicles come with this as standard equipment, so double check to make sure it is there and it works. You might also want to cache items like pepper spray or a weapon in the trunk, a knife or razor to cut any bonds you may be secured with. This way, if you are attacked and thrown into the trunk of your own car, you can get out. If tied up, you can get loose and then get out. If a trunk release latch cannot be installed, you need to learn how to open the trunk from the inside, which can be done with a screw driver. Then, you need to practice and stash the screw driver in the trunk. NOTE: If you are locked in your trunk, don't pop the trunk lid until you are ready to get out and run. An open trunk lid can cause a light to come on in the dashboard. So, you need to get out of the trunk when the car is stopped, slowing down to stop, or right as it starts accelerating. Open it, get out, and run like hell. You need to get out as soon as possible after being put in. It would do no good to jump out and try to escape if they have already driven to an area under their control.

You need to have fire extinguishers inside the cab of your vehicle front and back and in the trunk, the ones in the cab need to be mounted in some way either to the floor, on the side of the vehicle, or mounted to the seat. The one in the trunk also needs to be mounted to the vehicle in some way and the one in the trunk should be a larger size extinguisher. Remember that fire extinguishers are for PEOPLE first, not things. If for some reason your vehicle is hit and catches fire and you need to evacuate, get out and take the extinguishers with you. If each person is fine, THEN you worry about putting out the equipment or vehicle fire. The one in the trunk is for you to use if you come up on an incident, accident, etc., and need an extinguisher to put out a fire. Always use the trunk extinguisher for incidents that do not involve you or your vehicle; try to save the ones in the cab for your needs.

First aid kits should be kept inside the vehicle, small ones in the cab, larger one in the trunk. These kits need to have the items needed to treat a trauma wound like a gun shot, or shrapnel hit, and any medications needed to meet the medical needs of persons who will be traveling in the car, that is, if someone is allergic to bees, you should have a bee sting kit or medicine needed to keep them from going in to shock; if a person has a bad heart, you should have extra medicine he needs in the kits.

A survival kit may be necessary if your vehicle breaks down or you are forced to leave your vehicle and start moving by foot. Like everything else, smaller kits should be kept in the cab for immediate grab and go, and larger more in-depth kit should be kept in the trunk. Now, a survival kit is more than just food and water, you need to have an alternate means of communications, map, MONEY in both U.S. and local currency, etc. The kit should be made to meet the specific needs of the environments you will be working and traveling in.

An upgraded, heavy-duty suspension: If you have added armor to the vehicle, you have added weight; what equipment you are carrying will add weight also. Some factory suspension systems might not be able to handle all the extra weight you may now be traveling with, especially over rough roads or terrain. So, you should ensure that the vehicle has an upgraded heavy-duty suspension that can meet the needs you will be placing on it.

You must ensure that the vehicle you are using has an engine with sufficient power to allow you to quickly accelerate out of any crisis situation, incident, or attack area. If you have had your vehicle armored, make sure the vehicle engine is upgraded also to handle the extra weight. When you step on the gas pedal, you want the car to MOVE QUICKLY when needed. You also want to make sure your vehicle has sufficient horsepower to outrun most cars available to the threat, in case they begin chasing you.

Tinted windows can make it difficult for someone on the outside to look into the interior of the vehicle. With tinting, surveillance will not be able to tell how many people you have inside, where they are sitting, are they armed or not. Be aware that in some countries, states, cities, how much you can tint and how dark is controlled by local laws. Just be aware that it also gives some restriction to you looking out and you need to be aware that tinted windows will make it more difficult for you to perform a car bomb search, on the interior of your vehicle or for you to check your vehicle for intruders.

Vehicle alarms are a must: There are many types of alarms in the market that are affordable to everyone and have different means of activation. I know people say that everyone ignores them when they go off and these devices can be circumvented. But they do cause people to look at the source of the sound, and in some areas, parking garages, parking areas that have security. It will cause them to look and see what is going on: if it comes down to two targets for selection, one with a vehicle alarm and one without, who do you think they will pick as a target? They work as an excellent deterrent and will increase your security profile. NOTE: Cars with panic button on the alarm system can also be used in the house, keep the key fob by your bed and hit the panic button on it if you hear an intruder. The panic button can also be used in a dark garage. Just hit it and let it run for a minute to see if anyone is around; it should startle any people hiding there. But a remote can also work against you and help the threat. If you immediately hit the remote to find your car or unlock your doors before you are at your vehicle, the threat now knows where you are parked and which direction you are walking to get there. You have just told them you are on your way; you should always wait until you are at the vehicle to unlock it and get inside.

You need to keep your gas tank at least one-half full in the event you need to escape an attack site, have to take a detour if an incident has taken place on your chosen route, or you must evade pursuers. Running your vehicle until it is empty before refilling can cause you to run out of gas when you really need it.

You should also keep control of your vehicle keys and house or office keys at all times. If you have to leave your car with parking attendants or valets, you should just leave the key that starts your vehicle. All your other keys should be kept on another key ring; this includes the keys that are used to lock your interior compartments of the vehicle. This way the person parking your car cannot look through insurance or registration paper work and find out your home address. The same should be done with mechanics, oil and lube businesses, tire places, etc. You should always just leave only your ignition key. If you think about it, usually you have to give a phone number, home address, etc., at these places, so they know where you live or work. There is nothing stopping someone from making an impression of your house or business keys when they are out of your possession. If possible, you should always park your vehicle yourself instead of using valets. If the garage or parking lot won't let you do this, then ride with the valet or parking attendant while he parks your car and then take the keys from him. This way if something happens, and you have to leave the event quickly, you know where your vehicle is and you have your keys. If leaving normally, just return the keys and let them bring the vehicle out. Remember, once your keys are out of your possession, you have no idea what is being done with them.

You also need to keep your car in good mechanical repair. You don't want to be on a trip and have your car breakdown. This makes you vulnerable to attack by the threat and can leave you exposed until help arrives. If your vehicle breaks down and blocks traffic, this will also cause you problems such as drivers start to yell, cuss, start honking horns—or, in other words, drawing attention to you. If you keep your vehicle in good running condition, it will be able to perform when you need it too, so you know you can count on it.

Last but not least, license plates: You need to check and make sure you have them before you get into the vehicle, and the plates for the vehicle need to be secured to the vehicle with some type of locking device, zip tie, anti-tampering device, etc. This is so people cannot steal your license plates to gain access to restricted or secure facilities or parking areas if you have special plates that allow this. Also, it prevents people from using your plates when they commit a crime, especially in the states where people are now stealing them, putting them on their car, and then filling up with gas and driving off without paying. Since businesses normally record the plate number, the police will now come looking for you the plate owner. If you work at an organization that has special plates that allow access, there needs to be a system in place that people can report when theirs are stolen so that security can be on the watch for anyone trying to use them to breach the security perimeter.

IF YOU HAVE A DRIVER ASSIGNED

If you have a driver assigned to you for either business or personal travel, you will need to evaluate him before you get in the car with him. Look at his background and training. If he has not had any formal training in security or defensive driving, you need to ensure he gets the training needed by sending him to a driving school that will train him to meet the needs for the environment he will be driving in. Whenever you allow someone else to drive you or your family, you are putting your life in their hands!

When you have a driver, he should remain alert at all times focusing his attention on his one job of operating the vehicle in a safe manner and keeping his mind on his operating environment. He should know the traffic patterns of the operating area and the normal conduct of both pedestrians and other drivers; he should be the first one to notice anything unusual in these patterns. The driver should have experience and training because if or when a crisis develops, the driver's decisions and how he acts or reacts to each situation will influence the lives of the passengers, in other words, YOU.

A designated driver should be trained to be proactive and respond to any situation that may arise. His primary responsibility is to drive the car; many times drivers want to do or are asked to do other things such as adjust the radio, hold something, etc. If the driver is also part of your security, he may want to react with the rest of security to certain situations that may arise. But until the vehicle is brought to a halt, the driver should not use a gun, a radio, or any other device; he needs to concentrate on keeping the vehicle moving and finding the best routes away from any incident. The vehicle he is driving, in most cases, can serve as a weapon or tool for breaching any barricades and escaping. Many schools offer classes in defensive/antiterrorist driving. If these schools are inaccessible, there are excellent books and magazines that provide this instruction.

The driver should always maintain a cautious (and careful) attitude when he is operating the vehicle. He should be observing and visualizing his movement and the movement of other vehicles two or three blocks ahead, and he should be thinking about crisis response plans—and be constantly "what if'ing"—as the vehicle moves. Once the driver starts getting ready and the car bomb search has been completed, he should enter the vehicle, lock the doors, and then start the vehicle. Once he has the vehicle secure and ready to go, he can start adjusting the seat, the mirrors, etc. This way, if a crisis situation develops, the car cannot be breached, and he can drive off quickly. The driver, once he is in the vehicle and has it ready to go, should not exit the vehicle to open doors, the trunk, etc. If you have anything that needs to be stored, give it to him prior to the car bomb search; after he finishes, he can store it. You should exit your building and walk down and get straight in the vehicle, so that he can pull away from that static location as quickly as possible.

RULES OF CONDUCT FOR ASSIGNED DRIVERS

The driver must remain with the vehicle at all times when there is no trusted guard force or other oversight with direct observation of the vehicle. While he is waiting for your arrival at the vehicle, after you have left the secure area, the driver needs to get out of the vehicle and stand to the front or rear of the vehicle so that he can observe anyone tampering with it. If he has a secure parking area, he can stay in the vehicle. You can call him and tell him when to pull out to get you or set a designated time for him to pick you up. Remember, if your vehicle is under observation, the less amount of time spent with the vehicle waiting for you to get in or out, the less chance you will be considered a stationary target. Ideally, if you can, you should always enter and exit a vehicle inside a facility with controlled access such as a company parking garage or a building's underground parking. If you ever come out and the assigned driver is not at the vehicle when you approach, do not go any closer. Turn around and go back inside the secure area. Wait until you can contact the driver and find out why he was not with the vehicle; he may have had to use the bathroom, etc. If the vehicle was not under his or a trusted security force's direct observation during this time, another vehicle car bomb search needs to be done before you enter.

You need to have a set of prearranged signals with the driver indicating that it is safe for you to exit the secure area and to enter the vehicle (such as the driver taking his hat off or placing a pack of cigarettes on the dash). But, do not let your guard down or be complacent when approaching the vehicle. There is the potential for this safe signal method to fail if the terrorists have managed to get the drop and have a gun to the driver's head, found a way to blackmail the driver, or coerce him in some other way to cooperate with them—such as taking members of his family hostage. As you approach the vehicle, you should be checking for people loitering in the area, hiding behind the vehicle, etc., and always look inside the vehicle before you enter to ensure that there is no other people in the vehicle.

Depending on your security situation and working/living environment, you should never give your itinerary for the day, week, etc., to the driver. If he is an assigned local national, local company staff, you should instead give the driver a general idea of when to show up at your residence—for example, 0600, even if you don't plan to leave until 0630 or 0700. This will throw off any surveillance, cause them to expose themselves by staying in an area too long, and it makes you less predictable. You should inform the driver of your destination after he arrives in the morning, and if you are using him for business throughout the day, only after he starts the vehicle and you begin moving. You should know what route you want to take. If you have an assigned security element, they will take care of this for you.

Never allow your driver to have or use a cell phone during the work day. Not only is it distracting, but, if you do not speak the language he is using, you will not know if he is telling the person on the other end your route and destination. Your driver could be the most trusted person in the world, and he could just slip up when speaking to family or friends, that is, saying he can meet them for lunch, or to talk at a specific place because he is dropping you of nearby, etc. However, this gives a time and location for you to anyone who was listening; it also gives a time and place for the threat to find your vehicle if they didn't have it before. This includes taxis. I always ask taxi drivers to stay off the phone or radio if I don't speak the language he is using. This can prevent him from telling a threat either criminal or terrorist where I am going. In some countries, they have to give call outs so their business knows where they are going. Ask for them to wait until you have arrived at your destination; if you tip well, they will do it.

You should know who your diver is before they arrive, and you should always have the same driver assigned. Never leave a secure area and enter the vehicle with a substitute driver until you have checked his credentials with the people who are responsible for providing him. This means that when you call in, check his name and ask for a description—and if you have set it up prior to a safe word—he should use when identifying himself. The description is important; just because Bob is supposed to be a substitute today, it doesn't mean Bob is who showed up! Any driver or other type of help substitution should be prearranged; you should not be finding out about it for the first time when the substitute appears.

If an incident occurs during a crisis situation, will your driver be more concerned with saving his own life or yours? In some cases, drivers have left their vehicles and run to escape an attack, leaving the passengers there. Or they have refused to drive by or through a barricade when confronted by the threat, allowing the passengers to be taken. They have failed in their duties to protect their passengers in the past, allowing them to be killed or captured. When you first get a driver, you need to determine whether your driving capabilities are as good as your assigned driver or chauffeur's. If they are, dismiss him. Tell the company you don't want to use him and take the responsibility of your life into your hands.

YOUR BEHAVIOR AS A PASSENGER

For you being a passenger, there are certain things you need to be doing as well—active measures that will increase your security level and situational awareness. You are not going to be just sitting in the back reading the comics or drinking coffee. When you are a passenger in a vehicle, you must stay mentally alert at all times and keep situationally aware; riding is not the time to review reports or to eat your breakfast. You can add mirrors as discussed earlier, even a small mirror attached to the passenger's visor can help that passenger observe the rear, since the driver should be occupied with operating the vehicle. Use the extra set of eyes you have to spot any unusual activity and alert the driver to any dangers so he can take the appropriate action. Remember, "the more you see, the safer you will be."

You need to ensure your routes and routines are varied on a continual basis. You need to have at least three different routes to and from work to home and any other primary areas you travel to or use. Do not allow a routine of always taking the same route every day for convenience. DO NOT ALLOW your security detail or driver to get complacent either; they get lazy also, get sick, want to get it over with as quickly as possible, etc. It is YOUR responsibility to make sure they do their jobs; the moment you become PREDICTABLE, you become a target regardless of whose fault it is.

You should always drive with the doors locked, and your windows rolled up. With regard to windows, it does not matter if you have the best armored vehicle money can buy or have the best security practices, the moment you lower your window, you have broken the integrity of the vehicle's security. It doesn't matter why you did it: buying fruit or a newspaper from someone at a stop light, asking for directions. There is no sense in having an armored vehicle or having a high security profile if you allow someone to pull you from the vehicle and shoot you because the doors were unlocked, or you allow someone to throw a Molotov cocktail in, or just put a gun through the open window and open fire because a window was rolled down. You should also ALWAYS fasten your seat belts. This is not only for safety reasons but in case your vehicle has to outrun another vehicle or ram a roadblock. It will keep you from being bounced around the inside of the vehicle, and getting hurt that way, and stops you from interfering with the driver's concentration.

Other thing you can do to confuse any surveillance is to consider swapping cars with a friend or a co-worker. This can make them think you have a vehicle pool to draw from, making you harder to ID and predict. It can cause surveillance to think you have not left your residence or work because they are concentrating on your car. Then, when someone else gets in and drives away, they will not know what to think. When doing this, you just have to be careful about whose car you borrow or swap with; you don't want to swap vehicles with someone who is a potential higher priority target than yourself for the threat. You also don't want to swap with someone who is a soft, easy target that practices no security measures, and you don't want to swap with someone who doesn't maintain their vehicle in good condition, or who has a flashy or expensive car.

You can also consider carpooling to and from work. These types of arrangements can offer safety in numbers and confuse the terrorists as to which car you are using. However, if the terrorists decide to carry out an attack, carpools will offer a larger number of victims and possibly be a more valuable target to the threat. Carpooling also has some other problems; it is much more difficult to vary the routines of all the persons involved, and this also applies to varying the routes used. It will be very difficult to set up a system that rotates who will drive randomly without upsetting some people in the carpool, and others might not be very good drivers or keep their vehicle in good repair. They could be security complacent or have no situational awareness at all.

OTHER CONSIDERATIONS

Traffic accidents are a problem anywhere you drive; you need to come up with a plan to follow if you are involved in a traffic accident. First, you need to quickly determine whether or not it is a ruse to stop your vehicle; criminals and terrorist groups sometimes use minor traffic accidents as ploys to get vehicles to stop and to get the person to exit his vehicle to view the damage, then they are car jacked, robbed, kidnapped, or killed. If you think it is a ploy, you need to leave the scene of the accident and drive directly to the closest safe area, police station, etc.

You then need to report the accident, your involvement and explain why you left the scene to the local police as soon as possible. In some cases, you can or your company can make up laminated cards with COMPANY contact information on it and who to call to resolve the incident; each card should be numbered, and when you get to work, you report it to the right people, fill out a report, and let them deal with any accident claims. It is better to pay a ticket for leaving the scene of an accident, than to be mugged, shot, or kidnapped! If you do not think it is a ploy, stay in your car, doors locked, window down just enough to speak through. Call someone on the cell or radio and wait for law enforcement to arrive. Do not shut off your car engine; this way, if you are wrong, you still have the opportunity to drive away if anything is tried.

You also need to think about what you will do if you are halted by police; first, you need to find out what the local procedures are for law enforcement by going and asking. If you are being halted by the police, keep driving slowly with your emergency flashers on until you are in an area that has a lot of people and is well lit if it is night; do not get out of your car otherwise.

You should also keep your vehicle engine running and roll down the window just low enough to allow voice communication and the passing of documents, but not enough for them to reach into the vehicle. You need to stay alert for any unusual actions or behaviors on the part of the law enforcement officer. You should also call your residence or your business and inform someone that you have been stopped and where. Keep your awareness level high and if the situation changes, and you need to exit suddenly because of the officer's behavior, you feel uncomfortable, etc., you should proceed to the nearest safe area—the U.S. Embassy or other U.S. Military installation, the closest police station—and immediately report the incident.

You also need to use extreme care when approaching any type of roadblock, whether it is legitimate and a known one, or an unknown one in a different area—or a possible false one set up by the threat. If that is the case, and the roadblock is a ploy by the threat, they will have an advantage over you since they have some control over the environment you are in. Whenever you see a roadblock, you need to determine as quickly as possible whether or not the roadblock is an official one. You do this by studying the uniforms of the police or the military and looking at the overall setup of the roadblock to see if it follows local law enforcement or military standard operating procedures (SOPs). Most official roadblocks are set up with signs, cones to guide cars, and separate lanes. They are lighted so law enforcement can see and usually set up in a blind spot on a corner or over a hill so that people will drive upon the roadblock without knowing it was there and don't have the chance to turn around and go another direction. The uniforms being used by the personnel working the roadblock should match, and they should also have the same basic equipment. You need to look at the vehicles being used; they should be official vehicles with plates, paint jobs, lights, markings that match what the local police or the military use. If they are not official vehicles, the chance of the roadblock being a ruse by the threat is good. For the threat, this type of planned incident causes many problems because when the threat sets up an official looking roadblock, they have to steal their uniforms, which means they won't fit like they should, especially footwear. Many times, they don't steal or obtain everything they need and some parts of the uniforms will be different, such as belts, holsters, etc. You have to make the determination is it official or a ruse, is it safe or not safe, quickly so you can keep your vehicle as far away from the threat and out of any "kill zone" as possible. This gives you enough room to escape and evade as necessary; you should never allow yourself to be boxed in, trapped, or allow your vehicle to be completely stopped; this will limit the possibility of escape. NOTE: The above is assuming the threat will attempt to look official. In some areas of the world, they will set up roadblocks with no attempt to fool anyone. They do this for a variety of reasons: to collect tolls, money, intimidate people before elections, harass people, to show that local law enforcement or security forces cannot stop them, and to find people they think they can get ransom for. If you are approaching a roadblock like this, turn around; if you cannot turn around, be prepared to use some of your defensive drivers training to get away. If you know they just want "toll money," just go through and pay them. Do not draw undo attention to yourself.

When you are moving by vehicle, you should drive in the far-left lane as much as possible. This will keep a threat from forcing your vehicle to the curb. Another advantage of driving in the left lane is that it restricts the number of weapons an attacking vehicle can bring to bear on your vehicle at one time. Since few people will be firing a weapon over the driver, it only allows the rear passenger window to be used on that side. When you are approaching traffic control points such as stop signs or traffic lights, you need to stay in a lane that will allow maneuverability out of a crisis situation, usually one of the outer lanes; if you stay in the center lane, there is a chance you could be blocked in by the cars stopped on either side of you. You should also have at least 8–10 feet between your vehicle and the one in front of you (the rule of thumb is 1 foot of ground between the rear tire of the vehicle in front of you and the top of your hood as you are looking over your steering wheel). This will ensure you have enough room to get around the vehicle in front of you instead of being blocked in by it.

The driver and the passengers in the vehicle need to keep an eye out for persons carrying packages, shopping bags, large purses, or bottles that might be thrown at your vehicle. Remember to watch the hands anyone throwing something at your vehicle, he will have to transition from the non-threatening posture he is presenting to one where he is a threat, watch for this transition which starts with the hands. But there are ways to lessen the damage caused by a Molotov cocktail; first, you need to make sure your windows are closed at all times, which shouldn't be a problem since you are supposed to drive with your windows up. Many times, thrown bottles will often bounce off a vehicle without breaking, so there should be no problem anyway, but if your vehicle is hit by a fire bomb type device that does not penetrate its interior, keep the vehicle moving and allow the flames to burn out. The exterior paint on the car might be damaged, the temperature inside the car will rise no more than about 10 degrees Fahrenheit, and the flames will last only 10–15 seconds and die out as soon as the fuel source is used up. If your vehicle is disabled in the attack and cannot be moved, wait 8–10 seconds for the flames to subside before exiting, or wait for a follow-on vehicle to extinguish the flames before exiting. Remember, we keep fire extinguishers inside the car for interior fires. Whenever possible, after evaluating the situation, you should remain inside your vehicle even if it is disabled, you have some protection inside the vehicle until help arrives.

Roadside emergencies: Whether you have a flat tire, run out of gas, etc., you should try to make it to a well-light area with lots of pedestrian and vehicle traffic before attempting to change your tire. If it is someone else who is experiencing a roadside emergency, consider everything before you stop your vehicle and getting out to help. The threat has used such ploys before, to stop victims and separate them from their vehicle and they will continue to use them in the future.

PROTECTION MEASURES WHEN TRAVELING BY COMMERCIAL MEANS

Following are some protective measures you should consider taking when traveling by commercial means. This area will focus on commercial air travel but any of these measures can be modified and changed to meet the needs of using other types of commercial travel or mass transit systems.

Most people when we plan travel don't try to control our travel itinerary; many times we call a travel company to do it for us, going for the cheapest way possible. If it is work related, we rely on our companies travel office to handle the arrangements for us, once again usually the company goes with the fastest cheapest way to meet that goal. When we allow others to plan and dictate our travel itinerary, we are basically putting out lives in their hands. After all, they are not looking at the safest most secure way to get you to the destination, they are looking for the fastest, least expensive way. You need to become more involved in making your travel arrangements; remember all the research we do before we leave to visit another country and the research on the threats for those areas we are going to. We can also research and learn about what airline we should avoid flying on or flight route that has been targeted by terrorists in the past and we should avoid. You should look at and select airports that have a good security record to lay over in, change planes in or for your final destination (you usually travel out of the airport closest to your work or home, not much choice), so you also need to check up on and select an airline that has a sound security record, history of good performance, etc. This may add expense or time to your trip which may cause your company to protest the matter but this is just a matter of educating your superiors with facts and justifications of why you chose that travel itinerary, explaining the value and lessening of the threat against them and you by planning a smart route.

You should avoid flights that travel over high-risk areas, since you never know when a plane might have mechanical difficulties or a plane may be rerouted by a company to pick up passengers if it is not full. The scheduled flight is delayed or canceled and the airline you chose should not be one that has scheduled stops in high-risk areas, or with connecting flights that have come from high-risk areas. Not all airports in every country practice good security, not every airline follows the good security practices.

You should also purchase your airline ticket through a travel agency, get it from your company office, or pay for it online and then check in at home rather than wait at a ticket counter; this way, you can select your seat and get a boarding pass before you arrive at the airport. You should know that the primary security in airports does not start until after you enter the gate area. From the ticket counters to the street, there is little to no security in place and anyone can walk into the airport terminal. This means that airline ticket counters offer a wide selection of targets to any threat: there have been attacks at ticket counters in the past by terrorist organizations in 2002 at the Tom Bradley international terminal in Los Angeles, CA, and at the Los Angeles International Airport where a man used an assault rifle to kill a Transportation Security Agency (TSA) agent and wound others before being shot by local police.

You should plan your arrival at the airport so you can quickly move through to the counter or a kiosk and check bags, many places now allow curbside check in for bags if you already have your boarding pass, which can now be printed online or have it on your phone. This allows you to get back to the security checkpoint, and into the secure, protected areas faster, and, once you are there, you should spend as little time as possible in unsecured areas.

CONDUCT PRIOR TO BOARDING

Just because you are past the security checkpoints and in the supposedly secure area of an airport does not mean you should be complacent and let your guard down, NO SECURITY is FOOLPROOF. You must maintain your situational awareness and stay alert to what is going on around you, watching for any suspicious or unusual activities, such as anyone who walks away from their luggage, hand bag, backpack, briefcase, etc., leaving it behind. A group of nervous-acting people: people who are dressed in clothes that could conceal weapons, anything that makes you suspicious or nervous, you may not know why it does but if it does and you become suspicious or if you see anything unusual, then move to another area away from it. Then, find security or airport personnel and report the incident; it may be nothing and it will cause an inconvenience to someone or it may save your life and the lives of those around you.

You have to be careful about who you talk to and what you say when traveling; remember that anything you say to someone, once it leaves your mouth, you have no control over what is done with that information and it may be used against you. You should also be careful about who you associate with especially other passengers who are loud or who conduct themselves in a manner that will identify them as American, or someone who could be a valuable target. If the area is under surveillance by the threat, you could be picked as a target, just by the people you associated with. If an incident does take place either in the airport or on the airplane, one of those passengers you talked to could recall your identity and essential facts about you, he could then use that knowledge to shift the threat's attention to you off of himself. NOTE: This also goes for standing in line at banks, ball parks, sitting at the bar in your hotel, etc. You never know what the person you are talking to or the girl you are trying to impress is going to do with the information you give them.

You want to try and avoid long layovers; if you cannot avoid a long layover, somewhere you need to stay in the secure area of the airport, if possible, in a first-class or business-class lounge. If you are not flying first class or business, you can buy a day pass. If that is not possible, you should rent a hotel room and wait there until you need to return for your connecting flight; since your luggage is already checked and you have your boarding pass, you should be able to go straight through security. If the layover is expected to be short, but still several hours, depending on the services available there, you should leave the airport to eat or to shop. The idea behind leaving the airport is to separate you from what have been ideal targets for terrorists to attack in the past. It could also help you maintain a low profile, by having people assume you are just another tourist. If you cannot leave the airport, stay in a secure area and find a lounge or a restaurant to wait in; you should do a check of all the airports you will be traveling through to find out what services are available and the hours they are open; most of that information can be found on the web nowadays. Whatever you do, whatever your situation, avoid those dangerous areas such as ticket counters, restaurants, bars, and gift shops outside of the secure area of the air terminal.

You should also avoid traveling in uniform if you are in the military. Nowadays, the military wants its service members to fly in uniform; in the United States, this may be fine, but you should be careful when flying through other countries this way; depending on where you are flying through, it could cause problems. It could happen that a threat, a terrorist, a war protester, someone anti-American could realize the exploitation value of an American serviceman in uniform who becomes a victim. Remember, traveling in uniform just doesn't mean military or police one. Many companies have dress codes which are like uniforms in that, they designate what people have to wear a suit, what color, what type of shoes, etc., so if you two or three people dressed alike walking around together is like a uniform and people notice this. There are also those people who are going to work in those high-risk areas around the world, many feel they need to travel through all international airports wearing desert combat boots, 5–11 shirts and royal Robbin pants, with desert camouflage backpacks, this is another way for a threat to pick you out as a possible target. Kuwait, Jordan, Amsterdam, Frankfurt all have elements of a threat that would like to target Americans and especially those who are helping them fight the war on terrorism. Use common sense when traveling.

CONDUCT WHILE IN THE AIR

To begin with, you need to make sure you get a good seat security wise, so when you are choosing your aircraft seat, you need to select one in the "gray area" of the aircraft. What is the gray area? It is the middle third of the aircraft, seats against the body of the aircraft, so basically you want a window seat positioned in the middle rear of the aircraft. Whenever possible, you should choose the seat so you can be close to an emergency exit, so you can exit the plane faster in case of an incident or emergency. Incidents from past skyjackings have shown that when terrorists decide to make an example of someone, or to show they are in control and have the power, they choose an easily accessible person. This can mean that just walking up and down the aisles, and they strike people randomly to keep fear induced. They are not going to reach over two people to hit someone unless that person is doing something that they want to punish him for. You also want to avoid the front and the rear of the aircraft. For a limited number of people to be able to see and control the aircraft, they have to position themselves at the front and the rear. This allows them to see everyone and gives them the advantage to control a situation (this is true when you need to control ANY linear target, i.e., plane, train, bus, etc.); so, avoid these areas since they will be closest to the people with guns. The closer you are to them, the more likely you will become a victim of physical violence.

In the past, the actual takeover of a plane occurs 15–60 minutes into flight. This is because the plane has reached cruising altitude, still has a majority of its fuel, and routine radio traffic with the departure airfield tower is over with. This is also the time when the fasten seat belts sign is turned off, which means it is not unusual for people to get up, start moving around the cabin, and start getting things from the overhead bin. The stewardess will start preparing for drink and meal services, so they are not watching what the passengers are doing as closely as before. If you are on a plane when a skyjacking takes place, you need to return to your seat, sit down, and fasten your seat belt as quickly as possible. This is preparing you for any action by sky marshals, decompression of the plane, or if the pilots decide to do some maneuvering to throw the skyjackers off balance. After you are in your seat, you need to sanitize yourself and your belongings if you didn't do it before boarding; this means hiding any paperwork that could make you a target, official passports, government, military, law enforcement identification. If you have dual citizenship, keep your passport that is the most neutral and hide the other one, any papers, computers, or other articles that could make the threat consider you a good victim. You need to start thinking of what you are going to tell the terrorists if they ask you questions. Usually, you have to SANITIZE YOURSELF as quickly as possible, which means you have around 10 seconds to clear your wallet and your body of anything that could make you a target such as military affiliation. That's why, it is better to do this before you get on the plane. Remember to keep your wallet, driver's license, etc., basically all of your neutral identification, and place documents you want to keep out of sight in a secure hiding place, inside a used airsickness bag, under your seat in the pocket that holds life vests, etc., and even though placing your documents inside a magazine or under the seat is not the most effective method of concealing them, they are something that should be considered if you are caught unprepared. Once the skyjackers have control, they will ask for everyone's identification, so when asked to produce identification, show civilian identification (tourist passport/driver's license). You should never lie about your involvement with the military, government, and organizations but never volunteer information about your association; do not help them make you a victim. If you are questioned about your job or travel plans, tell them and explain the innocent circumstances that led to you being on the plane (plausible denial).

Another reason we want to be in our seats with seat belts fashioned is if an explosion or weapon discharge breaches the skin of the aircraft at a critical location, the side of the plane could rupture. This will cause rapid decompression to occur, resulting in severe flying difficulties for the crew, and all loose objects in the plane to go flying toward the hull breach, this includes people who are not belted in.

You should also delay your identification as being affiliated with the government, military, law enforcement, etc., for as long as possible. If you are confronted with facts, do not lie since it means they already know who you are and what you do. You also need to be aware of contradicting or compromising items you may have on you, such as military, government agency, or law enforcement coins, business cards, having a driver's license or passport photo of you in uniform, having military, government service, etc., tattoos visible, souvenirs such as military plaques, drinking glasses, etc. Remain calm, state your innocence of any wrongdoing, and do not get confrontational. If the terrorist doesn't know anything about you other than your nationality—DON'T HELP HIM by being belligerent.

If you are being held captive, you should at no time be a threatening image, become confrontational, or confront those holding you or other passengers. The threat whether it is terrorists or criminals will not hesitate to eliminate any possible interference to their control of the situation; they do this not only to get the threat out of the way but to instill fear in others so they will not do the same thing. If there comes a time and the terrorists decide to inflict punishment on someone as a warning to others, or those they are negotiating with, they will remember the troublemakers and those who challenged them and possibly select them as examples. Do you not try passive measures either, by making obscene gestures at the terrorists behind their back, mocking them, etc.; you never know when they will see you and you never know who is sitting around you or how they will react. Causing someone close to you to start laughing is going to bring the threat down to see what is going on. Remain calm and suppress any defiant attitudes.

Firearms are a bad thing to have on your person if you are not a sky marshal or other recognized law enforcement agent responsible for that flight. If you are authorized to carry a firearm, place it in your carryon luggage with all the equipment that goes with it and put it in the overhead bin, or you place it in your checked baggage. If you have your weapons, chances are still highly unlikely that you would be successful in an attempt to overtake the terrorists, who had planned for this. You have no way of knowing how many terrorists or if there are any "sleepers" mixed in with the passengers to watch them also. Such drastic action on your part could cause the terrorists to kill you, other passengers, and members of the crew. In the event of a shootout, a window or critical juncture of the aircraft may be hit, creating an emergency situation from which escape would be extremely difficult. If they have an explosive device, it could destroy the plane. You have to consider if there are air marshals on board, and they do not know who you are. When they act, they could see you as another terrorist. And how do you distinguish between terrorist and air marshal? Pilots are now armed; he will not know who you are either, and then you have rescue forces to contend with. If a rescue is attempted, and they see you with a gun, you will more than likely be shot. So, with all these things to consider and account for, it is better if you have a weapon when the takeover begins, hide it, as well as the holster. Pay attention to what is going on around you.

ATTITUDE TOWARD TERRORISTS

There is a problem with people being "cowboys" and standing up to anyone; there are always situations where this is not a good thing, such as when dealing with terrorists who have successfully planned and executed an operation like a skyjacking; there are certain ways to present yourself.

DO NOT give terrorists, those long hard looks and stare at them; do not argue with them about their goals, their beliefs, or about what they are doing. Since they just violated international law and are now fugitives from the world, do you really think you are going to talk them into changing their mind? Do not make obscene gestures. If you are enough of a problem or instigator, the terrorists could simply kill you as an example to the others. Or, they could kill the person sitting next to you to prove to you they can do it. Whenever you confront people in this situation, they will have to do something to maintain fear and dominance over those they have in their control. Don't force them into this action by being stubborn and stupid; it is not only your life in danger.

Because of September 11, and the events and flights involving the Pentagon and the World Trade Center, you may need to take action while on board the aircraft. This is a decision you make; no one can tell you what to do and when to do it. Ultimately, it is your decision to make based upon the circumstance of the situation taking place, and what you KNOW for fact before you act. Some things you want to consider are:

- Is a Federal Marshal on the aircraft? How many? If you know for a fact they are there, then stay out of it and let them do their job, but be ready to assist, do not rush forward volunteering; remember, he DOES NOT KNOW WHO you are or WHAT your intentions are when he is dealing with this threat.
- How heavily armed are the hijackers? What weapons do they have, what do you see? Do they have handguns and explosives? If they have knives or other weapons but no firearms and say

they have a bomb, consider the security you just went through to get on board, how good was it, could they off gotten a device on board, if so why couldn't they get firearms also?

- How many hijackers are there and do they closely monitor activities of passengers and air crew? Do they have enough people to watch all sections where there are passengers and air crew at all times, are they continual walking back and forth checking between passenger compartments, are they forcing everyone into one area? These could be signs that they don't have enough people to watch everyone at once.
- How are they conducting themselves? Do they look like they have a plan? A chain of command? With set goals, this means they are organized and probably have training of some kind.
- Are pilots left in control of the plane? The cockpit of the aircraft is lockable from the inside and cannot be breached. Are the pilots still in control and flying; if so, they are going to put the plane on the ground as soon as possible, let the authorities deal with it; if this is the case, you should allow this to happen as it increases your chance of survival and escape once down on the ground. If the door has been breached and the pilots and crew are no longer operating the aircraft, then you need to consider the option of trying to stop what is taking place.
- What are the hijackers' destination and other demands? Where do they want to go? This will give you an insight into who they are, is it a realistic goal? More than likely with the pilots still in control of the aircraft (secure cockpit), they will land at the nearest friendly airport, regardless of where the skyjackers want to land.
- Are the hijackers demanding ID from passengers? This means they have a specific agenda and are looking for people of certain nationalities, affiliations, or professions to target as their immediate victims; this why it is a good reason to always have a civilian form of identification. It could also mean they are looking for one specific person and/or his family. Do they start separating people by nationality? Job? Sex? etc. This could also give a clue as to what their agenda may be.
- Are passengers able to place calls to people on the ground? Without getting caught, either using cell phones or the planes phones. If so, this could be a large boost to authorities on the ground, negotiators, rescue team, etc., since now information can be passed from sources besides the skyjackers themselves about what is taking place and possibly some photos or film, allowing authorities to begin planning before the plane lands.

In the event of a skyjacking, you want to remain calm and comply with the directions of the hijacker, do not get confrontational, argue, etc. However, you want to continuously evaluate the situation as it plays out and react to things accordingly. One of the ways that will help you do this is to have an EMERGENCY PLAN OF ACTION (EPA): as soon as you know for sure you are hijacked, you need to take the opportunity to access all cover and concealment that is available around you, in case shooting starts. You want to pay attention to and watch the emergency exits, especially the ones closest to you; if you are on the ground, rescue attempts will start there as they are the only way into the aircraft; also, if an incident starts inside, this is your fastest way out of the plane, so have a plan to get to one and know how to open it. You need to develop Emergency Plan of Action (EPA) for all the different situations that can happen for being at altitude and on ground; one of your plans on the ground should be a plan to initiate EPA of finding cover and getting off the airplane as quickly as possible, if the terrorist begins mass killings or begins randomly firing into the passengers. NOTE: In the world today, attitudes and perceptions have changed drastically since 9–11. For many people, it means that they have the attitude of "not again," which makes them super aggressive and wanting a confrontation. Several military and law enforcement people I have trained in the past have said, "I am going to attack those F**kers anyway, screw'em." In these types of situations, it is a BAD idea to do this. There have been several instances of skyjackings after 9-11 that have ended with no casualties of either the skyjackers, but, more importantly. the passengers. A gung-ho, going to kill'em all attitude can not only get you killed, but everyone else on the plane. SO, REMEMBER THIS; IF THE PILOTS ARE FLYING THE PLANE AND THE COCKPIT HAS NOT BEEN BREACHED, DO NOTHING. Anything you do or attempt to do will only escalate an already dangerous situation. When there is no need, the pilots will land at the first sign of trouble at the nearest airport, and then the professionals will handle it. By attacking when there is no need, you could cause the skyjackers to fire their weapons, rupturing the skin of the aircraft or killing other passengers. They could intentionally set off explosives that they have placed on board, or you could cause them to do this unintentionally. Do not forget about other security or law enforcement personnel that may already be on the plane and have a plan of action, that you could potentially disrupt. You need to continually evaluate the situation, know who is in charge of flying the aircraft, and pay attention to what is taking place around you. ATTACKING the skyjackers is an OPTION OF LAST RESORT—when the cockpit has been breached and the air crew is no longer flying the plane but the terrorists are.

RESCUE ATTEMPT

At some time during the skyjacking, assuming it is not a 9-11-like suicide mission (what skyjackings used to be back in the 1970s and 1980s), the plane will have to stop and land somewhere for refueling. It is during this time on the ground that the authorities may initiate a rescue attempt. They will try negotiations first, but if that is failing and hostages have been killed, they will probably begin the rescue. This is not a safe time for being a hostage, as statistically, the rescue attempt is the most dangerous time for the passengers, since now you have two groups of people firing rounds, explosives, etc., in an enclosed space and the passengers have no protection.

To protect yourself at the first indication of a rescue attempt, use all available cover around you; cover is something that will protect you from bullets. In your seat, you need to assume the classic crash position (arms into your sides/head on your knees/fingers covering your neck), but you need to do a couple of other things for your protection. Raise your feet up so that no bullets or grenade fragments will strike your feet, ankles, and lower legs; this can happen when flash-bang grenades are thrown in the plane by rescue forces, or other explosive devices are used; the explosive path takes the path of least resistance which is under the seats. The same is true for bullet ricochets, so if your feet, ankles, or lower legs are hit, broken, etc., it will make it more difficult for you to run. You also need to keep your eyes open and on the closest terrorist in the event that he is going to start shooting in your direction. If this is about to happen, your choices are limited. At the very least, you should try to find more cover or run toward cover or an exit. Moving targets are harder to hit. If at the time the rescue attempt is started and you are not in your seat, find the closest cover you can that does not require much movement to reach, or stay low and make yourself as small a target as you as possible. You need to avoid any movement, especially sudden movements such as standing up quickly or running toward a rescuer. The rescuers are trained to focus on movement because it is a possible threat. Any movement attracts attention from them, and you could get shot; it also will cause the terrorists to look at the movement, and you could get shot by them as well.

You should NEVER attempt to help during a rescue unless specifically asked to do so by a member of the rescue force. The violence, noise, and confusion will make it difficult for the rescuers to determine whether you are friend or foe. Remember, they do not know who the good or the bad guys are yet. Not all bad guys will be visible, as there may be sleepers in the seats. So, the rescuers focus on the hands and quick fast observations of individuals. Generally, anyone making a violent gesture (throwing his arms into the air or trying to grab the rescuer) or carrying a gun will probably be shot or forcefully dealt with. It will be difficult, your hearing may be short from all the loud noises, but you MUST LISTEN closely for commands from the rescuers. You need to do everything they tell you to. One problem you may encounter is these commands may be in a language that you do not understand, so pay strict attention to any gestures and to what the other passengers are doing. If everyone else is putting their hands on their heads, you should too, etc.

You should expect to be handled roughly at first and handcuffed. Remember that they do not know who the good guys are or who all the bad guys are, so this is to ensure yours and everyone else's safety. You should also be prepared to be separated from family members while everyone is searched, They will probably separate you by gender. Once you are out of the aircraft and your feet hit the ground, move away from the aircraft either by going in the direction of the tail section (preferably) or from the nose section, This way, the terrorists will have little chance of acquiring a clear shot at you. You should be shouting as loud as you can, "Don't shoot! I am a passenger!" You do not want to be mistaken for an escaping terrorist You should also raise your hands in the air and follow the commands of those rescuers on the ground to greet you. During your observations, if you see something that is life threatening such as a fire, the terrorists start firing indiscriminately, explosions, and you must depart the plane or else risk being killed, then GET OFF THE PLANE. Don't wait to be told. This is the time you will initiate your preplanned escape through the nearest exit (this can be done faster and easier if you have rehearsed how to operate the exit mechanisms in your mind many times over). Move carefully outside the body of the aircraft, possibly onto a wing, and then work your way to the ground.

NOTE: You need to pay attention to what type of shoes you wear when traveling by air. I recommend wearing tennis shoes, running shoes, etc. Because flip flops, sandals do not offer any protection in case of a fire or other emergency and they impede your ability to run especially on a slippery surface or over debris if it is necessary. Hard-soled shoes, dress shoes, etc.: one of the escape routes in most aircraft is onto the wing of the aircraft, this surface is very slippery to hard-soled shoes and you will not be able to get traction to run, jump, etc. High heels: let's face it, you can't do much of anything in these; they are hard soled so you will not be able to get traction on the wings or other slippery surface; you will have to remove them to go down a slide for life, etc. Athletic shoes are your all around best bet in case you need to be able to move by foot during an emergency.

After the authorities have identified everyone and released you, it is vitally important that you cooperate with the authorities, especially if you are overseas. Try to maintain your calm. They are trying to help you but the law enforcement community in any country will need to talk to you to debrief about the incident. Overseas, you do not want to give the authorities a reason to detain you further, by being problematic or being that ugly American. COOPERATE! What you describe, what you remember before, during, and after the incident can assist law enforcement in their investigation, on how it happened, how to prevent it from happening again, and how to react better. Your cooperation will also speed your release from authorities.

BRIEF DEPENDENTS

If you are traveling to a high-risk area, or any area that can be considered high risk—or you are considered a high-risk individual because of your rank, authority, etc.—you are a possible target. Wherever you travel, you need to brief your dependents, other family members. and friends on what to say to media if your flight is skyjacked, you become a hostage, kidnapping victim, or are caught up in some other incident that makes the news. The best thing is to advise them not to say anything to anyone: period. Terrorists have been known to carry radios and portable TVs onto the aircraft or request that they are brought on board. With radios, the terrorists can receive instructions from the outside as well as monitor the amount of publicity and the types of information broadcast by the media. This includes interviews with members of your family saying things about you that you would prefer a hostage taker not to know—such as your job with the government, your military affiliation, how rich you are, etc. Then, now they know information about you that they didn't have before and that they might be able to use. Most people do not realize that radio and television is just as important for the terrorist as the other weapons he uses. The media can be his primary source of intelligence about an ongoing situation and it can make a terrific ally for the terrorist.

HOTEL SECURITY

Hotel security is going to be of vital importance to you during your travels for both work and recreation. It is important that you know what you should be looking for when picking your temporary residence during your movements, items you can travel with to increase your security, and how to conduct yourself to raise your security profile higher. First, you need to choose a hotel that employs active, VISIBLE security and practices proactive measures to their security plan and profile. You need VISIBLE signs of security. This includes the presence of guards, the use of cameras to monitor hallways and elevators and the outside of the facility, visitor sign-in rosters: these are all signs of VISIBLE security and points to the security conscious of the establishment. These are all deterrents to surveillance and anyone planning an attack. There are some downsides to having visible security because the threat, if they are determined to attack you regardless because of your status, can plan for ways to neutralize the security they can see. But, combined with the non-visible security measures, it should be enough to give them pause.

You should also look into the policy of your company on business trips, in regard to how they reserve hotel rooms for visiting personnel. They may house them in the same hotel that they have used for years, even reserving the same room or rooms on the same floor. This means that if it is known you are coming, the threat will have an excellent idea of where you are. If they are looking at an attack against any American or an employee of that company, they will know where you will be staying. This is especially true for airline companies; they usually have contracts with certain hotel chains for putting up their airline crews between flights.

If you have a hotel reservation prior to your arrival, with a designated room already assigned when checking in, you can request another room. Depending on how long that reservation has been in place and that room reserved, people will know which rooms have been set aside for you specifically or for incoming Americans. A hotel clerk might be completely trustworthy, but let slip that they have a group of foreigners supposed to check in at a certain date, or a VIP when talking to family or friends, and it could potentially lead to trouble.

If you have to stay at a hotel for an extended period of time, you should consider changing rooms and floors occasionally at random so that any effort to conduct operations or surveillance against you will require more time and resources. You may even consider changing hotels; do not make it easy for the threat.

When checking into a hotel, there are certain floors you want to avoid, because of their increase in risk to you and your safety. You need to avoid street-level rooms because they are easily accessible to illegal entry such as someone climbing in the windows, car bombs, and bomb attacks even if not directed at you. On the ground floor, the blast wave and secondary effects can enter your room, and in drive-by shootings, once again even if not directed at you, your room could be in the line of fire. You should also not stay in a room that faces the street; try to get one that faces to the interior of the hotel. You might not get a great view, but you increase your level of safety significantly. You should never accept a room above the seventh floor in any facility, including hotels. This is because most countries have limited or no ladders or bucket trucks that will reach above the seventh floor in case of a fire or other evacuation emergency. You need to stay off of floors that have shops, facilities open to the public. Don't stay on the floor with a vending machine area, ice machine, gym, or swimming pool, etc. Because there is a higher volume of pedestrian traffic who now have an excuse to be on the floor you are staying. And, you have no way of knowing if their excuse is real or not, they could be surveillance checking the area. On floors that don't have these types of facilities, it is unusual for people just to get off and walk around. Also, security will notice people doing this, being where they have no reason to be.

If you are paged over the hotel's system, or for that matter anywhere including airports or restaurants, do not answer the page in person. This could be a ploy from the threat that has your name but does not know what you look like. You should not be paged anyway; if you are there for business, then the people you work for should know what you look like and where to find you. If you are expecting visitors, sit in areas you can see the door and watch for them or have a prearranged meeting place. If you cannot find them, then you page them "your party is waiting in the bar." If you have been paged, go to one of the in-house hotel phones, which are usually located in all common areas, and inquire about the paging. With cell phones now so prevalent around the world, it's just another reason to be suspicious of someone paging you, since a business acquaintance or friend would just call or text.

You should keep your room key with you at all times. I know that many countries around the world now use the key cards, but in some areas, they don't—and they require you leave your room key at the desk when you go out. The key cards usually come in a small key holder where they put the room number on it. You should discard this or someone might see it; also, you should not disclose your room number indiscriminately. Telling people what room you are in, while in a public venue, means you can be easily overheard. Using your room number to pay for drinks at the bar or meals at the restaurant means that many more people—from the waiter to the checkout person—now know where you are staying. NOTE: Some magnetic keys are coded with your credit card information, name, etc., as well as the code to open the door. It is better to keep this and destroy it yourself rather than trust the hotel staff to zero it out.

When you are entering or exiting public rooms, halls, lobbies, or other public areas, be alert for anyone loitering in the area or who are carrying props or other objects that could conceal weapons, such large bags, shopping bags, backpacks, or are wearing concealing clothing that does not match the weather. You should avoid loitering in lobbies or public areas such as rest rooms and areas by the main entrance. These common areas could be the only area a terrorist has access to just by walking in off the street so they favor these locations for placing bombs and committing random acts of violence.

Whenever possible, change your routine at the hotel or other temporary residences; you can do this by using different hotel entrances, exits, elevators, and by taking the stairs. Many of us get complacent and always use the front entrance, because it is easier, but hotels usually have many different exits and entrances for us to use. Also, do not park your car in the same place at the hotel or park it by the entrance/exit you intend to use; this gives the threat knowledge of what door you need to come out to your car. Don't drive your car all the time: walk, take a taxi—make it harder for the threat.

Know the location of emergency exits on your floor and the ground floor and know how they are marked and if they work; you also need to know where the emergency equipment is located. You should learn how to operate the equipment and become familiar with the building's emergency plans. You should also check the equipment to make sure it is functioning. Some countries do not have the regular inspection schedule that they have in the United States for safety equipment. I have seen fire extinguishers that were zeroed out on their status dial and were 2 years out from their inspection date. You do not want to waste time running to get equipment that doesn't work to stop a fire, if you can use that time to evacuate safely.

You should always keep your room clean or at least picked up and your personal effects in a neat and orderly fashion; this will enable you to know when someone has been moving your things, changed things in the room, or added things, etc. You can also put up a do not disturb sign and tell the front desk that you do not want maid service unless you are in the room; most hotels will comply since they have a 24-hour staff. Then, you will know that no one was supposed to be in there, so if something is out of place or has been tampered with, it is a possibility that some threat has broken into your room.

You should also leave shower curtains, bathroom door, the closets, and any other area that has a door on it open whenever you leave the room; most of the time, these areas are usually close to the door to the room. When you leave them all open, you can check in the closet, bathroom, and shower without having to open anything to do so, and you can do this while holding the room door open, in case you need to run.

You need to make sure your doors and windows are locked when you leave the room; sometimes, they stick or the lock does not catch; depending on the hotel, many have installed latches that should not allow the window to open or block it from opening no more than a few inches. If the room has a safe in it, you might want to consider locking your valuables in it. If not, you should carry a lockable small container, put your valuables in that, and then lock that in your luggage. You can consider securing your valuables by placing them in the hotel safe, but this does not mean they will be there when you ask to retrieve them. Several instances have occurred in the Middle East and Southeast Asia; people have used the hotel safe or lockbox system only to find that when they went to retrieve their valuables from the hotel clerk and that they were gone, or told they never placed anything in them because the paperwork was gone, etc. Always travel with luggage that has zipper handles large enough to pass padlocks through.

While you are in your room, you should keep the door locked and use the security chain, even if these are not the best types of locks for security. There are a number of portable locks that can be bought for doors that will add to your security and will enhance any existing lock system. All you have to do is check online or visit some travel stores. If you don't want to buy something, you can use a chair by placing the back underneath the handle so that the door cannot be opened. You can also use the trick of screwing a thick screw into the space between the doorjamb and the lock. This will put a lot of tension on the lock bar itself and the door will be hard to open. If someone had an extra key to your room or a master key, the screw serves as a wedge, which would force the person to exert more effort and make more noise when opening the door. You can also use door wedges that are used to keep doors open; the kind that slide under the bottom. You can put them on the inside to also keep a door closed. No matter what you do, you need to remember the possibility of a fire and your need to get out of the room in an emergency; you don't want to trap yourself. If the threat cannot quickly and quietly enter your room to catch you by surprise, they might seek an easier target.

Another thing you can consider using are portable alarm systems, which can be purchased online or at many different stores. Again, this will not stop a determined attacker, but these items will make enough noise so that the attackers are aware of the danger of attacking a prepared and ready target.

Lights should always be left on in your room if possible. This makes it difficult for anyone who may be observing you to know when you are in your room or leaving your room. An example of how this would work is someone knows your room number, sees you turn Off your lights and the light from the room door opening, he now knows you have left your room, and him and the rest of the surveillance team can prepare themselves to follow you. Another example is there is no light in your room, so you are either not there or asleep. They could use this time to try to enter your room to cause harm since you will be slower to react coming out of sleep or to get into your room and set up a device for surveillance purposes or to cause you harm. By keeping a light on, you are always keeping them guessing; if you cannot sleep with a light on, take a small lamp and place it by the window and then close the shades around it, ensuring none of the drapes touch the bulb. Then, just leave it on; the lamp's light will wash out the entire window, so an observer will not be able to determine anything. In many countries, you cannot leave your lights on because you have to use your room key to turn on power to the room. You can then take flashlight and place it in the window leaving it on. It will also wash out the drapes just not as heavily. Or, you can ask for two key cards and use one to keep power on in the room. People do not realize that they set up a noticeable routine to outside observers with how they use the lights in their room, office, or at their primary residence.

You should never admit strangers to your room. This will allow them to know the layout of your room, which bed you are using, if there is more than one, and also what valuables and other items you may have in the room, such as computers, expensive clothes, etc. You should refuse unexpected deliveries. You do not want to open the door to someone you do not know. If the person is insistent, tell them to leave it with the desk and that you will come down to get it. Ask who sent it and then call the person and find out what's going on before you go to the desk and retrieve it. If you don't know who sent it, tell the desk you don't want it. Food deliveries such as pizza or other take out: you should never give your name or your room number. Just tell them when you order it, you will be in the lobby to meet them and have the correct amount of money ready. You do this because you never know who is listening or who will show up to deliver the pizza. So, you don't want them to have your name or your location.

If the hotel or facility you are staying at employs a security force, including guards, you need to familiarize yourself with their uniforms and the equipment they normally carry on them. You should also get to know them by name. Be friendly and start building rapport with them. They are more likely to provide help in an emergency or risk their life for someone they know, than they will a stranger. You should learn their schedules also, and what areas are watched and protected during the day and the night, since they might just lock off some areas or put them under camera observation after normal business hours. You need to know the proper procedures for obtaining their services also, who to call, etc.

If during your stay, there should be an explosion, gun fire, or a firefight between security forces and terrorists, you should stay in your room, on the floor, or in the bathroom. Stay away from the window and avoid the hallways and balconies. If you want to watch, watch it on TV. If you have weapons, this does not mean you get to involve yourself. Do not attempt to assist the security forces or law enforcement. Involving yourself in a gunfight where you do not know who is who is very bad for several different reasons. Not only will you have broken the golden rule of "out of sight, out of mind," and keeping a LOW PROFILE. When you appear with a gun and no one already involved knows who you are, you will become a hostile target to both the terrorists and the security forces. So, you need to remain in your room. If you have protective gear, get it on. If you have weapons, get them ready. Call your people and tell them what is going on and that you may be late to work and then wait until it ends. If they enter your hotel and are targeting you specifically, or just want to kill foreigners or VIPs staying there, then you should be prepared to fight, just make sure you always keep an escape route open. Exiting the hotel in these circumstances is similar to exiting a plane after an incident, get out hands raised and start screaming you are a civilian, so law enforcement has some idea who you are. Do not take your weapons with you; if you do this, when people are pumped on adrenaline and see a gun, they might shoot first and then figure out who you are later.

Taxi cab use: if you must use a taxi, do not take the first one in line at any location, or take one that is called by the door man. It is possible for the threat to be paying them to direct any Americans that come through and want a taxi to them, or the person calling the taxi forward could be a terrorist himself once again wanting foreigners, especially Americans, to enter his cab. Never get into a taxi that has more than one person in it. If it stops to pick someone else up, get out. Be aware of the danger involved when calling for a taxi or car when going out. If terrorists should intercept your call, they may send one to pick you up. You can just walk out to the street or down the street and pick one at random. These same cautions should also be used when using ride share services you can now order through apps on a smart phone.

Taxis are an excellent way to gain intelligence about movement patterns on people and on what their business is. They do this by just listening to conversations. Always be suspicious if all of the sudden you start running into taxi drivers that now speak English or you continually get the same one. Business intelligence is a big business and in some places that cater to business people, the taxis may be bugged to record any information that is discussed; sometimes, this is done with the knowledge and permission of the host country government. Remember, Air France was caught bugging the business class cabins to gain business intelligence.

You should also turn down the ringer on the telephone or phones in your room. This is a means where a threat could track down what room you are in by doing the following: they know your name but not your room number. They know what floor you are located on either by watching what elevator button you push or riding in the elevator to see what floor you get off on. Then, one of the threat actors will keep calling the hotel and asking to be connected to your room while you are gone. During this time, another terrorist walks up and down the hallway listening for it to ring. Once they find it, they know your room.

RESIDENTIAL SECURITY

This section will cover the selection of your residence. One of the most important things you can do when looking for a residence is to use a good site selection process. This process takes into account many different areas that should be considered for your overall safety and security. To do this, you need to use a list. I say this because people forget things, what to look for, what questions to ask, etc.; having a written list in front of you means you will not miss something that could impact you later on.

A checklist can be one you have written; it can be obtained from the security officer at the embassy or your company security office. If you cannot find a checklist that fits your circumstances or criteria, then write your own, using common sense deterrents for the threat. Remember, by using a WRITTEN checklist, you are less likely to miss an important weakness during the inspection process through an oversight.

When choosing a new residence or doing work to strengthen and secure your current residence, you must look at it from the threat's point of view. You do this by asking yourself questions like: if I got locked out, how would I get in? How long would it take me to get in? How easy would it be to bypass these locks?

You always need to compare all available options before deciding on your new home; these options are for the type of home you want. Do you want an individual family home? Will it meet your security needs? This type of home might be the least desirable option available to you since these types of residences can require a high degree of security to make it secure and safe for you, depending on the modifications required. Once it is done, it could end up giving you a high profile. Living in an area where there are other Americans—or friendly foreign nationals have been clustered together, such as a gated community—could provide a higher degree of security and peace of mind without causing a great deal of attention to be focused on you specifically. But remember, just living in such an area could cause you to become a target, and an living area like that might be a very tempting target to a terrorist wanting to make a statement. Condominiums and apartments offer some benefits that can increase your security profile such as having neighbors close so they could hear any disturbances and contact law enforcement and there will be limited entries and exits which are sometimes controlled to the building. But, they also offer semipublic access to the lobby and building, and unless each person is screened, you have no idea if you are living next to or around people who could be a threat to you or sympathetic to the threat's cause. Also, building maintenance people and outside vendor access is something else that is totally out of your control.

When you are out looking and evaluating properties for a residence, you need to avoid homes that have a limited number of routes into and out of your housing area. If you only have one street that runs from your residence out, then you have been automatically channelized and this makes you predictable. You need to have the ability to go different directions as soon as you leave your driveway; the more decision points you have along your various routes, the less predictable you are. You also need to avoid any residences that are on dead-end streets for the same reason. These types of restricted movement areas make you extremely predictable and that makes you a good target. So, find a residence that has several roads that lead to it; remember, victims are hit where they are most predictable. Also, with multiple roads in, if terrorists attempt to hit you at your home or near it, this will prevent them from being able to block you in a kill zone. You should also remember this for work buildings or offices as the same rules apply.

Many landlords even overseas ask for references and do a background check on prospective renters, leasers, or buyers, but almost no one checks on the landlord. You need to run a check on your prospective landlord. Get references, have the embassy run a check, have your company's security people do a check on him or her. After all, you do not want to rent from someone who has been convicted of a crime against foreigners or has ties to the terrorists or is otherwise sympathetic to their cause. You also want to collect information on your neighbors, if you can; they can have routines that could affect you.

Examine the neighborhood for the following.

After looking at the residence, you next need to drive around the neighborhood and the surrounding area trying to get a feel for them. You should also check out the local emergency services who will respond to your residence if called. You need to know how reliable the local police are. Do they have patrols? What is their response time, training, types of vehicles, uniforms, etc. You also need to know the same for rescue services such as fire department, paramedics, ambulance, and other rescue systems: where they are located, response time, training, uniforms, vehicles, how far are these different facilities from your residence? The location of these type of facilities can be a good deterrent for you if they are close to your residence. By being in close proximity to these facilities, the terrorists might consider the quick response from security forces in case of an attack, which may lead them to choose someone else. But, the flipside of this coin is that the police, rescue units, etc., might themselves be the intended targets of an attack. If your home is close enough to them, you could become a victim of the cross fires, the explosion, etc., even though they were not intended for you specifically. You also need to look around for late-night establishments in the area; restaurants, gas stations, newsstands, and the like are preferable to bars even if they are fast food places. If a community is able to have a late-night establishment open, this is usually an indicator of a good area, since, in a bad area, these types of places wouldn't stay open at night because of crime, local residents being afraid to go there at night, and other issues. You are wanting to find places like this because in the event of an attack on your home, or near your home, you can gather your family and proceed to a safe public place, or another known place you can tell your family to go to in case of an incident at the residence—similar to an emergency rally point, and from there, call for help. Because of the possibility of bad media exposure as a result of a public killing or injury to bystanders, hurting locals may deter the threat but that is not always the case. What do you perceive the attitude of the entire neighborhood toward any terrorist movements, criminals, gangs, and toward foreigners in general, especially the United States? You can check this by looking at graffiti that may be around the area, articles in local newspapers, attitude toward you as you are looking around, etc. It is important to try to determine the neighborhood attitude since it can possibly cause issues for you with your neighbors providing intelligence to the threat about you and maybe even participating in an attack. The reverse is also true; your neighbors might end up helping you, informing about people asking about you, or at least not providing any intelligence to the threat and calling for assistance in case you are attacked. During your drive through and study of the local areas around your residence, do you notice anything else that might affect the safety of your home and family, anything that stands out to you as being suspicious or out of place. Remember, this is based upon observation and perception, so you might want to take someone you trust who has lived in that area for a while so they can also give you their comments and perceptions.

LAYERED DEFENSE

A layered defense is recommended for the physical security of your residence. Concentric circles around your house will present different layers of barriers or defenses that a threat has to get through to conduct an attack. You need to understand that there are very few impregnable security systems. The layered defense is designed to give you warning and to delay the threat, providing time for you to react when an attack is underway; more importantly, it may motivate the terrorists to attack a less security-conscious target or softer target. This layered defense deals with the actual physical security of your residence, what things you use, build, etc., that will increase the physical security of the area and building. A big part of physical security that is forgotten by many is to information-proof your home against the threat's ability to conduct surveillance of you, your family, and any staff or vendors; the less they can find out about you, your residence, and your routines, the harder it will be for them to plan an attack.

Information

First, we want to information-proof the home and make it extremely difficult or impossible for the threat to gather any information about you or your routines. Information proofing a residence just means you are trying to protect your home for outside observation, which is conducted by hostile elements. You need to make sure that the body of your mail box is inside your fence line, so you don't have to exit the property to get it. It should also be away from the drive way and any pedestrian gates; if possible, it should be a locking box with a slot that only takes letters. Any communications lines should have their junction box for your residence inside the fence line to prevent tampering, and you should have an unrestricted view of it from the pole or ground terminal where it originates. All of the trash from the home stays inside the fence, where it can be protected, until it is picked up by your trash man and disposed of. Remember to shred all paper. You must keep in mind that the more information they can find out about you, the easier it is to find a pattern they can exploit to get to you. It doesn't matter if it is a servant taking a note, a child throwing away a calendar, etc. You need to deny them as much information as possible. You also need to ensure that you password protect all your wireless routers and other electronic items that can be hacked or exploited.

OUTER LAYER

The outer layer is that area from the physical walls of the residence to the outer perimeter wall itself; this is the layer that will help limit observation and intelligence gathering, physically restrict hostile movement against you, give you early warning to protect yourself, and will slow the attack down so that you can put your emergency plan of action into effect. The outer layer should consist of but is not limited to the following:

High walls or fences should be placed so they will limit the view of the residence and grounds; this will hopefully prevent the threat from direct observation of your home activities, routines, and any other information they may try to obtain such as photos of your family, servants, visitors, vehicles and any inner security measures you have in place. The walls and fences you have in place may also be able to prevent the terrorists from performing a drive-by attack on the residence since they will not have a clearly defined target to aim at. There are many ways to build walls and fences around a residence: solid walls that act as a physical and visual barrier to the grounds, but these types of walls do not allow anyone to see in. This could include the police and security forces, who might not be aware of a crisis situation taking place at your residence if they do not have a clear view of your house, buildings, or the grounds. You can consider constructing a wall that is solid at the base with a fence for the rest, and you can also consider placing barbed wire or broken glass on top of your walls or fences (if local laws allow) to deter intruders from attempting to climb over. You need to ensure that any items such as tree branches, poles, and trash cans or other items found outside your fence line are placed or removed from the area so that they cannot be used as a tool to gain access to your residence grounds and help in bypassing the wall or fence. Any breaks in the fence or wall such as vehicle and pedestrian gates should be sturdy, in good repair, should have limited visibility into the grounds, be closed, and locked when not in use. You should always have more than one gate, and they should be situated in different areas around the perimeter to offer alternative ways out of the compound in case of an incident.

You need to look at the placement of trees and shrubs inside the fence line and outside; tall trees and shrubs serve as a screen to anyone trying to observe into the grounds or can work as a climbing aid and allow people to bypass the walls or fences. They can be used as entry points onto your ground or into your residence; they can also be used to hide attackers or explosive devices near gates or other points of entry. So, inside the fence line on the grounds, all shrubbery near the home that could conceal a threat should be trimmed down and cut so it is at least 3 feet from the wall of the house or should be removed. You should also trim any shrubbery and trees on the outside perimeter near the walls, fences, and gates; once again, it should be at least 3 feet from the wall, cut down so it will be difficult for someone to use it as cover. To enhance your ability to see people or objects that may be trying to hide in these areas, you need to make sure there is a good contrast in color between the bushes, trees, etc., and the wall: paint the walls white or another bright color, so any shadows or outlines will stand out that much more. For improving night time detection, along the base of the wall or fence, and around the residence, low-level lights should be placed at the base of the wall with the light shining out through the shrubbery, trees, or bushes so that anyone hiding or anything placed in them will be outlined.

Having a dog or dogs: it does not matter whether the dog in the outer layer is big, timid, or small and viscous as long as it is loud. A dog is just an early warning device, and although a trained guard dog might cause fear and hesitation in many untrained intruders or amateur criminals, even a trained animal will pose little or no problem to a determined professional who knows he has to deal with the threat. Remember to get a dog that barks and is loud and use it primarily as a four-legged alarm system.

Warning signs should be used on your perimeter wall, fence, gates, and house; this sign should give warning of some of your active security measures but not all such as advertising the presence of a dog or an alarm system; this type of advertising may cause the threat to choose another target, but you must remember they just won't read the sign. They will want to ensure these measures are in place, so test the alarms every so often and let the dog or dogs be seen or at least heard. You also need to find out the local requirements for posting these signs and ensure they are posted in the local language. If there is a low literacy rate in the area you live, you can also post signs in the local language plus use drawings to specify the dangers.

You need to have outside security cameras that are visible to go along with any of the signs you place on the perimeter fencing. They will be a further deterrent to anyone with hostile intentions. You can even purchase fake cameras from different stores or retail outlets that rotate and have red lights that run off of batteries, which is fine since the threat will have no way of knowing if the cameras work or not and will have to work off the assumption that they do. REMEMBER they only know what they can see, and when they can see it, it becomes a visible deterrent. Not all cameras or other security measures need to be visible; remember, a visible security measure is a deterrent, but the threat can also come up with a plan to neutralize it. Some security needs to be visible and some needs to be hidden to give you a good comprehensive security system. Another technique with outside cameras is not placing them all inside your perimeter looking out, because this can limit your view of the area and what is taking place outside your fence line. Place a few on the outside looking toward your fence line and house, such as across the street on a pole or in a tree. They should be hidden from observation. These cameras will give you a great view of the exterior of your walls, the street outside your residence, and the areas around your gates. This way, you can see any vehicles parked there, people lingering along the wall or gate area, people placing things by the gates, and any other suspicious activity, and few people check outside the target property area for cameras to try to avoid, since they are focused on the property itself, its fence, and its security.

EXTERIOR LIGHTING

You should have lighting around the outside of your residence and along the walls, fences, and shrubbery; some people consider continuous lighting the best way to accomplish this. Continuous lighting is basically as soon as it gets dark, turning on the outside lights illuminating a given area during the hours of darkness. Your security lighting should be designed to expose low-contrast targets that may be visible for only a few seconds, so any areas with dark backgrounds will require more light than those areas with lighter backgrounds. This type of lighting allows you to see, but you have to be physically watching somehow to determine whether anyone is moving around outside. It can also create shadows where a threat could hide. You must make sure that your lighting overlaps; this will also ensure coverage of all areas in case a light goes out and prevents your perimeter from having an unlit area.

You can also set up your lights so that they provide protection from visual observation into your zone of protection; this is called glare protection; you set your lights up in such a way that they are positioned slightly inside the perimeter, usually facing to project against the fence or upward out over the fence or wall. This makes it extremely difficult to see through the fence; you can also place the lights so they are pointing out over the wall; this also makes it difficult for the threat to see or take photos through the glare and into your zone of protection.

The use of controlled lighting is another option you have. This is when the light width can be controlled so that those areas outside the zone of protection are not illuminated. The major drawback with this type of lighting is that it may silhouette the guard force or others, allowing the threat to notice things like routines, numbers, etc. This type of lighting is usually mounted high so that it shines downward and overlaps other lighting.

Other options you can use are lights that come on automatically such as those with photoelectric cells that come on at dusk. Or, you can get lights that are motion activated and come on when they sense movement in their detection field. I prefer a mix of motion with fixed lighting to have overlapping coverage. I use low illumination lamps for the continuous lighting, with high illumination lamps for the motion lighting; this allows a smaller guard force and will direct the attention of the security force to an area where motion is detected by increasing the illumination in that area. A good mix and combination of lighting will provide the best coverage, but remember any type of outside lighting will be a major deterrent to the threat.

Night Watchmen/Roving Patrol

If your housing area or apartment has a current night watchman or roving patrol, you should conduct security checks and news media checks on the company or individuals before hiring them. If you are moving into an area that already has them, you should still run a check on them. Do not assume that, just because they are in place, they have no connection to the threat or criminal organizations—or are a competent or reputable company. If you feel one is needed, you should talk to other homeowners in the area to discuss the group hiring of a guard service to watch the area.

The host nation and local law enforcement are usually helpful in arranging for private guards, recommending companies, etc. When you are looking at and considering these different options, you need to remember where you are, because although these are recommended guards, they probably have few standards and little training, dedication, and are generally not competent by U.S. standards. Just the presence of a security patrol/guards acts as a visible deterrent to the threat, because even if the threat knows they are incompetent and can easily be defeated, it will still give you an early warning like the barking dog. You should not, however, use them as your primary means of defense, ignoring other protective measures.

Once the decision is made to use guards, either just a few you employ directly or a company to handle security, there are some things you need to ensure happens to increase their effectiveness in protecting you. You need to make sure to avoid 12-hour shifts for the guards, even if they have breaks. Many companies try to push this as the most efficient way to use guards. But it is just one of the cheapest ways and provides no benefit to your security since past experience shows us that watch tours in excess of eight hours will degrade effectiveness of the guards—especially when the guards are working another job or are moonlighting law enforcement. Everyone needs time to rest and recuperate; don't let the company talk you into believing this is a good idea. You need to check on the guard's training and experience since they are there for your protection and they need to be briefed and trained on how to respond/react to emergencies. There should be a set of SOPs for the guard force to follow, ensuring everyone will follow the same agenda. You also need to make sure they have successfully completed some type of protection training program before allowing them to work. There should also be continuation and some type of refresher training as well as drills.

When you have an armed guard force, you should ensure that strict compliance with local laws is met. More than likely, if any laws are broken, you will be held responsible. If they do have weapons, you need to check and make sure that the guards have been trained in the use of their assigned arms and in weapons safety, especially around you and your family. The guards should all show a professional attitude and demeanor around your family and when dealing with the public. How they interact will reflect on you, especially in social and business areas. One of the areas that local guards need to be warned about is flashing weapons in an unprofessional manner, to bully or intimidate people. If you also use roving patrols around the residence grounds and around the outside of the perimeter such as a neighborhood watch, you should also research and check to find out what their response times are at different hours of the day and night and to ensure roving patrols are not establishing patterns and routines. IF YOUR GUARD FORCE HAS A PATTERN OR ROUTINE, THEN YOU HAVE A PATTERN OR ROUTINE THAT CAN BE EXPLOITED BY THE THREAT!

INNER LAYER

The inner layer of protection is that area inside the residence and those measures that are done to the interior of the residence itself, including all openings such as doors and windows. This inner layer should consist of the following:

First, you have to look at each opening (doors and windows) and consider its overall strength and security as an individual item; you have to consider the strength of each door and each window both when it is opened and when it is shut and locked. A solid door is needed to increase your security at these entry points; it can be a steel door, solid hardwood door, or a wood door with a steel core. It should have no windows in it, not even iced or glossed over since that will still let the person outside know when someone is in front of the door.

You also need to change the existing locks in your new residence, even if the person you are buying it from says that you have the only available keys. He has no way of knowing if every person that has lived or worked at that place made spare keys for the family, etc. Also, many new homes have what are called builders or contractor locks which have a master key and are very easy to bypass. So, change the locks put in a good security locks. Number the keys and keep a log of who has what key.

Determine how strong each of the locks and latches are. Each entry door should as a minimum have one dead bolt lock with a minimum of a 1-inch throw into the doorjamb, and this will prevent a pry bar being used to pry the door away from the doorjamb popping the dead bolt out. You should also consider having a push-button lock system on the doorknob itself; this will allow you to activate the lock quickly if an emergency should occur, instead of having to turn to lock or use a key. You should install a locking dead bolt on the inside of each door that can only be accessed from the inside. This gives you an added security by allowing you to secure your door from the inside in such a way that it cannot be defeated from the outside.

Windows are also entry points and should be properly secured. Usually, they are the weakest link in someone's home security plan. Your windows, like your doors, need locks. Most people confuse the latch that comes with the window with a lock, but it is not. There are many ways to bypass a latch. There should be a lock or a form of deadbolt that will allow the window to be locked in place so it cannot be used. You should consider tinting to limit visibility into the residence and possibly adding a layer of Mylar film coating to all window surfaces; this gives added protection from bullets being fired through it, or people trying to break the window, but also from shrapnel and other secondary blast effects from bombs or other explosives.

The next thing you need to do when looking at the entry points into the residence is to evaluate the effort required to force entry. So, you need to consider the following: All entry points into the residence should be equipped with heavy-duty hinges, if it is required, such as a door. These hinges should have at least four attachment points to the door frame, and the hinge pin needs to be on the inside so it is protected from being removed from the outside. All the entry point frames which are around your doors and windows should be as strong as possible. Many people never fortify or harden the framing around an entry point after they complete an upgrade on the doors or windows. But, you should know a new solid door with the best security lock available will offer no protection if the threat can kick the door down because of a weak frame. You also need to ensure that the correct mounting hardware for doors, windows, locks, and hinges is used; many installers or contractors use the cheapest materials necessary because they buy in bulk and these items will do the job of holding it in. But, that doesn't mean it is secure. You need to choose the strongest material available since it's your life that depends on it, not the installers! Whenever you are looking at mounting hardware, the screws for locks and hinges should enter into the framework at a minimum of 1 inch; ideally, they should enter to a depth of 3 inches. If you use window air conditioners, they should be reinforced in such a way so that they cannot be removed, thus allowing someone to gain entry through the openings. You can do this by building a cage around one, a reinforced frame, etc. NOTE: Attached garages, garage doors, garage windows, and the entry way from the garage into the house; these doors are usually overlooked when it comes to doing a security evaluation but they can be easiest way for a threat to gain entrance into a residence. You need to look at these doors the same as all the others; the entry way into the house from the garage needs to be as strong as the door at the front of the house; you should consider alarms for the garage and doors and a way to turn off your garage vehicle door when you are home, so it cannot be opened. Remember, once they get inside your garage, they can take as much time as necessary to do what they want since they are out of sight, DO NOT FORGET THIS AREA.

If you want to add bars and/or grills to your windows or doors, then they need to be installed correctly or they will not do the job. When you plan on installing bars and grills, you need to ensure the mounting hardware is not accessible or at least not easily accessible from the outside. No entrance should be barred in such a way that it cannot be used as an exit in case of an emergency, so the bars or grills should be placed on hinges so that they can swing out. To mount them for the most security, the hinges should be inside the bars, so that when closed, the two sides of the hinge are on top of each other and not accessible from the outside. You should use bolts instead of screws with the nuts placed inside of the house. The closing latching devices for the grill should be inside the house, and it should be locked in such a way that it can be opened quickly from the inside but cannot be manipulated from the outside. Don't forget when mounting these types of devices that limit movement that you have to make provisions to allow quick exit during emergencies. This includes making sure everyone in the household, including children and servants who might need to use these exits, know how to unlock them to get out. You want to ensure they are included in any alarm system you put in, or you have another way to ensure the grills or bars are always closed and locked. NOTE: Grills, screens, and other security devices that are not used on a daily or weekly basis should have tamper seals on them. This will let you know if someone has used that entrance/exit at some point since it was sealed.

Drapes and blinds are an important part of information proofing your residence and for providing another level of physical security. They will limit visibility into your residence if they are used, and they offer protection from fragmentation and other secondary blast effects during an explosion. The heavier the drapes and blinds, the more protection they give. You can also buy fire-retardant drapes, or sometimes they can be treated with chemicals to make them fire-retardant, and this will add more protection. In some countries such as Germany or in some areas such as Florida, homes are constructed with built-in shutters which are usually made of steel or other strong materials. These are placed at openings, and they usually have the ability to be locked. This allows you the option of keeping them secured. You can have such shutters installed in any residence as a security precaution. You need to remember that while some shutters can be electrically operated, you must have a battery backup power supply for each one or you have to be able to operate them manually if necessary.

Interior lighting is just as important, if not more important, than exterior lighting. How you use lights in your house can inform someone watching what you are doing and what routines and patterns you have for different activities. The proper use of interior lighting cannot be overemphasized both for denying information to the threat and for increasing your security while providing a visible deterrent for any possible personnel with hostile intentions.

Just like your exterior lighting, the lights you set up as security lighting inside the residence should be designed to expose low-contrast targets, especially around entry points where they may only be visible for a few seconds when entering. Any walls, drapes, brick areas that are dark will require more light than those areas or entry points that have a lighter background. In relation to the entry points to the residence, how easy they are to access, can their physical security features be defeated or bypassed, etc., will help you determine the required security lighting levels for each one. They might not all be the same, and any lighting you use needs to be installed, so that it overlaps in case of the loss of one light, lamp, bulb—that this will not leave an area totally in the dark. How we use lights in our house tells those who might be outside observing what we are doing and where we are. We turn off lights when we go to bed. We turn them on when we get up and move from room to room. Since most of us don't like to sit in a dark room, they know where we are sitting, reading, even watching TV since the TV itself creates a flickering light pattern. They can watch your progress through the house, if you need to turn on lights to answer the door or phone in the middle of the night, etc. So, what needs to be done is have regular room lighting used for illumination that can be used for normal activities and have security lighting set up with timers. Have some lights on at all times, usually in front of the window, making it more difficult to see clearly into a room. These lights should be spaced around the house so that anyone observing from outside will not know which room you are in or whether you are up or asleep. This should make it very difficult for anyone to pinpoint what room you are in during the hours of darkness. For areas such as hallways and in all your rooms, you should have small plug-in motion-activated lights. They are inexpensive and can be purchased online or at many retail stores; these will alert you when someone is in a room you thought was empty or if someone is walking down a hallway.

You should strongly consider an alarm system for doors, windows, and other possible entry points into the house and motion alarms that cover the hallways. A good effective security system allows you to enter or leave from all primary entrances while keeping them monitored or secure. Any alarm system you get needs to be equipped with an emergency panic button; in some systems, there is a portable panic button that you can carry with you at all times. All the systems enunciators such as external horns, sirens, and bells need to be loud enough to get people's attention and alert the neighbors. You should also consider mounting a bright flashing light on the house or on the gate or fence so that it can be easily observed by law enforcement or emergency personnel who are responding to the alarm, since in an urban environment, or another type of clustered living area, the alarm's noise might be difficult to pinpoint the exact location of the residence. You should have audio and visual indicators to wake up the people inside the residence; your alarm system should be monitored by a police station or private security enterprise so they can respond more quickly, instead of waiting for you or a neighbor to call which might not happen. If you cannot do this or there is no way to have the system monitored, then the alarm enunciators and lights are that much more important, especially to those inside.

The only alarm that must be monitored by security or law enforcement personnel is the duress alarm system, which must be connected to a police station or a private security station. When using an alarm system that is monitored, you must ensure that it is monitored locally to get better response times and to ensure continuity of service. Some alarm companies monitor everything from one central state or location and do call ups for local security personnel or law enforcement, this is fine as long as the phones are working, no bad weather, etc., but a trustworthy local company will know the situation in the local area and have a faster response time. To protect your system against tampering or loss of power, check the alarm system periodically. This should also be done so that any surveillance watching the residence will know for sure you have an alarm and not just the signs saying so. You also need to have a battery backup in place. This will provide an electrical source in the event of a power failure, and a wireless transmitter as a backup to the landline system will ensure it cannot be cut or tampered with. Don't forget to post signs around the outside of the fence that you have an alarm also. NOTE: Alarms only work if they are used, turned on, etc. Many people pay big money to get an alarm system and then they never use it because it is inconvenient or because they feel it is a waste of time or feel it should only be used at night. There was a series of robberies in Florida several years ago where the robber just walked in the front door of houses and took what she wanted; 90 percent of the residences had alarms, but she said none were turned on. If you are going to have an alarm system, it needs to be used all the time ALL DAY; it needs to be TURNED ON. Once you develop this habit, it will no longer be inconvenient for you.

Once again, the use of a dog or dogs on the inside is a good idea and can work in conjunction with the dog or dogs on the outside. The inside dogs are there to warn intruders, that someone in the house might be awake, and they will be warned because the dog is barking and making noise. This acts as one of those visible deterrents and an inside dog will serve as an alarm for the residents. Usually, with dogs of this type, you have a smaller dog inside, but inside or outside does not matter as long as it makes noise; once an outside dog starts barking, this usually warns the inside dog who runs to the window or door to start barking also. Since dogs have better hearing even if you don't have an outside dog, your inside one will hear more and react to those sounds by investigating and then barking or by going to you and barking. Either way the threat now does not know if you are awake and ready for him.

The use of closed-circuit television (CCTV) on the inside is just as important as on the outside; if they are available, by all means use them. You can control the cameras and the recordings, and at least, some of them should be visible especially at the primary entry points into the residence; that way, if someone is using a ruse to try to gain information about the interior of the house, they will see the camera while at the entry point. If you do not want real CCTV cameras, you should consider using dummy CCTV cameras on the inside, placed in the same way. Remember, this act as a visual deterrent also. And do not forget to post signs that you have cameras in use.

You need to put in and use optical viewers and intercoms for the primary entry points (doors). The use of optical viewers and intercoms will allow you to identify who is outside your door without opening it and exposing yourself directly to the possible threat. There are several doorbells available now with cameras and audio, so you can see and talk to whoever is at your door from any location. You should use wide-angle optical viewers (peepholes); there are several types available, some with a 3-inch width viewing lens so you can stand back and see who is there; you don't have to be right on the door to see out. This brings up another point; you need to exercise care when using an optical viewer, because when your eye is placed close to the viewer to look out, it blocks the light so the person on the outside knows someone is right there on the other side of the door. The attacker may decide, since he knows your location, to start shooting through the door (or detonate an explosive), injuring or killing you, a servant, or a family member. So, instead of standing in front of the door when answering, you should approach the door from the side if possible—or at least off center. Then, you can raise a book in front of the viewer and ask who is at the door to see how they react to the light in the viewer going dark. Or, you can place a piece of electrical tape or other movable cloth that will block the light through the viewer all the time; that way, it will always look dark and the person on the outside will see a change on his side. You can also offset these optical viewers; nothing says they have to be in the door. You can place one there so that is where a person at the door focuses his attention, but you can also place another one to the side of the door for viewing, with something to partially conceal it. You can even place a small video camera outside or mount it in the door with a wide-angle lens, like a viewer, so that you can view who is at the door on a monitor.

Using intercom systems is very similar to viewers and you need to exercise the same precautions, since most people who have intercoms mount them right next to the door. Sometimes, in the door, the inside unit is directly behind it, so when you are talking, they basically know you are behind that flimsy plastic face plate, which can easily be shot through. So, when installing an intercom system, you need to run the intercom wires so that the speaker boxes are offset from each other on the right or left side of the door or away from it on a wall somewhere. This way, if the threat shoots through the intercom box on his side of the doorway, he won't hit you. You could also install a wireless system, so you could place your inside speaker anywhere in the house or even have it as a portable unit you could carry with you.

Just like having fire escape routes in place for your family, you need to have evasion and escape (E&E) routes out of your residence. You will need to establish a primary and an alternate E&E route out of the residence leading to a pre-selected family gathering point or a safe rally point.

You need to rehearse going through your E&E routes during both daytime and nighttime activities, and if you have children, they need to know how to do this themselves if they are old enough and can get around sufficiently on their own. If you have servants, nannies, etc., they also need to know these plans and rehearse them since they may be the only people with your children or spouse. When developing your plan, you need to make plans for secure ways to exit from the second and higher floors; to do this, you might need portable ladders and ropes, and all family members should rehearse using them. This includes any staff. They also will need to know how to open windows, security grills and bars, and any gates or doors to the rally point. You will also need to have a plan for what happens once you are at the rally point and the rehearse actions that need to be taken once you reach the rally point. You might have a cell phone stashed there or a charger, have list of numbers to call, account for everyone, etc.

Safe havens or safe rooms, sometimes called a panic room, are areas in your residence that you can go to in the event of any attack. They are protected, secure areas with enough supplies to last so you can wait until security or law enforcement personnel arrive to neutralize the threat and retrieve you. If you have the ability, you should establish a safe haven/safe room on every floor. These rooms should not be easily accessible from the outside at all. There should be no windows, or doors—nothing that leads to the outside of the residence. These designated safe havens can be rooms that are used for other things and are modified to function as a safe haven in an emergency. They need to have more than one entrance and exit, and the doors must be made as strong as possible. and it needs to have sturdy locking system, using a door length dead bolt that can be put in place when they are used. Since you will need this room in an emergency, it will mean a threat has gained entrance into your residence to do you harm. They will probably attempt to shoot through doors or walls to kill you if they cannot capture you, so you will need to use armor or sandbags in the event of a siege. You can put armor on the walls of these rooms, or you can hang Kevlar blankets. The door itself needs to be locked and barred in such a way that it cannot be breached by destroying the locking system or mounting system. You can make a small area inside this room out of sandbags, so you can get in there in case they start shooting. Or, you can put sandbags along the walls and angled in front of the door so that it will still open to allow you entrance while still protecting the room. Sandbags add a lot of weight to a structure, so ensure that the floors can take the weight. You can redo the walls of the room with half-inch plywood underneath the dry wall and then, in the wall space between the studs, fill that with sandbags or shredded rubber. If you only have the resources to do minimal armoring of the rooms, ensure that each room has personnel protective gear, bullet proof vests, helmets, and eye protection so that you can put this on when entering, for an extra layer of protection. You also need to ensure that each safe haven is stocked with emergency items such as water, food, flashlights, candles, fire extinguishers, blankets, first aid supplies, specifically required medicines, weapons, and ammunition which should be stored in secure containers. Do not put anything explosive in there as a stray round could hit something like an oxygen bottle and cause an explosion. You need to have a communication system that is reliable under all conditions and is able to contact security forces or contact the police. You should also have the means to activate any exterior alarms from inside these rooms, by placing a duress alarm or panic button in each one. During any attack on the residence, there is the chance of fire either unintentional or intentional to try and smoke you out. You need to make sure fire extinguishers and ventilation systems are in place. Remember, this is a temporary safe haven for you, so you only need to design it to last as long as it takes emergency services, security, or law enforcement to arrive—2 hours at the most. You also need to come up with a safe word or verification word or phrase so you know that it is the real security responders outside and not the threat attempting a ruse.

Your residence needs to have some means of reliable communication and, ideally, will have several. On each handset for the phones, you should have the emergency telephone numbers of police, fire department, and rescue services. If you have them on speed dial, you should still have the numbers written out with their speed dial number. If you or your family does not speak the local language, you should write out key phrases in the language of the host country, to ask for assistance. For any phone you have, you need to understand that the landline could possibly be tapped by terrorists, or for cordless and cell phones, they could be listening in with a scanner, so be careful of the type of information you pass. As part of your emergency SOP, you need to have a phone available away from the residence. So, you need to locate a public phone or a neighbor's phone near the house, and then you let your domestic household and family members know of its location for emergency use. You also need to consider recording all incoming phone calls to help you keep a record of any calls that are suspicious. If you have radios in your home in order to contact security forces, law enforcement, etc., then each member of the household to include children and servants or other domestic help must know how to turn it on, what frequencies if it is not preset, and any call signs and code words. Trusting servants or domestic help is a determination only you can make. In many instances, they will be spending lots of time with your children if you have any. So, decide whether to trust servants or guards with the location of the radio, frequencies, call signs, and codes. All of the children should be taught to use any radios, but be sure to inform the people on the receiving end of the radio that children may use it because kids are often ignored in serious incidents; any possible contact with security forces could be considered a prank, delaying the reaction time of the security force. In building your emergency contact system, it should be developed so that when you use it/you are talking directly to someone who can get you help to your location as quickly as possible should you come under attack. Having a system that contacts someone, who contacts someone else, who then initiates the security response will waste time in an emergency. So, any system you select needs to allow direct contact with the response force, your office—to someone who can initiate an emergency response—or your neighbors who are closest and can provide immediate assistance. Any communications plan you set up should have primary, alternate, and contingency means of communications. Your primary system should consist of an alarm system or panic button, a cell phone with the required numbers on speed dial; an alternate system would be landline telephone, radio, or even computer; and the contingency will be things such as a loud horn, audio alarms, etc. You might also have or want a covert system if you are in your safe room or panic room, so as not to scare off the threat so security or law enforcement can deal with the threat right there. If you do come under attack, you should activate as many systems as possible to ensure your call for help gets out to those intended to receive it. You can never call for help too many ways. You also need to actually test your communication system frequently, not just you but anyone intended to use it. This will give those with the least familiarity with the equipment a chance to practice with it.

So, you might have the chance to own weapons and keep them in the house; if so, you need to make sure you know and understand all the laws surrounding the types of weapons you have before you get there. Remember to check into the non-lethal weapons status; some countries regulate pepper spray and stun guns. Ensuring you are following the local laws is especially important if you have firearms in a personal residence. If guns are kept inside your residence, you need to ensure that local laws governing their use are followed, and the weapons must be legally registered. This includes weapons used by private security companies or guards you employ, since you will probably be held responsible if they break the law. If you feel the need is sufficient that you need firearms or other weapons, then they should be loaded and stored in a secure place that is easy for you or any others who you want to have access to them to get to. They need to be accessible to those who need them without endangering children and those untrained in their use. If you cannot keep a gun in the house because of local laws or personal reasons, consider using stun guns, mace, baseball bats, other clubs, etc. Whatever weapons are kept in the residence, there is always a risk of an accident, so safety procedures still have to be employed for the user's safety. You also need to make sure the chosen weapons systems are looked at on an annual basis and have the required maintenance done on them to keep them working properly. You need to set aside time for anyone who will be using the weapons to train with them; this training needs to be more involved than just reading the instructions. If you are not proficient in the use of particular weapon you are allowed to keep at your residence, then train with someone who is. Find out before you deploy and attend a school; there are many available, and after you have received hands-on training, there are many books and videos that can also demonstrate the proper techniques in detail. However, you still need to do as much hands-on training as possible, not only to make you and others who may use those weapons more confidant, but if any threat surveillance sees you and others practicing with weapons, they will move you to the hard target category. You also need to make sure that the guard force or security personnel you use train with the weapons they have, and if they have firearms, they have them loaded; it does no good if they have these weapons to protect you and they are not loaded or they cannot get them to function when they are needed.

But the MOST IMPORTANT is having the PROPER MINDSET: which is, if you feel threatened enough to pull a weapon out for protection, YOU NEED TO USE IT! If you are pulling it out to intimidate someone, you are in the wrong, especially in your residence. If you are not willing to use the weapon to protect yourself or your family, then the weapon will now become a danger to you, since they can now take it away and use it on YOU. There are many stories in the news of people having a weapon to defend themselves or in the case of pulling a weapon to defend themselves, and they hesitate or don't use it. And the weapons is then taken away and used on them by the threat. If you are not willing to use the weapon you pull, doesn't matter what, stun gun, pepper spray, ball bat, firearm. then do not even pick it up, or let the threat know it is there. DO NOT BECOME A STATISTIC WITH YOUR OWN WEAPON!

BEHAVIORAL ASPECTS OF THE FAMILY

You need to make sure you educate and train all your family members in personal security, since you will not be with them all the time. They should have situational awareness, local cultural education, and training in personal security just as you do. You need to make sure they understand why IPM is important—for you to try and cultivate an interest in IPM and attract participation from all family members in the overall security effort, while enforcing the need to practice this for their own personnel security also. For planning purposes, there are behavioral aspects concerning family members that you should take into account, to help the overall security profile and security plan for the family.

There is a need to know where family members are at all times. This isn't to micromanage their day, but it is necessary in case of an incident or the threat of an attack, and not necessarily at the residence. If you know, for example, that your spouse is going shopping and which store, if there is an attack in the city at a store, you will be in a better frame of mind if you know it was not the store your spouse uses. This is also the same with children; if there is an attack at a school, mall, movie theater, if you know where they are and it is not at the incident site, this will allow you to deal with the situation and contact them and let them know what happened so they can raise their security awareness level. You might even send security to make sure they get home okay, but you can't do any of this if you don't know where they are. And, it will increase your fear, anxiety, which will hamper your ability to deal with an emergency situation if you don't know. With the advances in technology, this can be accomplished by tracking them through their cell phone or other electronic means so it does not become inconvenient for them to participate. Always set this up when possible.

Just like you during your day, it is also vitally important that family members not establish any routines or patterns either. You need to ensure this and explain the reason why; if your family develops a family pattern, then you are now PREDICTABLE. This happens because people get comfortable doing certain things, especially family things such as attending church services at the same time and place each week. Many times, parents establish specific times and locations for dropping off and picking up their children for school or extracurricular activities, and this extends to provided services such as school bus or shuttle services which are traditionally routine in nature since they have certain routes, locations, and times they have to be.

You need to brief all family members on your IPM plans; you should sit down at least once a week and go over them. Everyone in the family needs to thoroughly understand their role and responsibilities in the security plan. Is it possible for a threat, either criminal or terrorists, to get to you through your family? Of course, it is. Very few people could stand being coerced if a family member was kidnapped and threatened, and that is why everyone needs to practice good IPM and understand why it is important and know the threat against them.

SERVANTS

If you are someone who needs to have domestic help, and in many cases, people living overseas do by employing gardeners, cooks, drivers, guards, cleaning people, nannies, etc. You must ensure these servants are trustworthy and then you need to make sure they are trained in personal security measures since once they are at the residence, they need to be incorporated into the security plan.

You need to check on any servants who work at your residence and make sure they have had background checks run by the company, local law enforcement, and the security office at the embassy (if they will do it); no one should be hired unless they have undergone this background check and verification. Do not assume that because these people worked for the person you replaced that he did a check, or that just because they are working there when you arrive, they have been checked already. If so, get a copy and have everyone rechecked, circumstances could have changed since their last check which could prove to be a security risk to you.

The servants you have working for you in the residence can be either a vulnerability to be exploited by the threat or that can be an asset who contributes to the security profile of the residence and the people who live there. When you have them checked out and verified if you consider them trustworthy, you can incorporate them into the security plan of the residence for the time they will be there, some may only work days, or certain days of the week, while others may live there, so regardless of the time they spend on site, with the proper training and motivation, they can be a positive aspect of security.

You need to have a procedure for visitor control at your residence. Everyone should know what to do to include family and servants, but you need to make sure that you brief your servants thoroughly on this subject and that they understand what you want done. Since it is more than likely that a servant will answer the door during the day, if you have family members at home, you should have the servant rather than any family members answer the door. Help the family maintain a low profile. You should instruct servants not to admit any strangers, poll takers, repairmen, or police officers without getting specific approval from you or your spouse. The door should not be opened or unlocked until the visitors have been properly identified and authenticated as having business there. You should have the visitor slide an identification card through the mail slot in the door or slide it underneath the door or get identification data through the intercom. Check the number given by the visitor against his company or business number in the phone book and then call the visitor's office using the number obtained from a telephone directory or another verifiable source. Do not use the one he gave you or that is on his card (he could have another bad guy on the other end to vouch for him). When it has been determined the visit is legitimate by you, and he is vouched for by his office, he can be allowed in. The visitor should be escorted at all times and just taken to those areas in the house where the business is to be conducted; he does not need to see any other areas of the residence; the visitor should not mind the inconvenience of being verified or of being escorted. If you have a preplanned visit expected, then you need to brief servants as to the expected time of arrival and purpose of visit so that only the proper parties are admitted. You should also make sure they know where the visitor can go and what information they can give him. Controlling the information about your house, how it is laid out, where everything is, etc., is all part of INFORMATION PROOFING it against the threat, who will use any means, any ruse necessary to gain the information they need to plan a successful attack.

If the servants you have are from the area you are living in, they can provide in-depth knowledge as to what is unusual or suspicious that you will not otherwise notice because you don't have the history of living there. This type of information can be very helpful in stopping or identifying threat surveillance and other activities that might seem natural to you but is not right for that area. Because your servants will have this history of knowledge of the area, especially day-to-day activities and demeanor, you should instruct your servants to inform you of all suspicious or unusual activities. You can even give them a notebook and ask them to keep a daily log of such activities with an explanation of why they thought it was unusual; in some instances, you can even give them access to a camera so they can try to get pictures of the person or event, which will enhance your understanding of what took place, and increase your long-term knowledge of the operating environment in your living area.

How the telephone is answered is also important because it can confirm where you are or where you are not. Most servants are used to answering the telephone with the family name, but you need to train them not to. Instead, brief your servants against this procedure and tell them they should not give any information over the phone until the caller has been identified as someone known. How do they do this? Well, they can answer by just saying "Hello, May I help you," or with the phone number, when asked specific questions such as: is Mr. Smith there? Reply "He is unavailable can I take a message," by not saying NO or YES, she has not confirmed he is there or he is not there. This is the best way to respond to a question over the phone—as generically as possible and to give out no information on where someone is or isn't.

Remember, we already talked about why you should not have mail or packages delivered to your residence, so you need to explain this to your servants and instruct them not to accept any mail, especially packages, at home. You should have your mail sent through your company office, a local post office, or, if possible, through the embassy. The staff at these locations are trained to recognize suspicious packages and to deal with a possible bomb. If an unexpected package arrives, never accept it until it is opened. So, ask the deliverer to open the package at a safe distance from your residence, but at a point where you can still observe. If a package is just left, tell the servants not to move it, touch it, etc., and to call you immediately. People who know you should know you do not accept mail or packages at your residence, so you should not be receiving any.

All domestic help, servants that work at your residence need to know how to react in case of any incidents or emergencies, so you will need to instruct servants on the proper procedures for any in-house emergencies, such as a fire, an injury, or a terrorist/criminal attack. You should set up practice drills for each; they need to be taught to summon help using the residence communications system; this may mean for those who don't speak English that you have an English cheat sheet with key words written out for them; you need to make sure they cannot only take the necessary actions to protect themselves but your family as well. Remember, they may be the only person home with a family member during an incident.

SERVICE PERSONNEL (REPAIR PEOPLE)

You need to ensure that service or maintenance people that you call to your residence or are sent by a company have had a background check conducted on them and have been cleared. Plumbers, electricians, and general house maintenance personnel have a remarkable amount of freedom to work in a residence since you are not going to go into the crawl space with them or climb around in an attic. They will usually bring some type of work truck inside your secure area so they have access to tools and replacement parts, and they will have a toolbox or bag with them so they can do the work that is required of them. This would give the threat an opportunity to breach your security and conduct an attack, place explosive devices in your residence, or other devices such as smoke bombs to force you out. They could set up listening and other surveillance devices to help gather intelligence on you or they could set up ways to bypass your security and electricity, leaving you helpless. Have them checked and, if possible, always have them escorted, have someone check their work bags or toolbox and search them to ensure they only have what is necessary to complete their work. Do not allow them to have cell phones or other picture-taking devices with them inside your house and take them directly to the area where the work is, do not allow them to wander around your residence gaining intelligence. If possible always use the same company and only allow the same persons into your residence to work, anyone new or any strap hangers or extra personnel need to be checked also.

BEING ABSENT FROM THE RESIDENCE

Whenever you are going to be away from the residence for an extended period of time, you need to create the appearance of occupancy; if you have servants, this will not be a problem, but for those of us who do not, there are several ways to accomplish this.

- You can ask your neighbors to place garbage in your garbage can and make sure it is set out for pick up, just as it is done when you are there; this will prevent the disposal service from knowing you are not at home.
- If you do have mail delivered to your residence, arrange for someone to pick it up daily for; if you normally have mail in your box, leave some with the neighbors to mail for you. This will keep the postal employee from knowing you are not home. Remember having mail delivered to your residence is not a good security practice, nor is putting outgoing mail in an unsecured mail box; you should avoid this if possible.
- You need to set timers on lights, televisions, radios, and other noise-producing appliances to turn off and on at different times, to give appearance of being home. This light and noise should coincide with your normal living patterns; if you have a light in the kitchen on at night, you need to make sure you have one on when you leave; the noise producing devices are necessary because living in a house produces not only light but noise, phones ringing, music playing while reading, or watching the evening news on the television; you need to try to produce the same type of noises while you are away that you do when you are home.
- If you maintain your lawn yourself, you will have to find someone to do this maintenance and other services for you, so they will continue on a regular basis, just as if you were home; this includes watering the lawn at night if that's what you normally do.
- You should not discontinue newspaper delivery; if you have it, you should have a neighbor collect the papers daily. Having a newspaper delivered to your house can also be a dangerous practice; it can set up a pattern when you will leave the residence to retrieve it, and it gives a reason for someone to approach the

residence to collect money. You do not want to discontinue the service because that means the paper delivery person will know you are not at home.

- You should turn down the telephone ringer and unplug the telephone and answering machine; this way, they will not be able to tell if you are home or not because the machine will not pick up, or they will not hear the continuous ringing of the phone, with all the lights and living noises being made. So, they will not be sure if you are home or not. You should not discontinue phone service because this will let someone at the phone company know you are not home. NOTE: You should have your phone ringers turned down anyway, just like in a hotel room. If the threat is having trouble pinpointing what room you are in before an attack, they can call your house and listen for the phone to stop ringing; if you are like most people and only have one or two phones, they now have your location down to one or two rooms.
- You should inform the local police, area security guards, and your neighbors (if trustworthy); you should also let your work security office know that you will be away from your residence.
- If you are not taking your vehicle, you need to park in a safe and secure place, like in your garage; if you do not have a garage, you need to either park it in a secure area at work or at a friend's house. You can consider loaning the car to a friend or a neighbor, just be sure they practice good security measures also, so that it will prevent terrorists from planting a device on your vehicle while you are away. You should not use airport parking or other public parking venues where anyone can enter; this leaves your car vulnerable to the threat.
- Use your alarm systems. We discussed this before, but there is a big problem with using alarms, and this is most people DO NOT TURN THEM ON. Any alarm system you have for your home or vehicle will only work if it is turned on, so remember to arm the alarm system when leaving.

PROTECTION MEASURES IN THE OFFICE

Many people have a feeling of comfort and safety at their office or place of work, they feel that once there, they are out of danger for some reason, but you must not discount the office as a terrorist or criminal target. To the criminals and terrorists, especially in foreign countries, a company office symbolizes American or a foreign presence in the area, which automatically makes it symbolic and a potential target. In the past several years, there has been an increase in the number of U.S. facilities, companies, and embassies being targeted for attacks, and we should not forget about these same facilities on U.S. soil; they are still symbolic targets to some domestic terrorist organizations, foreign organizations operating inside the United States, so you must not relax your guard even when operating in the United States. In most facilities, regardless of their location, the overall security is probably someone else's responsibility such as a Security Manager or Security Director, but you and other employees are an important link in the security chain that protects the facility and the people working inside. Since you arrive and leave work to go to lunch, go home, etc., your actions and those of your fellow employees are unpredictable, so as you are moving through the neighborhood around the workplace, this gives you the chance to identify and report suspicious activities, vehicles, and personnel to your facilities security element and allow them to follow up and deal with it. Security in an office building is everyone's concern because, let's face it, if the building is attacked or bombed, you may become a victim.

There are things you need to do to increase the safety and security of those in your office, or the facility as a whole. You need to make sure that the interior of the office is arranged so that the occupants do not sit next to, directly in front of, or work in a direct line with the windows. This is because if there is an explosion outside such as a car bomb, the windows can shatter, sending glass and other fragmentation throughout the office with lethal force, doing possible fatal damage to those in direct line of the windows. To lessen this danger of glass fragmentation, you need to use heavy drapes and blinds in front of the windows, just as you do in your house. I know everyone likes to have a view outside when working, but you should try to keep the drapes and blinds closed whenever possible. If cubicles are used to divide the office up, you should place their walls so that they face the window. They can absorb fragmentation and will offer protection to personnel who are seated. You can also consider laminating the windows with plastic sheeting that darkens, tints, or mirrors the windows; this will restrict the view into the room and add extra strength to the windows. It will also limit the ability of gunmen and snipers to look into an office and pick out one specific victim to shoot or from picking random personnel as targets. NOTE: Security usually comes down to two things: MONEY AND CONVENIENCE. When you stop people from having a window view, it will upset people even though it raises their level of security.

One of the keys to security is to deny information to the threat; you do this through information proofing your home and you should do it for your office also. The best way to do this is to limit and control access, so you need to inform security if a visitor is expected outside your normal work hours, give name, reason for visit, etc. This information will let the guards know whether a visitor is supposed to be there and who to call; this protects you in several ways: it will give law enforcement investigators an approximate time, place, and a name should someone be taken or kidnapped from the office outside normal work hours. It also gives the same information if the attack takes place inside and a bomb is placed or someone is killed. NOTE: A good policy for security at any building is to make copies of the identification visitors and vendors use to gain access to the building and keep them on file, or take a digital photo with name and who they are visiting on file.

You should also not allow loiterers in or around your building, parking areas, parking garage, gate, etc. It may be necessary to post a guard as a deterrent and a show of force for the outside areas. Your security desk or position at the entrance to the facility should provide deterrence to anyone entering the facility as well. The security desk in the lobby or entrance should be positioned so that anyone entering the building must walk past it, and security personnel can see out to the front of the building. You should also consider having everyone, workers, vendors, visitors, sign in and out of the building; this will allow you to know who is inside and where they are located. This will give you a proper headcount of personnel in case of an emergency or evacuation; many businesses have started using access identification cards which people can use to enter or leave a building and the computer logs them in or out. If you have an office with a secretary, they should be trained in IPM and be security aware also; you should also install a buzzer so that in an emergency the secretary can summon security and alert the occupants of the building.

Receiving mails and packages at work can also be dangerous, so your office should have a mail room. Or, if not big enough for that, there should be people designated to receive all mail and packages for everyone in the office. Mail should all go to one room or area, and the people working there should have received training to handle incoming mail and packages and screen them for possible threats, especially bomb detection. This area should have a place it can set aside any suspicious packages or letters until law enforcement and explosive ordnance disposal (EOD) can be notified; this holding area should not be a smaller room, closet, or a safe; places like this increase the effectiveness of the explosive by tamping the explosive's pressure. A small area will also increase the amount of fragmentation caused by an explosion and limit the damage done to the building; once an object is identified, it should be carefully set in a large drum filled with sawdust or another type of device that will limit any destructive force of a bomb. Another reason you want mails and packages to go to one designated area or person is if a package appears on your desk and you have no idea what it is or who it is from. You can call one place or person and find out when it was delivered or from whom;

otherwise, something could be placed on your desk and you would have no idea how it got there or when.

Inside any facility or office building are usually many rooms that are not locked during the day such as broom, storage closets, maintenance areas, etc., and along with these, most of the time, rooms such as offices, break rooms, and rest rooms are not locked at night or after normal working hours. This can be a major problem for security in case of a bomb threat or incident in the building since each unsecured area needs to be checked for a threat. After normal work hours, which is the easiest time for the threat to gain entrance and plant a device, it increases the areas they have to choose from. So, you need to ensure to lock all unoccupied utility areas, offices, and rest rooms; this will prevent anyone from hiding or placing a bomb in these areas. The types of locks you need to use are double cylinder dead bolts which require a key on the inside or outside to open or lock it; this will negate the ability of someone hiding in there and locking the door. All keys need to be kept by security and signed out to the cleaning crew or maintenance as needed so they cannot be taken off site and duplicated.

You need to ensure that the building has contingency plans for emergencies (fire, bombing or bomb threat, hostage taking, etc.); if it is an office building with different companies in it, you still need to have building contingency plans and make sure that each company occupying it also has one and practices it on a regular basis. These plans should be updated regularly and briefed annually to all personnel and briefed for each new hire as part of the in-processing. An important thing to remember is the information proofing of your building; many facilities, buildings put up their evacuation routes and assembly areas throughout the building for anyone to see; you should limit the areas where these are displayed to non-public access areas, such as the lobby. This will allow a threat to know where to place secondary devices or where you will assemble outside the building. You should avoid setting a pattern when conducting drills, such as rallying at the same location each time: telephone booth, front of building by gate, certain sections of the parking lot, etc. If the terrorists know where the designated rally point is, they can call in a threat to an office or the building, wait until a crowd of office workers gathers at the rally point, and then detonate an explosive device at the rally point.

SOCIALIZING

Socializing is another area where people tend to let their guard down and relax their situational awareness to mix into the environment of meeting and speaking with new acquaintances or when meeting friends. Many times, this happens at office parties or get-togethers sponsored by the office, other friends, or night clubs where you frequent. You need to make sure you meet each new person with an open mind but be aware of the questions or attention you are getting, try to look for the hidden agendas that may be present in others meeting and getting to know you. What do I mean? Well—as an example—if a young, attractive woman is talking, dancing, and flirting with you and you are a middle-aged man whom this NEVER happens to you, ask yourself why is she paying you that much attention? The same is true for women. Why would that younger great-looking guy be doing it? Remember that information is extremely vital to the threat and their efforts against you, your company, your business, and possibly people you know. One of the best ways to get some of this information is to extract the information during a seemingly normal and innocent conversation from a person without them realizing what is taking place. This is called elicitation and is used by the threat all the time. So, when you do meet people and they express an uncommon or surprising interest in you, you should start paying attention to your conversation and what is taking place. People trying to gather information in this manner will try to not control the conversation but steer it in a direction toward the information they are trying to find out. If you get off subject, they come back to it with subtle reminders. Remember, they are looking for information sometimes very specific and they need to determine first if you have access to the information or know about what they are seeking. Then, they have to see if they can get the information out of you. Be aware of how alcohol affects you and limit your consumption when you are not in a place where you personally know everyone. You need to be constantly aware of how you are feeling physically; many drugs can be placed in drinks even it if is only water that will loosen you up enough to talk or to leave with someone you have just met. DO NOT think that no one would be interested in you for stuff like this because you don't know anything; they could want you for just your identification or access card, which could allow them to carry out their intended attack. So, have a plan when you go out, how much you will drink, what you will talk about, etc., know when you are going to leave or have a good estimate. This is not meant to scare you into never talking to people you don't know, but you MUST know the threat is there.

NOTE

When out drinking and socializing be aware, there are many ways to place drugs into a drink to incapacitate a person. If possible, when ordering drinks, order from the bar so you can see where it came from. Order bottled water, unopened; squeeze it when you get it to look for leaks and then check the cap to make sure it was sealed. If ordering a soda, order an unopened can; if they do not sell cans, watch where the glass comes from and ask for ice on the side. Never leave your drink unattended, take it with you if you move from the bar or table.

CHAPTER 8

Riots and Protests

The last several years have seen a rise in protests/riots that, in some instances, can turn to extreme violence. These protests destroy businesses and private property with the local and federal governments reticent to intercede. Such protests can be mobile or stationary, which can then turn into a moving protest. In several instances, these criminal organizations bussed in people from out of the local area to participate because there was not enough local support for their actions.

STATIONARY

These usually consist of picking high-volume vehicle traffic areas or urban areas, picking key transportation lanes and blocking them with no consideration to those who use these lanes of traffic for going to work or conducting personal business such as doctors' appointments. The protesters don't care; they only care that they are blocking a road. Their purpose is to cause disruption to bring attention to their cause.

Many such incidents of peaceful protests have turned violent at the instigation of the protesters. In some instances, they have set up hedgehogs, a version of a tank trap, and wired bicycle gates and other items together to block traffic. When people attempt to get through these protests, there vehicles can be mobbed and beaten on, windows broken, etc.

MOBILE

This is when a protest is a group of people that starts moving through an area to protest their cause. In a majority of incidents that have taken place, these can sometimes turn violent for no reason, with the violence seemingly having no point. They will move down an urban street and destroy store fronts of business, start fires, benches, vehicles parked there, statues, etc. This is another one of those instances where local government or law enforcement has often been reluctant to, or chosen not to,

 DOI: 10.4324/9781003292647-8

interfere. This moving riot is unpredictable in that you never know what side street or alley they will turn down, whether they will start blocking streets, or—more importantly—how destructive they will get.

For both types of protests, the protesters generally have cameras recording, as they are attempting to get video of people interfering with them or someone fighting back. Remember that the media will air any such footage provided for them to help in justifying their cause and calling out resistance or threats directed at them.

WHAT YOU CAN DO

Listen to local news or a police scanner to find out if protests are planned in your area or the areas you need to travel through. Most stationary protests or road blocks start early because they need to be in place before a heavy volume of traffic starts. Once you find out if any are taking place, go to extremes to avoid those areas, even within a few blocks because they could spill over. Just avoid the entire area. Make sure to let your family and friends know of these areas also so that they can avoid them.

If you come upon a protest that is taking place when walking, just turn around and leave the area as quickly as possible. This is not the time to get video to show your friends; just leave if you can. If you cannot, then find a building or a safe area you can get to, such as a bank or another business, that has established physical security measures in place. Stay there until it is over or use an alternate entrance that is off-street from where the protest is taking place to avoid it.

If you come upon a protest taking place when driving, this can be more difficult. If you do not react quickly enough. you could get blocked in from behind and not be able to back up and leave the area. If traffic is stopped make sure your windows are up and you have your cell phone out to record if need be. If you can find a parking spot, then park, lock your car, and leave the area immediately; your safety is paramount. This is the same if you can find a parking garage. Get in, go as high as possible, and park your vehicle. Ensure the doors are locked. (You must remember whenever you place your vehicle in park, that in most vehicles produced today when you place a vehicle in park, it automatically unlocks the doors). Any open alleys or avenues you can take to remove yourself from the protest is what you want to do as long as it will not trap you in any way.

If you cannot avoid the protest, and traffic is moving forward even if it's slow—or you are in the front and decide to move forward—you need to consider and do a few things to increase your safety. Often incidents of vehicles moving forward through a protest has turned violent on the part of the protesters against the vehicle and its occupants; be prepared for this. There are multiple videos online that show the tactics used. It includes jumping on your car to block the windshield, so you cannot see. They may stand in front of the vehicle and try to push against it. They may knock off your side views mirrors or beat on the car and windows, sometimes breaking them. If you are moving the vehicle forward, go slowly. Give the protesters a chance to move, while moving forward slowly. Instead of staying in a straight line, turn your wheels and zig-zag forward. This causes the protesters to move more since, instead of backing away or walking beside, now they have to follow your vehicle left and right and then they will have to move out of the way as it moves the other direction. Continue this until you are free of the protest. Then, go to the nearest police station or officer and try to file a damage or vandalism report. This is why you also want a dash cam or your phone video going, so that you have evidence of the people who damaged your vehicle; you might need it to dispute the narrative that what happened was your fault. Another thing to do, if you have a working horn, is just honk it and stay on it. This will make it difficult for those outside the vehicle immediately around you to communicate.

You always want to move forward as slowly as possible to allow people to move but keep moving forward. If windows start getting broken and severe damage to your vehicle, then you have to make a decision about your safety and if you need to move faster. This is only a decision you can make at the time of the incident. This is another reason to video record everything, if possible, from your point of view. Because, if you decide to speed up and this injures a protester, they are going to post their own videos and say you did it for no reason. With your own video you can show what caused you to fear for your life and take those actions that you thought were necessary at the time to protect yourself and your family.

A word of caution, whether on foot or in a vehicle, do not approach any law enforcement stationed at the riot. They do not know you; they do not know your intent. Just as your safety and your family's safety is the most important to you, their safety is very important to them. Do not force them to react to you as a possible threat, even if you are approaching just to talk with them.

Being caught up in a protest can be a highly emotional experience; do not let yourself get caught up in the emotion of the protesters. The safety of yourself and your family is the most important thing.

CHAPTER 9

Active Incident

ACTIVE SHOOTER

An active shooter is someone who is trying to kill or attempting to kill people—in a confined space such as an office type building, school, or an open populated area such as a park. According to the FBI, there is no pattern or method in how an active shooter selects their victims. This makes an active shooting incident unpredictable and hard to end, which can result in a loss of life and injuries to those victims of the incident.

WHAT YOU CAN DO?

There are potential warning signs that can be observed; these include but are not limited to the following:

- Increasingly erratic, unsafe, or aggressive behaviors.
- Hostile behavior based on claims of injustice or perceived wrongdoing.
- Drug and alcohol abuse.
- Claims of marginalization or distancing from friends and colleagues.
- Changes in performance at work.
- Sudden and dramatic changes in home life or in personality.
- Financial difficulties.
- Pending civil or criminal litigation.
- Observable grievances and making statements of retribution.

Be situationally aware of your surroundings and any of those people who you interact with on a daily basis.

DOI: 10.4324/9781003292647-9

WHAT YOU SHOULD DO IN CASE OF AN ACTIVE SHOOTER?

Run: This means to move immediately away from the active shooter if he is visible, or moving away from the sound of gunfire, if not visible. You should know how to get out of your place of employment, school, business, etc. by multiple means. Many people are so used to going to work and leaving work by one route that they do not know or are unfamiliar with other routes out of the facility. When moving look for exit signs, or other people who are moving away who might know where the nearest exit is. While moving, if possible, keep cover between you and the active shooter, and do not get trapped in a dead end or a place where you cannot get to an exit. Most exits are marked; look for this while moving. Many places have evacuation route maps on the walls, stop and look at this to find the nearest exit. Your best chance of survival is getting out of the area, out of the building. If you are outside and an active shooting event starts, again run away, do not run in a straight line, zig-zag, look for cover to place between yourself and the active shooter. Find a building you can get into and keep moving away from the entrance and windows. Again, your best chance of survival is to put as much distance between you and the shooter.

Hide: If you cannot get out of the area and away from the active shooter you need to find a hiding place that will afford you protection from being seen and from being shot. This room or area has to be securable, or access can be blocked, doors can be locked, etc. If the entryway is lockable, lock it, and then block it by placing furniture or other items in front of it to help deny entry. Turn off the lights and silence any cell phones to limit the shooter's ability to see or hear you. Do not peek, do not look, and do not open the door until you hear from more than one law enforcement officer. A shooter could pose as law enforcement to try to get people to open doors or come out of hiding.

Fight: If hiding fails, your last resort is to fight; do not go to the active shooter. Make him/her find you. Prepare yourself and find objects to throw and strike with. Stay hidden until the time of your attack, throw things to startle him, blind him, etc. Then, move closer to strike either with a weapon you have picked up or your hands, rake the eyes, and go for the weapon to push it in a safe direction. Use your knees and free hand and continue striking until the attacker is down or others arrive to help subdue the shooter.

KNIFE ATTACK

Knife and machete attacks are also a very real threat depending on your location and the environment you are moving in. Knife attacks happen more than people realize in the United States and are commonplace in several countries overseas due to many firearm ownership restrictions. Some crime statistics show that more people are killed by knives than are killed by firearms in the United States. People using a knife to attack a person means the individual has to get close to be effective; the active shooter guidance for a person to run first, hide if they cannot get away, and fight if they are trapped will also work with this type of attack.

Be situationally aware of your surroundings. After all, someone carrying a knife with an exposed blade in their hand while walking around is unusual anywhere.

Run: In this instance, it means to stay out of the range of the attacker; run to get as far away as fast as you can. If you loiter in the area to observe, you might end up a victim; these attackers can move quicker than you think. When moving, it is also good to place obstacles between you and the attacker; this will make it more difficult for him/her to pursue you. Even if you are an initial victim and are wounded, move away as fast and as far as you can.

Hide: Hide means hide, if you are moving from the attacker, especially in an enclosed space, find a place where you can close the door, lock it, barricade it, etc. A person attacking with a knife will move on to easier victims since s/he does not have the means to breach a barricade or locked door.

Fight: If you have no other option, you have to confront the attacker, with an edged weapon you must be prepared to get cut. Just like with an active shooter, throw things to allow you to get closer and have a striking weapon to hit with; this could be your backpack or briefcase, a tree branch, or anything to cause pain or incapacitate. It is important that if you have to fight, you try and gain control of the hand/arm the attacker is holding the knife in. If you can control the arm/hand, you can prevent him from doing damage; this might also allow others nearby to render assistance and help disable and disarm the attacker. Do what you need to do to survive in this instance. On February 12, 2016, during a machete attack at an Ohio deli, when he attacked, patrons started throwing chairs at him. The man fled and was shot by law enforcement later that day.

VEHICLE USED AS A WEAPON

This basically just means using a vehicle to hit people deliberately. This is not a new type of attack used by terrorists or domestic terrorists in the United States. There is no way to predict or determine when this type of attack will occur. The location has to allow access to a motor vehicle of any type. Terrorist organizations have been calling for their followers to conduct vehicle ramming attacks, using modified or even unmodified vehicles against areas with a large amount of pedestrian traffic, especially around sports arenas or other venues, against crowds, and even buildings.

This type of attack is an unsophisticated attack because anyone who can drive can do it, with no other training necessary. There are some potential indicators that law enforcement can look for, but, for you as the average person, visiting one of the potential attack sites would not notice. As always, just be aware of your surroundings and listen. A vehicle that revs its engine or starts moving toward unprotected pedestrians without giving any type of warning, such as honking a horn to alert bystanders, is intending to hit people. After the initial contact, if the vehicle continues on or maneuvers the vehicle so as *not* to avoid people, but to strike them, he is using his vehicle as a weapon.

WHAT YOU CAN DO?

Run: Like what we have talked about before, run from the attacking vehicle but ensure you run perpendicular to the path of the attacking vehicle. You are not trying to outrun it, you are trying to avoid it, let it get past you.

Hide: If you cannot run, then hide. You need to find a barrier that can stop or deflect the vehicle basically anything that will prevent the vehicle from striking you, this could be a tree, an actual vehicle barrier, another vehicle, stairs, etc.

There is no fight here as a pedestrian; once you are safe, you need to vacate the area as quickly as possible to avoid any follow-up attacks or this could be the start of a complex attack with the vehicle being the lead in and people will exit the vehicle with weapons of some type to carry on the attack.

One option if you are in a vehicle witnessing this attack take place, you can strike the attacking vehicle with your vehicle; this will cause the airbag to go off and trip the fuel cutoff switch, making the vehicle stop. Most modern vehicles come equipped with a fuel cutoff switch for safety reasons. In case of a collision or impact, this activates to stop the flow of fuel to prevent fire.

CHAPTER 10

Domestic Terrorism

Terrorism is defined as:

Homeland Security Act Definition of Terrorism, 6. U.S.C. 101(18)

- Involves an act that:
  - Is dangerous to human life or potentially destructive of critical infrastructure or key resources
  - In violation of the criminal laws of the United States or of any State or other subdivision of the United States
- Appears to be intended:
  - To intimidate or coerce a civilian population
  - To influence the policy of a government by intimidation or coercion
  - To affect the conduct of the government by mass destruction, assassination, or kidnapping.

Domestic Terrorism is referenced in U.S. Code 18 U.S.C. 2331(5)

- Involving acts dangerous to human life that are a violation of the criminal laws of the United States or of any State
- Appearing to be intended to:
  - Intimidate or coerce a civilian population
  - Influence the policy of government by intimidation or coercion
  - Affect the conduct of a government by mass destruction, assassination, or kidnapping
- Occurring primarily within the territorial jurisdiction of the United States

Domestic terrorism is the unlawful use, or threatened use, of violence by a group or individual based and operating entirely within the United States (or its territories) without foreign direction, committed against persons or property to intimidate or coerce a government, the civilian population, or any segment thereof, in furtherance of political or social objectives.[1]

DOI: 10.4324/9781003292647-10

The problem with defining domestic terrorism is that it is such a politically charged issue, how to separate criminal acts that take place during protests and riots with acts of terrorism. After all, many of these acts meet the above definitions of domestic terrorism, but law enforcement, politicians, and news media do not call them domestic terrorists. Also, most criminals use terror to achieve their goals: a robber uses a gun or other weapon to scare people enough so they will hand over their valuables, but he is not a domestic terrorist.

But there has to be a definition of domestic terrorism that we can use to help us understand it, without all the political and other concerns interfering.

Domestic terrorism is a criminal act. It is violence, or the threat of violence, used in such a way to create fear and a sense of alarm in the general population. This fear or alarm is created to make others take actions they would otherwise not take, or stop them from taking actions that they want to take. Domestic terrorists target the civilian population, trying to influence them with an interruption of their lives, with violence, or threats of violence to get the civilian population to either support them or not interfere with them in their goals of creating the changes they want to benefit themselves. The criminal acts they commit are intended to influence the population as a whole, sometimes done with the help of the news media and social media.

Hopefully, this will help you when trying to distinguish between a domestic terrorist and a criminal, allowing you to take measures necessary to protect yourself from either one.

LONE WOLF

A lone actor is a person who commits an act of violence alone, is not part of any terrorist command structure, or is otherwise without assistance from a terrorist group. They have many motivations that are similar to terrorist groups or they may have other motivations such as personal reasons for committing the criminal acts that they do in order to gain revenge, or in their eye's, justice for themselves or a cause.

It is impossible to predict or determine who will commit a criminal violent act as a lone wolf or a lone actor; there are not set traits or information that allows us to do this. Nearly all lone actors have a personal or political grievance that they feel is not being addressed. Their perception of reality may be that these grievances have caused harm to them or to society as a whole and that they are taking matters into their own hands to make it right.

Many of people who conduct these types of actions finally act out because of either their personal grievances have reached a breaking point, or because of their ideology, which may be in line with other terrorist organizations but is unique to the individual.

Lone actor terrorism accounts for approximately less than 3 percent of all terrorist incidents, though they are often in the public eye more because they are sensationalized by the media. The thing that prevents this type of attack from being stopped is the fact that often no one knows of such individuals' plans to commit violent acts until it's too late. This in turn makes any form of pre-incident interdiction impossible. Without being linked to a terrorist organization in any way, there is little to no ways to track the persons radicalization or discontent, unless these are expressed in conversations, online postings, or other media. That's what makes these types of attacks so devastating; they are such a surprise to everyone, leaving people shocked not only of violent attack, but because of the person who committed it.

WHAT CAN YOU DO?

Just as with the active incident chapter, be situationally aware. Know the people you work with, go to school with, play with, and when their attitudes are changing for the worse. Warning signs can include being perpetually angry, talking about their grievances, getting more and more violent or extreme in their speech. When a violent incident starts, take those actions you need to stay safe.

NOTE

1 James F. Jarboe Domestic Terrorism section chief, counter terrorism division FBI, before the house resources committee, subcommittee on forests and forest health 12 Feb 2002.

CHAPTER 11

Fire Used as a Weapon

Terrorist groups—both international and domestic—have always had a specific interest in using fire as a weapon during the events they create. This is due to many reasons but primarily the low cost associated with performing the act and no training or other expertise required. So, any member of the organization can perform this act. The return for the terrorist is that this type of attack has the potential to cause large-scale damage and destruction to property and possible deaths of persons. It will also, depending on the size and placement of the fire, use resources of the first responders, most notably fire department, police, and rescue personnel that might be needed in other places. Then, there is the economic damage that can be caused by destroying government centers, retail establishments, restaurants, and other businesses. And, as previously discussed, it will also generally get media attention.

Using fire has several advantages over other terrorist tactics and methods; it is a relatively inexpensive tactic to use, little or no training is required, the duration of the fire, the long-term effects of the fire damage for people to see, the media coverage generated, and the use of limited resources to control the fire or put it out will ensure that this tactic is always feared by people and governments. And it is almost impossible to detect or intercede pre-incident because all you need is an ignitor (match, lighter) and something that catches fire. These materials are common in all areas of the world.

Fire as a weapon can also be used to distract and draw the attention of building occupants as well as security away from the primary duties. This can allow the attackers to exploit other vulnerabilities, including entering the structure while everyone is distracted by the fire. Fires cause evacuations, forcing people out of a building into the open where they can become more vulnerable to another means of attack. It is effective in helping terrorists perpetrate other attacks, such as using direct fire weapons, bombs, even bladed weapons while people are focused on the fire. Likewise, fires can utilize first responders to block streets or routes, slowing the response to an attack at another location.

 DOI: 10.4324/9781003292647-11

Urban areas are especially good targets for the terrorist: residential buildings mixed with commercial buildings and the density or closeness of these structures could mean the fire spreading past the intended target area and creating more damage. Structures that do not have good fire evacuation infrastructure such as fire escapes or fire alarms/detectors—or firefighting equipment—are prime targets because the number of persons that can be lost. Urban areas that have limited firefighting equipment, that can reach the heights of the tallest structures, can also be targeted, knowing that the responding agencies cannot cover them all, thereby creating more damage.

Sometimes, specific structures are targeted for their symbolism, or because of a specific grievance. In these cases, there could be sabotage associated with the employment of fire. Such sabotage can include disabling the fire detection and fire protection systems, or setting ambushes for the first responders as they start fighting the fire or facility residents as they exit.

Many times, during protests or riots, fires are started as a secondary effect of what is taking place. The use of Molotov cocktails against police barricades or structures limits movement. Molotov cocktails can be against locked store fronts or vehicles parked along the line of advance they are using. Another way fires are being started as a secondary effect is using fireworks during these protests and demonstrations, firing rockets and other flammable devices at law enforcement, other first responders, buildings, barricades, or vehicles. These devices have the potential and have caused fires.

Terrorist use fire as a weapon and will continue to do so in the future, so you need as an individual to learn how to best prepare yourself for this threat.

WHAT YOU CAN DO?

When traveling, have a fire extinguisher in the cab of your vehicle and in the trunk, the one in the cab is used to make sure you can get out of the vehicle safely and away. The one in the trunk is for use when helping others. Check them and ensure they are in good working order, so they are ready if you ever need them.

NOTE: A quick note about Molotov cocktails when used against vehicles. These devices burn off the fuel that is inside the bottle being thrown. Then, it needs to find another fuel source, most motor vehicles have only rubber that is flammable and the paint of the vehicle. So, unless one makes it inside the cab of the vehicle, you can continue to drive and wait for the flames to die out on their own once the fuel source is gone.

At home, make sure your fire detection system is in working order; make sure you have fire extinguishers available and everyone knows how to use them. Make sure you have set aside fire extinguishers for use outside the home, such as in a front closet, in case a fire starts outside near the house or your vehicles. While a hose and water will also work, you have to make sure the hose is hooked up, the water is on or available, and the hose will reach the fire. With a fire extinguisher, all you have to do is pick it up and go. Ensure that you and your family know how to get out of the family home safely from different directions, since you will never know where a fire will start or be started—and practice these drills. DO NOT FORGET YOUR PETS, but remember, people first. Make sure you have a location that everyone knows to go to for accountability in case you get separated.

At work, make sure your place of employment has in place an emergency action plan for fires and evacuation and accountability locations are practiced. That they perform maintenance and tests of the fire detection and prevention system. That fire extinguishers are available in the facility and are up to date and inspected. That the parking structure, if there is one, also has fire detection and either fire detection or fire extinguishers are available, tested, and inspected ready for use.

Always remember that a fire could be a tool being used by the terrorist to breech the security of your home or office; be aware when you are outside for follow-on attacks or attempts to cause more harm. These could include bombs placed outside the structure, waiting for people to come out, or for first responders to show up before being detonated or direct fire weapons (people shooting at you). Once people start exiting, this can cause people to run back inside the burning structure. Always be aware of your surroundings during these types of incidents and be prepared to act to protect yourself and others if needed.

CHAPTER 12

Cyber Awareness

WHEN ONLINE, HOW TO PREVENT DIVULGING CRITICAL INFORMATION?

In today's world, everyone needs to be cyber-aware. The threat will use cyberspace to find out who to target. Once a target is selected, they will find out as much as they can to make sure you are an easy target.

Common cyber threats against persons include, but are not limited to the following.

PHISHING AND SPEAR PHISHING

Phishing is when someone uses an email or message to deceive you into providing personal information. It can put you and your family at risk. Spear phishing is generally targeted toward a specific individual, section, or group of people that work together, school together, or of a certain age group.

There are things to watch for that should raise your suspicion when receiving emails or messages:

- Use of email, text messages, or other message service only.
  - Could have improper grammar, misspelled works, and/or generalized greetings.
  - Could be using your email name, a nickname on your message service, or your real name incorrectly. Such as calling you Mr. Beright there, and your email is beright there.
- The request for information will come from a position of authority or a company you do business with; your employer, a bank or credit card company, an online payment provider, or some government organization. This is an attempt to create fear if the information is not provided something bad will happen.

DOI: 10.4324/9781003292647-12

- This request will ask you to update information or validate information, usually banking password, and will provide a link.
- Says it will direct you to a website that looks legitimate.

Directed phishing or spear phishing is the same but targets specific groups or individuals. These are usually a higher level of scam and will appear to come from an associate or acquaintance. It might even include other people you know in the address line. It is just an attempt to get you to give information about you, your family, or your business—that cannot be obtained by other means—for the use of this scammer or threat.

Both of these are considered social engineering attacks.

What you can do?:

- Delete any suspicious emails, from unknown senders (you can click for more details and it will list out the sender's complete email address so you can know for sure where it originated).
- Do not click on any links (you can run your cursor over the link and it will show you the entire address before clicking; if it does not look right, report it.).
- Contact your company security office or system administrator and report it, ESPECIALLY if you clicked a link.
- Make sure your anti-virus software is up to date.
- DO NOT open attachments.
- Never provide the information requested until the source is verified.

MALICIOUS CODE

This is software that does damage to a computer or a network and can create unwanted security breaches or side effects. These can include viruses, trojan horses, worms, keyloggers, spyware, rootkits, backdoors, and other destructive items that are being created every day by the threat.

Things to be on the lookout for that can contain malicious code include:

- Email attachments or links.
- Downloading files without knowing who sent them or what they contain.
- Visiting sites that are infected and viewing files at the site (porn, gaming sites, free software sites).
- Removable media—especially USB-type devices that you get from other people or find and put them into your computer.

What you can do?:

- Only view emails in plain text; use caution when opening an email.
- Never use a preview pane to view emails.
- Scan all attachments before you download; you can set your virus scanner to perform scanning before download so it is done automatically so you do not forget.
- Never use automatic download as a setting.
- Never click on a link without viewing the link address first (placing your cursor over it should make the full link address pull up without clicking it).
- If someone who never sends you links sends you one in a texting or messaging service, contact them to see if they sent you something or if they were hacked.
- If someone who never sends you attachments in texting or messaging services sends you one, contact them to see if they sent you something or if they have been hacked.

Just because you have received an email or message from a friend, coworker, or family member does not mean it is safe to open without taking precautions. After all, any one of those people could have been hacked also and could be sending out infected files or links, perhaps without sending it themselves.

Many people follow all the rules, but co-users of their devices do not. People allow children and spouses to use their laptops at home where they receive mail or their cellphones or tablets. If you do allow others to use your computers, tablets, or cellphones, ensure they know about cyber awareness. Also make sure you have your security settings set in such a way that they cannot be changed by other users; this allows your device to have some protection regardless of who is using it.

What you need to do to protect yourself and your devices from websites?:

- First DO NOT GO to websites that you do not know or want to load large amounts of cookies or other things on your device.
- Set your computer security settings to block malicious links and IP addresses.
- Make sure your device is current in its operating system updates and virus software updates.
- Most software browsers have security settings that will automatically block or require you to confirm accepting things from any site. Make sure your security settings are set to protect you and your device regardless of who is using it.

WEAK PASSWORDS

Many people have weak passwords, and they try to pick something easy that they can remember. Others use the same password for everything because we are required to have so many of them, such as bank, credit cards, mortgage, utilities, work, social media sites, new sites, etc. Having a weak password means that if someone can figure out your user name, they can get into the site they are trying to break into.

What are weak passwords?:

- People use passwords out of a dictionary. The issue with this is brute force attacks where hackers have a tool loaded with dictionaries and it tries every word until it finds the one. If you are going to use a word only, you can misspell it, so these type of brute force attacks will not work; just remember how you misspelled it.
- Public knowledge type information such as names of children, spouses, parents, pets, birthdays, graduation days, etc. Other significant information to you that can be found by the threat.
- Lack of special characters, numbers, or upper/lower case; this makes the job of a hacker using a program or brute force tool easier by limiting the characters they will have to search through.
- Using only numbers; this is done by many older people and children because they are easier to remember and fast.
- Default passwords or pre-installed passwords; many people never change the passwords that came with programs or devices they have purchased.

Please remember that if you let multiple people use your device such as children, significant others, friends, co-workers … your password strength is only as good as the weakest of those using your device.

These types of weak passwords can lead to you or your organization getting hacked or exploited by the cyber threat, giving them access to information they would otherwise be unable to obtain.

What you can do?:

- Use a combination of characters, numbers, and special characters, 10 characters or longer.
- Never use personal information.
- Never use fad words or phrases because you think they are cute (children).

- Use a password locker or some other device or program to store your passwords, so you do not forget them.
- Never save your username or password in your browser, to make it easier for you to get in (make sure other device users do not do this also).
- Never let someone else use your password.
- Create passwords for your children to use on their devices for games and learning, do not let them create their own.

REMOVABLE MEDIA

Removable media is everywhere nowadays, and all different sizes. Basically, it is any device that can be plugged into and removed from a device while it is running to download or upload information or other items. These devices can be used by the threat to gain access to your device or system by having executable programs, malicious code, or other things on them that will hack or give access to your device and system. Types of removable media include thumb/flash drives, external hard drives, CDs, DVDs, etc. Some removable media can now be accessed by Bluetooth without having to actually be plugged in.

The way this is accomplished is the threat will leave removable media in places that people will pick them up in order to find who they belong to, such as work cafeterias, restrooms, break rooms, smoke areas, and meeting rooms. For children, they will leave them on playgrounds or play areas in malls. Many people will pick them up and plug them in to see who they belong to, to return them, especially if found at work. Sometimes, they are turned into security who may also just plug it in to see who it belongs to in an effort to return it. Another way is that they will give removable media away as a gift or a free item at a trade show or mail to someone as a free product trial with them wanting your opinion.

These devices can contain various codes or programs that will run as soon as they are plugged in or have access to your device. Many computers have an automatic function on USB ports or CD/DVD drives that read them as soon as they are set; this setting can be changed to require input from the user first. You should be able to set up your virus scanning software to automatically scan all removable media placed in your computer or tablet. These codes or programs can corrupt files or destroy/modify information; they can load programs giving hackers access or they can sabotage systems. Basically, they can do anything the threat needs to accomplish their goal.

What you can do?

It depends on your company or your personal preferences; you can disable all USB ports and CD/DVD drives so they do not operate.

- Do not use removable drives when you do not know the origin or who has had access to it.
- Scan all removable media before accessing any files or programs located on it.

BLUETOOTH

Another item that people tend to forget or ignore is that you can grant access to your devices, phone, laptop, or tablet through Bluetooth—especially if you allow your devices to be found. This is an avenue into a device that can be exploited by hackers. There are various reasons that people leave Bluetooth on: so it can sync with their new fitness watch, so the phone can link to the car, so their watch and cell phone are synced, and they can receive messages on the watch.

What you can do?

- If you have a fitness-worn device or watch, it does not need to be linked to your cell phone 24/7, when I wore one, I linked them when going to bed to see my information for the day, then turned the Bluetooth back off.
- I also link my Bluetooth to my vehicle for making and receiving calls, but I only do it when I am in the car. I get in, turn on my Bluetooth, link, and then go; when I reach my destination, I turn my Bluetooth off and exit the vehicle. Not only does it keep me safe from the Bluetooth standpoint but it means I always know I have my phone with me and did not forget it.

Just be aware that any access you give to your device can be exploited. Always check your devices to ensure your settings are correct, especially if you let others use them.

CHAT ROOMS, GAME ROOMS, ETC. AND CHILDREN'S DEVICES ONLINE. THE DANGER OF SOLICITATION

This is one of the easiest ways for the threat to obtain information not only from you but from your children. There are multiple chatrooms that deal with work, games played on the Internet, and groups of similar interests such as comic books, or cars. Even some games themselves have chat capability between multiple players, and you never know who you are actually talking to.

People will strike up conversations trying to build rapport and then start asking minor, then more in-depth, questions, trying to obtain personal or business information from their selected target. This could take place over weeks with the threat building their rapport slowly over this time trying to raise any suspicions. These attacks work especially well against the elderly and children who, in this age of social media and online gaming/dating, can be too trusting.

You need to be aware and make your family and co-workers aware that not everyone they meet online is their friend, and that giving out information—particularly information that was specially asked for—can be highly dangerous.

Conclusion

This book has the purpose of giving you a basic understanding of terrorists and terrorist organizations and the information needed so that you can begin making yourself UNDESIRABLE as a target for anyone and UNPREDICTABLE to any threat that you may encounter regardless of your location. No matter where you are, any time you suspect anything, REPORT IT to someone. Whatever suspicious activity you see, it needs to be reported to someone, do not hesitate or think someone else will do it. How many times have we seen on TV where someone would say, "*I thought something wasn't right*," "*he just didn't act right*" after an incident has taken place? I want you to use the things discussed in this book to move the threats crosshairs off of you as a hard target.

And finally, you always need to remember we as potential targets always want to be INFORMED about the threat, be as LOW PROFILE as we can be, as UNPREDICTABLE as possible, and always be ALERT to what is taking place around us.

DOI: 10.4324/9781003292647-13

Index

Pages in *italics* refer figures.

For Product Safety Concerns and Information please contact our EU representative GPSR@taylorandfrancis.com
Taylor & Francis Verlag GmbH, Kaufingerstraße 24, 80331 München, Germany

www.ingramcontent.com/pod-product-compliance
Ingram Content Group UK Ltd.
Pitfield, Milton Keynes, MK11 3LW, UK
UKHW021724240926
475702UK00030BA/2659
9781032274164